Exploring Civil Society

Political and cultural contexts

Edited by Marlies Glasius, David Lewis and Hakan Seckinelgin

LONDON AND NEW YORK

First published 2004
by Routledge
2 Park Square, Milton Park, Abingdon, Oxon OX14 4RN

Simultaneously published in the USA and Canada
by Routledge
270 Madison Ave, New York, NY 10016

Reprinted 2005

Routledge is an imprint of the Taylor & Francis Group

Typeset in by Sabon by Bookcraft Ltd, Stroud, Gloucestershire
Printed and bound in Great Britain by TJ International Ltd, Padstow, Cornwall

British Library Cataloguing in Publication Data
A catalogue record for this book is available from the British Library.

Library of Congress Cataloging-in-Publication Data
Exploring civil society: political and cultural contexts/edited by Marlies Glasius, David Lewis and Hakan Seckinelgin.
p. cm.
Includes bibliographical references and index.
1. Civil society. I. Glasius, Marlies. II. Lewis, David, 1960 June 2–
III. Seckinelgin, Hakan, 1969–
JC337.E97 2004
300–dc22

2004001293

ISBN 0-415-32545-5 (hbk)
ISBN 0-415-32546-3 (pbk)

Contents

Contributors

Ṣọlá Akínrìnádé is Professor of History in the Department of History, Obafemi Awolowo University, Ile-Ife, Nigeria.

Helmut Anheier is Professor in the Department of Social Welfare and Director of the Center for Civil Society, University of California, Los Angeles (UCLA).

Leonardo Avritzer is Professor in Political Science at the School of Liberal Arts of the Universidade Federal de Minas Gerais, Brazil.

Jerzy Celichowski is Deputy Director of Government–Citizen Communication, Open Society Institute, Budapest, Hungary.

Neera Chandhoke is Professor of Political Science at the University of Delhi.

Bernard Dreano is Co-chair of the Helsinki Citizens' Assembly, and president of the Centre d'études et d'initiatives de solidarité internationale (CEDETIM), Paris.

Sabine Freizer is a research student in the Department of Social Policy, London School of Economics and Political Science.

Chris Hann is Professor and Director, Max Planck Institute for Social Anthropology, Halle/Saale, Germany.

Jude Howell is Professor of Social Policy and Director of the Centre for Civil Society at the London School of Economics and Political Science.

Marlies Glasius is Lecturer at the Centre for Civil Society and Research Fellow at the Centre for the Study of Global Governance, London School of Economics and Political Science.

Deborah James is Reader in the Department of Anthropology, London School of Economics and Political Science.

Mary Kaldor is School Professor and Director of the Centre for the Study of Global Governance, London School of Economics and Political Science.

David Lewis is Reader in Social Policy, London School of Economics and Political Science.

Ronnie D. Lipschutz is Professor of Politics in the Department of Politics, University of California, Santa Cruz.

Ebenezer Obadare is a research student in the Department of Social Policy, London School of Economics and Political Science.

Bhikhu Parekh is Professor Emeritus of Politics at the University of Hull and a Fellow of the Royal Society of Arts and of the Academy of the Learned Societies for Social Sciences. He is a member of the House of Lords.

Ali Paya is a Senior Researcher in the National Research Institute for Science Policy (Iran) and the Centre for the Study of Democracy, University of Westminster (UK).

Jenny Pearce is Professor of Latin American Politics in the Department of Peace Studies, University of Bradford.

Hakan Seckinelgin is Lecturer in International Social Policy in the Department of Social Policy, London School of Economics and Political Science.

Salma A. Shawa recently completed a PhD at the Centre for Civil Society at the London School of Economics and Political Science and is now a Lecturer at the College of Southern Europe, Athens.

Frank Trentmann is Senior Lecturer in Modern History, Birkbeck College, University of London.

Hilary Wainwright is Senior Research Fellow at the Centre for Labour Studies, University of Manchester, and Editor of *Red Pepper.*

Part I

Introduction

1 Exploring civil society internationally

Marlies Glasius, David Lewis and Hakan Seckinelgin

The concept of civil society, which has its origins in early modern West European thought, was reinvented in Eastern Europe and Latin America in the 1980s and found its way into the policy language of international development agencies during the 1990s. Subsequently, the concept of civil society has travelled to all corners of the globe, through intellectual exchange, activist discourse, and the official policies of development donors and politicians. Taking a wide range of local, national and regional contexts from around the world this book considers the questions of whether and how the concept of civil society is being translated into different political and cultural contexts, and the impact of using the concept on the political development of different regions. Other important sub-questions and debates follow from this central concern. Is the civil society idea simply part of a neoimperialist project of imposing Western hegemony? Or does the ever-increasing talk of civil society instead reflect important and progressive trends in the radicalization of democracy and the redistribution of political power? Does the Western bias implied in the formulation of the civil society idea as secular and formally organized prevent recognition of local but different forms of civil society? Is it beneficial, finally, to be thinking of a 'global' civil society as a normative concept that embraces notions of non-violence, solidarity and active world citizenship?

We have organized the presentation of the contributions on a geographical basis. Beginning with an overview section that picks up key strands of the history of the civil society debate, we then move on to the contexts of Eastern Europe and Latin America, which can in a sense claim 'ownership' of the revival of the civil society idea in the 1980s. The focus then moves on to Europe and North America where there has been a process of rediscovery of the home-grown but long forgotten concept of civil society (cf Comaroff and Comaroff 1999). From there we move on to Asia and Africa where there is an uneasy coexistence between local and imported or imposed versions of civil society, ending our global tour in the Middle East, where the 'desired' nature and role of civil society are particularly contested at present. The volume concludes by pulling away from national and regional discussions with a section on the idea of global civil society.

Three sets of interrelated issues emerge from the papers presented in this book. The first is the exploration of the politics of civil society across different contexts in the light of the shifting interrelationships and blurred boundaries between civil society and state. The second is the challenge of examining the relationships that link civil societies with wider institutional contexts and the dynamics of power embodied in such relationships. The third is the importance of place and recognition of a need for an empirical and theoretical engagement with the various forms taken by civil society in different contexts.

Civil society and politics

Politics is clearly central to discussions of civil society and is discussed here in many forms. Some chapters directly address the issue of political participation, while others focus on the importance of political context in the analysis of civil society. It is possible to discern two main trends. For some authors, it is clear that the impact of existing political institutions in a given country context has played an important role in framing the space that exists for civil society. For others, it is equally or more important to pay attention to the fact that civil society itself is a political agent. While civil society is constituted within a particular political discourse, it also in return influences the way this discourse is transformed.

One way of dealing with this paradox is by identifying different 'ideal-types' that show the ways in which civil society and political context have developed symbiotically. Avritzer (this volume) identifies liberal, participatory and 'uncivil' forms of civil society, which he locates predominantly in Argentina and Chile, in Brazil, and in Peru and Colombia respectively. The liberal form 'is related to the reconstruction of a rights structure and to forms of collective action aiming to secure accountability and the rule of law ... civil society triggers social action only when the political system fails to fulfil its proper role within the liberal order'. The participatory form 'challenged a central aspect of the process of mediation between political society and the state'. In the uncivil model, 'civil society constitutes itself without the guarantees that are part of the pacification of the political space' and 'the many forms of collective action that exist in the region are subordinated to the destructive dynamics of state politics' – or, Avritzer adds, market politics. Many of the categories he uses resonate with those of other authors. Anheier (this volume), for instance, identifies the United States of America as the homeland of the liberal prototype but points out that this is not a very explicit self-identification, and is so ingrained in the fabric of social and political life that it makes it difficult for Americans to see that this is but one of several possible manifestations of civil society.

Pearce (this volume) distinguishes between a liberal and a radical view of civil society in Latin America (or 'builders' and 'critics' of democracy), but her radicals appear to be close to Avritzer's participatory model (see also

Howell and Pearce 2001). Rather than locate either type in particular countries, she sees an unhelpful polarization between the two across Latin America, arguing that both are needed in order to counter 'the growth of the authoritarian and populist impulses that remain strong throughout the region'. Wainwright (this volume) describes how Western social movements such as the women's movement have also engaged – albeit without much theorization and with limited success – in developing more participatory models of relations between civil society and the state.

Avritzer describes his model of 'uncivil society' primarily in terms of citizen 'self-help' in the absence of state provision of public goods such as personal and social security. Despite the use of the term 'uncivil', he does not condemn civil society self-help, but deplores the circumstances that have forced this defensive form of collective action. This phenomenon turns out to be by no means exclusive to Latin America. In Bangladesh, a mosque-organized 'community initiative' in Dhaka successfully reduced organized crime by violent means (Lewis, this volume). James (this volume) describes how vigilante groups in South Africa have sprung up in response to inadequate policing, but makes it clear that the methods and membership of these private 'crime-fighting' initiatives all too easily become criminal themselves. Echoing Avritzer's contradictory label 'uncivil civil society' she wonders whether one can speak of a 'civil society' in the face of such a basic lack of functioning of the state.

Since the attacks of 11 September 2001, a new political challenge has emerged for civil society at global and domestic levels in the form of the so-called 'war on terror', which is, among other things, undermining progress achieved with the entrenchment of human rights and weakening the effectiveness of UN processes and institutions. This process is refocusing some elements within civil society to question anew what 'protection of human rights' may or may not license states to do, including the unfettered claims made to justify unilateral intervention in the international arena to *protect* people through violent means. As Kaldor (this volume) warns, the new policy environment may contribute to a 'roll-back' of gains made by global civil society processes during the 1990s.

Civil society linkages and relationships

The accounts given by authors in this volume of relations between local civil society actors and the wider world mainly fall into two groups. The first group comprises those describing horizontal contacts, dialogues and experiences that have had an inspirational or emancipatory effect. The second group focuses on vertical relations, arguing that all too often there has been an unhelpful imposition of a particular external view of an 'appropriate' vision of civil society, which is one based on neoliberal policies, sweetened by the provision of funding, but without regard for local conditions.

In the first group, Paya (this volume) describes how, as early as 1906, when Iran experienced the Constitutional Revolution, 'greater exposure of the Iranian society to Western ideas or models resulted in greater demand for sociopolitical reforms'. While he emphasizes that civil society, conceptualized as a buffer and breathing space between the individual and powerful social institutions, has deep roots in Iran, he conceives of outside influences on Iranian civil society primarily as benign. He concludes that, due to the permeation of new ideas through globalization in general and the fall of the Ba'ath regime in Iraq in particular, Iran is on the way 'towards emergence of a more robust and effective "civil society"'. Freizer (this volume) describes how, in the early years of glasnost, the emergence of an environmental movement in Central Asia (and elsewhere in the former Soviet sphere of influence) was influenced and strengthened by the global environmental movement. In China, the Beijing Women's Conference spurred the growth of autonomous women's organizations, tolerated by the Chinese government (Howell, this volume).

However, most of the instances of 'positive influence' cited here did not travel West–East or North–South, but through more complex trajectories. Dreano (this volume) argues that the political heritage of migrant intellectuals has had an energizing and democratizing effect on French civil society. Wainwright (this volume) describes how Central East European dissidents provided a theory to fit the existing practices of West European activists. She then discusses how this theorizing was weakened by the neoliberal interpretation of the fall of the Berlin wall, how the 'language of civil society' was instrumentalized by 'third way' governments such as New Labour in the UK, and finally how certain local political initiatives in Western Europe are inspired anew by Brazilian examples of participatory politics. James (this volume) suggests that postapartheid South African activists are successfully counterposing a newer, global struggle to the ANC reproach that they were not part of 'the national struggle'. This goes beyond rhetoric, and indeed beyond urbanized civil society: the landless movement in South Africa has allied itself to the same movements in Brazil and Palestine. Moreover, the World Conference Against Racism and the Earth Summit provided opportunities to raise the profile of this new South African civil society internationally.

In the second group of accounts, it is useful to differentiate neoliberal perspectives on civil society from liberal perspectives. At one level there are obvious similarities, such as an emphasis on voluntaristic self-organization outside formal political circles. However, liberal perspectives on civil society are primarily concerned with increasing the responsiveness of political institutions, while neoliberal approaches to civil society are more focused on the reorganization of political space in order to minimize the role of the state.

The impact of neoliberal policies on civil society is seen by many authors as strongly conditioned by the manner in which such policies have been introduced by international policy-makers since the 1980s. A 'blueprint' model of civil society based on the construction or support of certain organizational forms can be observed throughout the world.

Some authors are concerned about particular neoliberal policy prescriptions such as privatization and decentralization, while others object primarily to the introduction of non-governmental organizations (NGOs) within such policy frameworks, considering them as unwarranted foreign interventions into their sociopolitical context. Hann's contribution (this volume) for instance points out that much of so-called civil society in Eastern Europe is simply the result of international aid funds channelled to a set of Western-style NGOs and is associated with modern managerialist values and a close familiarity with the English language.

This provides us with a further analytical possibility by differentiating the existence of NGOs in general from the ways they are incorporated into a particular agenda within international neoliberal frameworks. Although some observers suggest a close link between particular international policies and the increased number of NGOs as well as expansion of a particular form of civil society, NGOs *per se* do not represent a perspective that is naturally neoliberal. There is no doubt that as actors in civil society NGOs of all kinds take part in numerous political debates, but this needs to be distinguished from the instrumentalized use of NGO forms, which has led some to suggest the abbreviation is better understood as standing for 'not grass-roots organizations'.

Although many proponents of neoliberal policies would consider their interventions less political and more social (in other words, as interventions in support of the social institutions of a given country) their position is underpinned by an implicit vision about the relationship between the social and the political (Seckinelgin 2002). Furthermore, in considering the mechanisms that are used in introducing these policies, the authors identify an international political context that is influencing political debates in individual countries. This influence is not only related to the main political actors in a given context but is also closely linked to existing forms of traditional, or already existing, civil societies (Lewis 2002). Tensions between civil society motivated by the neoliberal formulations and that based on more 'traditional' structures and resources therefore constitute an important political problem in many countries. Freizer, writing in this volume about Central Asia, identifies two further ideal-types, which have much resonance elsewhere in this volume: the communal and the neoliberal forms of civil society.

The question of culture and tradition is considered by some authors here, but there is little support for arguments that the civil society concept is culturally alien to non-Western societies. The oft-cited position of the anthropologist Ernest Gellner (1994) – who argued in his analysis of Islamic contexts that civil society is an essentially Western concept, which cannot apply elsewhere in the world – finds few supporters among the contributors to this volume. Chandhoke's chapter (this volume), which explores aspects of the forms of linguistic exclusion within civil society that disadvantage India's indigenous people, might be used to lend support to such a view in its argument that only the language of 'legal and political modernity constitutes the modern domain of the state and civil society in India'. But what emerges from most of the contributions in this volume is the surprising extent to which both the concept and the actually existing forms of civil society are evolving and adapting in ways that are both diverse and unpredictable. The construction of civil society 'others' appears to be proceeding apace.

Civil society and place

While civil society is discussed by most authors here in relation to the state, the rediscovery of the term took place in a late twentieth-century context that involved broader processes of urbanization, migration, democratization, state disintegration, privatization and globalization. It should come as no surprise therefore to find that the connections and conflicts of civil society with other actors are much more complex and multifaceted than any simple national state/national society dichotomy would suggest.

A purely abstract political analysis of civil society can only take us so far and it is clear that 'place matters'. The volume therefore takes a geographical rather than a thematic or political-theoretical approach to the subject. However, it has attempted to avoid the 'stamp-collecting' tendency (Shaw 2003) of comparative politics, which would be to compare the situation in country A to that in country B to that in country C, as if each country and its society were discrete and homogeneous entities. While the authors in this volume do typically take particular geographical locations as their point of departure, these include not only nation-states (Akínrìnádé, Anheier, Freizer, James, Lewis, Paya, Seckinelgin), but also provincial towns (Hann), global cities (Dreano), subnational regions (Chandhoke), supranational regions (Celichowsky, Hann, Obadare, Trentmann and Wainwright), entire continents (Avritzer, Pearce), and not-quite-state entities (Shawa on Palestine). They all consider outside influences, whether these have been emancipatory, problematic or downright destructive.

Naturally, a volume with a global remit of this kind must make difficult choices, and will necessarily exclude whole areas of the globe. In making our choices, we have tried to privilege relatively unknown regions and perspectives over those which have already received attention in the literature. We have, for instance, given relatively little attention to the oft-told story of the rediscovery of civil society in Eastern Europe and Latin America, with just one contribution from the former region and two from the latter, all of which concentrate on how civil society has fared since the celebrated triumphs over authoritarianism. We have ignored the whole of Southeast Asia and focused instead on China and Central Asia, and devoted a whole section to the Middle East. Unlike some earlier works focusing on 'non-Western' contexts, we have explicitly included Western Europe and the United States in our explorations.

The rise of civil society is often associated with urbanization. In the Western historical context, it is linked with ideas about 'civil', 'polite' behaviour, including norms of toleration and non-violence, which were necessary for relative strangers, possibly of different religions, to live side by side in an urban setting (Elias 1994; Keane 1996). In his historical contribution, Trentmann (this volume) makes the point that understandings of civil society often did not go much beyond religious toleration, and did not carry any of the present-day deliberative or activist connotations. Moreover, such toleration was firmly anchored in a Christian, rather than a secular, tradition.

Beyond its Western origins, Mamdani (1996) has famously described civil society in a colonial setting as being the reserve of a small urban middle-class population, and permanently excluding rural populations. Authors in this volume provide a rather different and more complex picture by tracing how forms of associational life emerged in various local settings. Interestingly, they do associate this with urbanization, but not in the form of gatherings of 'polite strangers'. Akínrìnádé (discussing Nigeria), Freizer (Tajikistan and Uzbekistan) and Seckinelgin (Turkey), all this volume, each describe the ways in which people (generally men) arrive in the city and then begin to form mutual support networks based on their ethnicity or region of origin. These forms of association were new and voluntary, but based on earlier rural relations. Such observation updates longstanding anthropological interest in these themes (such as Banton 1968; Little 1965). James (this volume) shows how, while Mamdani's differential treatment of the urban and the rural realm was indeed the intended policy of colonial rule and, later, apartheid, it never entirely succeeded, due to labour migration: 'Africans who were "subjects" at the rural pole of their existence were more like "citizens" in an urban setting as a result of their experiences as members of the unionized workforce, supporters of political parties, Christian town dwellers, and the like'. Naturally, they took their political experiences back to the countryside with them, which had an emancipatory effect on politics there.

Such urban–rural movements of people were never just a national phenomenon, but now more than ever borders and, often enough, continents are also crossed. Akínrìnádé (this volume) describes how, even in the colonial era, Yoruba, Ibibio and Ibo communities in Nigeria organized to send students to the UK, Ireland and the USA, which 'made nonsense of the position of the colonial government that there was no real need for the provision of higher education in the country'. While deprivation at home and opportunities abroad are usually the driving factors behind migration, they also contribute to the release of civil societies from the restraints states placed on them (Kaldor 2003; Keck and Sikkink 1998).

States, of course, have not given up trying to control their civil societies, even after migration. Seckinelgin (this volume) cites a Turkish general who suggested that Turkish diaspora groups should set up an umbrella group in order to coordinate policies to defend Turkish national interests. A recent Bangladeshi newspaper article carried a discussion of roles that could be played in the country's development by 'non-resident Bangladeshi non-governmental organizations' (NRBNGOs).

Dreano (this volume) on the other hand provides a picture of the effect of migration on a host city, Paris. He does not take up the familiar, depressing theme of cultural, economic and political conflicts between indigenous and migrant populations. Rather, he shows how the influx of migrants, particularly African, with their own fresh experiences of civil society, has popularized and re-energized the idea of civil society in France, which was traditionally populated by intellectuals with a preference for statist solutions to social problems.

Conclusion

The contributions to the book show that here are multiple interpretations of civil society and that these depend more on political configurations in different parts of the world than on cultural predilections. To return to our opening questions, there is plenty of evidence for the idea that civil society is an idea imposed by Western institutions in many parts of the world (the term 'westoxification' used by conservatives in Iran is an extreme version of this view: Ali Paya, this volume) but there is also plenty of evidence that shows links between civil society and political radicalization. For example, many contributors differentiate the notion of civil society as a ground of political contestation from a different, though often coexisting, depoliticized, neoliberal definition of civil society as simply the realm of 'non-governmental' or 'non-profit' organizations. Indeed Lipschutz (this volume) emphasizes the need for 'bringing politics back in', in his concluding chapter on global civil society.

By moving away from the 'either/or' forms of analysis that characterize much of the international civil society debates we hope to show in this book the need to recognize civil society as a site of struggle, multivocality and paradox. One of the important messages from the multiple voices collected here in this volume is that the power of the concept of civil society depends less on abstract definitions than on the extent to which it is grounded in actual experiences from around the world and embedded in local realities.

The relationship between authoritarian regimes and the rediscovery of civil society has now been commonly accepted. However, the end of most authoritarian regimes did not mean the end of history: civil society continues to respond to new threats from the dominant institutions that are now mostly located at the international level. As Obadare and James both point out, it is precisely in those countries most severely affected by neoliberal interventions that civil society is refocusing its energy on challenging this ideology. The fight against privatization of public services, campaigns to define the provision of medicine as public good, and the agendas of the Social Forums are all manifestations of this new focus of an increasingly global civil society.

At the same time, the boundaries between civil society and state have always been blurred. In Eastern Europe, South Africa and the Philippines, a number of civil society activists and NGO leaders found themselves moving into government positions, after the velvet revolutions, the end of the apartheid regime and the fall of the Marcos dictatorship respectively. More widely, the permeability of these boundaries and the wider embeddedness of civil society actors are increasingly highlighted within recent work (such as Hilhorst 2003; Lewis 2004 forthcoming) and may be a more prominent feature of the institutional landscape in years to come.

References

Banton, M. (1968) 'Voluntary associations: anthropological aspects', *International Encyclopedia of the Social Sciences*, 16: 357–62.

Comaroff, J.L. and Comaroff, J. (eds) (1999) *Civil Society and the Critical Imagination in Africa: Critical Perspectives*, Chicago: University of Chicago Press.

Elias, N. (1994 [1939]) *The Civilizing Process: State Formation and Civilization*, Oxford: Blackwell.

Gellner, N.Y. (1994) *Conditions of Liberty: Civil Society and its Rivals*, London: Hamish Hamilton.

Hilhorst, D. (2003) *The Real World of NGOs: Discourse, Diversity and Development*, London: Zed Books.

Howell, J. and Pearce, J. (2001) *Civil Society and Development: A Critical Exploration*, Boulder CO: Lynne Rienner.

Kaldor, M. (2003) *Global Civil Society: An Answer to War*, Cambridge: Polity Press.

Keane, J. (1996) *Reflections on Violence*, London: Verso.

Keck, M.E. and Sikkink, K. (1998) *Activists beyond Borders: Advocacy Networks in International Politics*, Ithaca: Cornell University Press.

Lewis, D. (2002) 'Civil society in African contexts: reflections on the "usefulness" of a concept', *Development and Change*, 33(4): 569–86.

——(2004 forthcoming) 'Reflections on accountability issues in a Bangladesh NGO: bringing in society, culture and politics', in E. Weisband and A. Ebrahim (eds), *Global Accountability and Moral Community*, Cambridge: Cambridge University Press.

Little, K. (1965) *West African Urbanization: A Study of Voluntary Associations in Cultural Change*, Cambridge: Cambridge University Press.

Mamdani, M. (1996) *Citizen and Subject: Contemporary Africa and the Legacy of Late Colonialism*, Princeton: Princeton University Press.

Seckinelgin, H. (2002) 'Civil society as a metaphor for Western liberalism', *Global Society*, 16(4): 357–76.

Shaw, M. (2003) 'The global transformation of the social sciences', in M. Kaldor, H. Anheier and M. Glasius (eds), *Global Civil Society 2003*, Oxford: Oxford University Press.

Part II

Setting out the argument

2 Putting civil society in its place

Bhikhu Parekh

There is today an almost universal consensus that civil society is a vital component of a good society, and that the stronger and more developed it is, the better governed and more stable the wider political community is likely to be. This belief underlies the widely held view that Western societies are vibrant, free and democratic because they have, and the erstwhile communist societies came to grief because they did not have, a civil society, and that if the developing world is to avoid the fate of the latter, it should foster civil society. Large and well-meaning Western foundations devote huge resources to helping the developing world do just this, and Western governments and international institutions make it a precondition of their aid. The fact that the consensus has acquired the status of an intellectual orthodoxy is a good enough reason to subject it to a critical scrutiny. The further fact that it has profound consequences for the lives of large parts of humankind, and that similar recent orthodoxies such as the Structural Adjustment Programme of the International Monetary Fund (IMF) have turned out to be deeply problematic, reinforces the need for scrutiny. In this chapter I do two things. I briefly outline the historical discourse on civil society and tease out its central features. I then analyse its explanatory and normative strengths and weaknesses, and suggest its proper place in a well-ordered political community.

What is civil society?

Although the concept of civil society (*societas civilis*) goes back to the Romans, who contrasted it with the 'natural society' of animals and used it to refer to the rational and law-governed society of humans, the concept did not become dominant until the seventeenth century (see, for example, Cahoone 2002; Ehrenberg 1999; Keene 1998). Hobbes was one of the first to articulate it with great clarity, followed by such other writers as Locke, Grotius, Puffendorf and Montesquieu. For them human beings were by nature free and equal and endowed with the capacities for rationality and self-determination. They could not flourish in the unregulated state of nature and needed a well-ordered society that ensured them maximum freedom to pursue their self-chosen purposes. Such a society had a public or civil authority entitled to take and enforce collectively binding decisions. The authority was derived from the consent of its members, did no more than protect the basic rights of its members, and governed according to general laws. Its subjects were free to lead such lives, pursue such purpose, and enter into such relations as they thought proper within the limits set by the laws. Hobbes, Locke and others called this 'civil society'.

Civil society referred to a group of individuals held together, and forming a single society, by virtue of subscribing to a consensually based public authority and sharing in common the practice of civility. Civil society was a human artefact, created, sustained and capable of being changed by human beings. It was not an organic expression of human sociability as Cicero and Aquinas argued, nor a teleological requirement of human nature as Aristotle maintained. It was a rational and artificial institution, growing, no doubt, out of the natural desire to live but in no way dictated or sustained by it. It called for its own distinct institutions and practices, as well as virtues and motives that it sought to cultivate in its members by educational and other means. Civil society was not separate from the state nor one of its institutions; rather it was a way, and for Hobbes, Locke and others the only proper way, of constituting the state.

Writers of the Scottish Enlightenment, who were particularly influential in popularizing the concept of civil society, shared their predecessors' view of it. Although they added minor novel touches, they did not radically depart from it. In their view human beings were inherently social, and the concept of the state of nature made neither logical nor historical sense. They contrasted civil society with 'savage', 'primitive', 'rude' or 'militaristic' society, and equated it with civilized society (Ferguson 1767). Civilized society was distinguished by increased wants, division of labour, growth of the arts and sciences, self-restraint, moderation, rationality, liberty, gentle and refined manners, and respect for the law, all of which were believed to be enabled by and closely tied up with the development of commerce. A civilized society was above all a commercial society, and was constituted as a civil society based on a civil authority governing by means of laws and maintaining the basic rights of its citizens. Only a civil society was believed to create the framework necessary for the development of a civilized and commercial society. Non-European societies had remained backward because they lacked such a civil society, and had no hope of turning the corner without developing one with or without European help.

Hegel marked an important stage in the discourse on civil society. He too shared the earlier view of civil society, and his originality consisted in giving it a new orientation and probing its philosophical foundations. For him, as for his predecessors, civil society or *bürgerliche Gesellschaft* referred to a legally constituted association of free and equal individuals pursuing their self-chosen goals. It was characterized by subjective freedom, personal autonomy, individual rights, mutual respect and recognition, satisfaction of needs, a system of exchange, rational legal norms, abstract morality, and a minimum structure of public authority. Unlike his predecessors, Hegel argued that civil society was inherently unstable. It threw up acute contrasts of wealth and poverty, created a rootless and discontented 'rabble', and was ridden with tensions and conflicts that it could not itself regulate. It also lacked collective self-consciousness, capacity for collective self-reflection, and a sense of moral direction. For these and related reasons, civil society was incomplete, pointed beyond itself, and required the institution of the state. While nurturing civil society, the state also regulated it, gave its atomized members a sense of community, and provided a higher and fully rational level of social existence. For Hegel, the state could never be constituted as civil society as the earlier writers had maintained. It included civil society as its necessary moment, but transcended it and provided it with a rationally and morally necessary wider framework (Taylor 1975). While most earlier writers had equated civil and political society and used the two terms interchangeably, Hegel drew a fairly sharp distinction between them.

For Hegel, civil society occupied a space between the family and the state. The former was based on love, unselfish concern for its members, overlapping selves, and so on, and represented an organic unity of reason and nature. Civil society was the realm of differentiation, in which free, independent, and otherwise unrelated individuals pursued their self-interest in a spirit of mutual respect and within the limits of the laws. The state embodied individuals' dialectical unity, and represented objective rationality, rationally regulated sentiments of love and disinterested concern for the whole, pursuit of collective well-being, and a non-instrumental view of public authority.

Karl Marx represented another stage in the developing discourse on civil society. He too shared the earlier view of it, but differed from his predecessors in his analysis of the nature and dynamics of civil society and its relation to the state. As he put it, 'material conditions of life are summed up by Hegel after the fashion of the English and the French of the eighteenth century under the name "civil society"'. For Marx civil society referred to the 'whole communal and industrial life of a given stage', 'all the material relations of production possible within a definite stage of the development of productive forces' (Marx and Engels 1973: 362–3). Although Marx sometimes suggested that civil society existed in all historical epochs, his considered view was that it was unique to the modern bourgeois society, especially in respect to the autonomy and the freedom from moral and communal constraints that it had currently acquired. For Marx as for the earlier writers, civil society was characterized by individualism, rights, pursuit of self-interest, satisfaction of needs, liberty and equality.

Following Hegel but far more so than him, Marx saw civil society as the realm of conflict, indeed a state of war between organized classes. Being inherently unstable, it needed the state to sustain the prevailing economic order. Unlike Hegel, Marx argued that the liberty, equality and so on that lay at the heart of civil society were deeply distorted and rendered vacuous by the class structure of the capitalist society. Workers had no choice but to alienate their labour, and were not really free. Lacking the necessary opportunity and resources, their rights too remained largely formal and empty. This was just as true of equality and individual choice. Unlike Hegel, Marx argued that the state did not and could not transcend civil society. Being the product of and inextricably tied to the class conflict inherent in civil society, it lacked the capacity to act autonomously. The universality that it claimed to represent was nothing but the particular interest of the dominant class masquerading as that of the society as a whole.

For Marx civil society was not a moment of the state as it was for Hegel, but its basis. Once the classes were abolished and the civil society was radically reconstituted, the state forfeited its rationale. People would reclaim the power they had hitherto alienated to the socially transcendental state, and govern their collective affairs democratically. Civil society would be replaced by a planned economy based on the principle of 'from each according to his ability and to each according to his need'. Marx called such a society 'communist'. It represented the dialectical unity of civil society and the state. It was not collectivist, as it became in the hands of the Soviet communist regime, for example, and was more like a socialist version of Locke's civil society. Individuals were its basic units, but they were socially conscious and motivated, not egotistical and self-interested. They enjoyed maximum freedom, but used it to expand their human powers and enrich their being rather than to accumulate wealth or increase consumption. While the concept of civil society dominated Marx's early writings, it virtually disappeared from the later ones, where Marx preferred to talk of 'material relations', 'relations of production', the 'economic' 'structure of society' and so on in contexts where he would earlier have used the term 'civil society'.

Within the Marxist tradition, the term 'civil society' played a limited role until Gramsci reintroduced it and made it one of the central categories of his thought. Since he drew heavily not only on Marx but also on Hegel, Croce and other Italian idealists, his usage was both inconsistent and richly suggestive. For Gramsci, 'it is not the economic structure which directly determines the political action, but the interpretation of it', or what Marx had called ideology. He therefore shifted the focus of attention from the material relations of society to the 'cultural and spiritual' agencies that shaped the consciousness of its members, and called them civil society. In this broad sense, civil society was not peculiar to the bourgeois society, and existed in the middle ages, where the 'church was civil society' (Gramsci 1971: 170). Civil society referred not to the economy but to the realm of free associational activity, and included the family, universities, the press, trade unions, cultural institutions, working men's clubs and publishing houses. Unlike the state or the political society, which exercised 'direct domination', or coercion over society, the dominant class used the institutions of civil society to mobilize popular consent in favour of the prevailing economic order and to establish 'cultural and spiritual supremacy' or 'hegemony' (Gramsci 1971: 12, 53, 125). Working classes and their organic intellectuals needed to contest this by carrying on the class struggle not only at the economic level but also in the civil society.

Gramsci's vision of the classless communist society was very similar to Marx's. People would reclaim the power they had hitherto abdicated to the state, and all social institutions including the family, the schools, the universities and the state would be run democratically. 'Coercive elements of the state would wither away by degrees', and individuals, now liberated from all unnecessary constraints and inequalities, would enjoy maximum freedom (Gramsci 1971: 263). Such free, equal and socially conscious individuals would spontaneously carry out the laws they had given themselves, and the external discipline of the law would be replaced by the internal pressure of morality. Since people would readily appreciate the legitimacy of the prevailing economic and political order, their consent to it would be genuine and spontaneous, and would not need to be manufactured. Gramsci called such a society an 'ethical state' or 'civil society' (1971: 263). Unlike the capitalist society in which the institutions of civil society were manipulated to generate consent for a hegemonic social order, the communist society represented the 'reabsorption of political society into civil society', and symbolized the full flowering of the latter with free and equal individuals autonomously forming their views (Gramsci 1971: 253).

In recent years the term 'civil society' has experienced a revival and found favour among people of different ideological persuasions. The current usage draws heavily not only on the European discourse but also on the American, especially the Tocquevillian, account of the vital role of voluntary associations in American life. For Tocqueville, American democracy was dominated by the idea of equality, which had its great virtues but also the tendency to isolate and atomize individuals. The only way to hold such a society together and forge bonds of solidarity was to create an extensive network of voluntary associations. Drawing on this tradition of thought, Robert Putnam (2000) has in his influential writings stressed the value of a thick associational life in building up trust, social capital and solidarity.

Michael Walzer (1994) blends the two and captures the current usage well when he says that 'the words "civil society" name the sphere of uncoerced human association and also the set of relational networks formed for the sake of family, faith, interest and ideology that fill this space'. As an area of uncoerced associative life, civil society includes such associations as the family, trade unions, universities, the press, professional bodies, churches, non-governmental organizations (NGOs) and social movements. It excludes the state, which is seen as an inherently and exclusively coercive institution. Political parties are also excluded, largely because, although voluntary, their purpose is to capture the state and use its coercive resources to realize their objectives.

In the light of our brief historical sketch, the discourse on civil society displays a remarkable consistency. It refers to what I might call the area of associative freedom, that is to the freedom of individuals to enter into relations with others, pursue common purposes, and form intrinsically or instrumentally valuable associations. It refers not to freedom *per se*, nor to how individuals lead their personal lives, but to the active exercise of freedom in forming networks of social relations. The concern with associative freedom arises out of the belief that as free, equal, rational and self-determining individuals, human beings desire to, and should be able to, form such social relations as they please. Since coercion violates their dignity and rational nature, it is inherently undesirable, and should ideally be avoided. However, since human beings sometimes fail to act rationally, some more than others, coercion becomes necessary. However it should be minimized, placed in the care of a legitimate public authority, and exercised according to clearly stated and rationally defensible laws. The basic idea behind civil society is to minimize all avoidable forms of coercion and to maximize the area of associative freedom.

Since different societies have different histories, the idea of civil society plays a different part and acquires a different degree of urgency in their political discourse. In the erstwhile communist countries, the state was an overpowering presence in society and stifled all areas of life. Not surprisingly, when communism collapsed, the demand for the long-suppressed associative freedom dominated popular consciousness and the concept of civil society became the central category of political discourse, especially among creative writers, trade unionists and political activists, who had suffered the most from its absence. Asian and African experiences were different. Despite its brutality, the colonial state there was not unduly oppressive, and left considerable space for associative freedom. At independence the idea of civil society did not therefore dominate their political discourse. Their primary concern was how to organize and structure their political life so that the state pursued developmental goals and remained accountable to its people. Insofar as they thought of civil society, they looked to the state to nurture it and, where necessary, to create its preconditions.

Since different societies hold different conceptions of human life, they take different views on the role of coercion in social life and what areas should or should not be subjected to it. In deeply religious societies, the economic life is regulated by moral and religious norms enforced by religious organizations and social pressure. It does not enjoy the autonomy that it does in the modern bourgeois society, and is not generally seen as part of civil society. Again, in different societies different social institutions limit associative freedom. In some it is tribes, in some others castes, in yet others religion. In each case the struggle to create a civil society involves different targets and strategies, and the resulting structure of civil society has a different character. We should not therefore make the mistake of thinking that civil society must have the same shape and form the world over, or that an institution that forms part of civil society in one country must also form part of it in another. Rather than universalize the Western history and model of civil society and expect all others to conform to it, we need to take different views of it and appreciate its diverse forms. It is odd, even self-contradictory, to take a monistic view of the very area of life that is supposed to be the home of plurality.

Critical assessment

Civil society has much to be said for it, and the associative freedom that forms its constitutive principle is an essential part of a well-organized society. Freedom, including associative freedom, is an emblem of human dignity and sense of self-worth. By freely associating with others in pursuit of personal and common purposes, human beings also express and cultivate their sociability, discover themselves, develop civic virtues, and grow to their full stature. Economic, professional, neighbourhood, civic and other associations arrest the atomization and feeling of helplessness inherent in modern industrialized society, generate multiple centres of power, cultivate moral and social discipline, provide formal and informal spaces in which to interact with others and rise above one's subjectivity, and foster social cohesion. They also provide a vitally necessary counterweight to the state and limit its power. All states have a tendency to become remote and arrogant, and need to be checked by citizens' movements and NGOs. Furthermore, power accrues to the state through its functions. As citizens assign more and more functions to it out of inertia, apathy or indolence, it acquires more and more power and legitimacy. It cannot be controlled merely by means of an internal system of checks and balances, because that only regulates its *exercise* of power and does not *decrease* the amount of power and moral status it enjoys. We need to limit its range of functions by fostering the spirit of self-help among its citizens and encouraging them to undertake as many of them as possible through voluntary associations. A vibrant civil society ensures that citizens accept the responsibility for their shared life, and do not alienate their power to and help create an overbearing state.

While these and other virtues of a vibrant civil society are obvious, much of the discourse on it exaggerates its importance and gets it out of perspective. The discourse has a built-in bias against non-voluntary associations. As we saw, it is based on the deeply held belief that as free and self-determining agents human beings should not be subject to the authority of associations they have not themselves created and which they cannot leave at will. Associations based on traditional allegiances, ties of blood, inherited loyalties or the 'accident' of birth – such as castes, clans, tribes, and ethnic and religious communities – are viewed with disfavour. They are to be discouraged, even dismantled, in order that their members can be fully free, and civil society can emerge in its purest and uncompromised form. Where they are not dismantled, for prudential reasons, their presence is regretted, and their members are seen as unfree, truncated and even inadequate human beings.

This bias against non-voluntary associations is unjustified. They do have their obvious drawbacks. They sometimes have rigid norms, oppressive practices and structures of authority, limited mutual contacts, and encourage frozen social identities and narrow loyalties. However, they also have their strengths. They are often historical communities with deep bonds based on shared collective memories of struggles, achievements and failures. They encourage a strong sense of social obligation, mutual commitment, and spirit of self-sacrifice. They provide a readily available network of support and represent a valuable resource for their members and an asset to the wider society. Since they are not deliberately created and cannot be dissolved or left with ease, they have tenacity, are free of volatile individual impulses, tend to strike deep roots in the lives of their members, and evoke strong attachments and loyalties. They are narrow but deep, demand much but also offer much, and make up for some loss of liberty by offering a sense of existential security and rootedness. They can certainly corrupt public life by encouraging nepotism and narrow partiality, but voluntary associations are not free from these vices either. While ensuring that they do not become oppressive and deny exit to dissenting members, we should value the contribution they make to the good life. Not all voluntary associations are inherently good, nor all non-voluntary ones inherently bad.

While voluntary associations form civil society, non-voluntary associations form community. In civil society we meet as strangers, colleagues, neighbours, fellow professionals, fellow trade unionists, and citizens; in a community as friends, kin, fellow ethnics, Jews, Catholics, tribespeople, and speakers of a common language. Civil society is based on reciprocity, distance, respect for rules, loyalty to institutions, and so on; community on intimacy, affection, warmth and mutual concern. Civil society nurtures associative life, community communal life. In civil society we share common interests and hobbies and 'bowl' together, to use an evocative image of Robert Putnam's (Putnam 2000). In a community, we celebrate common festivals, grieve together, holiday together, or spend Christmas together. 'Bowling alone' represents the decline of civil society; grieving or spending Christmas alone that of community.

In many Western societies, traditional communities have largely disappeared, and almost all social relations including the family are cast in the mould of civil society. This has brought both gains and losses. While individualism, the adventure of self-creation and civil society have flourished, communities have declined. The voluntarist spirit that drives civil society has a tendency to encourage expectations, attitudes and values that militate against the inherited loyalties and acceptance of non-contractual obligations and traditional bonds that lie at the heart of communal life. In many non-Western societies the opposite is the case. Communities of different kinds remain strong, but civil society is weak. While they need to foster civil society, there is no obvious reason why they must be expected to declare a war on communities. They can create a space for civil society by loosening up and restructuring rather than destroying these communities, as Indians are doing with castes, African societies with clans and tribes, and Muslim societies with their religious institutions. The Western model of civil society is culturally and historically specific and has its obvious limitations. It should not be held up as a universal norm and used to mould the rest of the world in the Western image, as is currently done by many enthusiastic governmental and non-governmental champions of civil society.

The second limitation of the discourse on civil society has to do with its failure to give an adequate account of the nature and role of the state. This is so because it considers coercion inherently evil, identifies the state with it and civil society with its absence, and aims to maximize the role of civil society at the expense of that of the state. The distinction between the coercive state and the non-coercive civil society is too crude and sharp to do justice to either. The state certainly uses coercion, but it also does much more. It plays symbolic, inspirational, educative, facilitative and coordinating roles. It symbolizes the unity of society, fosters social cohesion, and gives society a sense of historical continuity and depth. It enshrines certain norms and values in its institutions and practices, and embodies a particular vision of the good life. It nurtures formal equality and encourages the ideas of fair trial and procedural justice in a society that might be wholly innocent of them. It can use its coercive power to challenge vested interests, remove unacceptable inequalities, fight pockets of coercion in different areas of social life, and increase the freedom and opportunities of its citizens.

Just as the state is not exclusively coercive, civil society is not wholly non-coercive. It does, of course, ensure associative freedom, this being true by definition, but the freedom is not and cannot be without constraints. All associations affect public order and public interest, and the state cannot be indifferent to their structures and practices. It may rightly ban associations that incite religious, ethnic or racial hatred, and require that they should not discriminate against blacks, untouchables, gays or women, or impose unacceptable cost on their dissenting or departing members. Civil society does not precede or exist outside or behind the back of the state. Instead it is made possible by the state, which both permits and protects associative freedom, and exists as a moment, a space, within it.

Although associative freedom is most valuable, or rather precisely because it is so valuable, we must avoid the mistake of dissociating it from its wider context. As Marx highlighted, the formally equal civil, political and other rights are unequally enjoyed in an unequal society and even used to legitimize and perpetuate it. This is just as true of associative freedom. Although it is in principle equally available to all in a well-ordered society, in practice its exercise is highly uneven. The poor and the marginalized are often too atomized and overwhelmed by a sense of powerlessness to have the confidence to set up vibrant associations. They also often lack the necessary skills and resources, and do not understand the complex mechanisms of the modern society well enough to target its weak spots. It is hardly surprising that civil society in almost all societies is dominated by the middle classes, and even the organizations of the oppressed and marginalized are often set up and led by the middle classes. The powerless find it difficult to organize and, since organization represents power, their failure perpetuates and intensifies their powerlessness.

Associative freedom, further, can be used to legitimize state inaction. Since the state is expected to ensure maximum space to civil society it is required to pursue minimum goals and to intervene as little as possible in economic and social life. This is how Oakeshott, Hayek, Friedman and others justify a libertarian state in the name of civil society. For these and related reasons, we should not make the mistake of idealizing civil society in the abstract. We need to ask how it is constituted, who exercises and benefits from associative freedom, and how we should restructure civil society so that all citizens and groups can exercise it equally. Since the state can play a vital emancipatory role here, we should not allow it to be undermined by an uncritical ideological commitment to the maximum autonomy of civil society.

Voluntary associations, social movements, and so on that comprise civil society lack historical continuity, and are often issue-based and unable to take a long-term and comprehensive view of society. They are not popularly elected and accountable, and sometimes they are authoritarian and remote from their members. Their decision-making procedures are not always transparent, and their decisions open to public scrutiny. It is wrong to assume that just because an association is voluntary, it is democratic or speaks for all its members, or that a protest movement against the policies of the state necessarily serves public interest or even that of those in whose name it claims to speak. We should not homogenize the civil society, which encompasses a wide variety of networks, interests and associations not all of which are equally welcome. And nor should we take the naïve view that all coercion is inherently undesirable. Coercion tends to spring up subtly and stealthily in so many different areas of life and forms of social relations that the coercion of the state often becomes necessary to monitor and deal with it.

The civil society and the state are based on different principles and play a complementary role. Neither can replace nor should be privileged over the other. A varied and vibrant civil society gives the state moral depth and political vitality, even as a justly constituted state creates the conditions in which all its citizens can build a rich world of networks and associations. Rather than set up an abstract opposition between the two, a well-considered political theory should establish a partnership between them on terms that are relevant to our times. Locke's and Adam Smith's reduction of the state to civil society disables it from dealing with corporate capitalism and grave social and economic injustices. Hegel saw the importance of both the civil society and the state better than any other writer, but made the mistake of romanticizing the state, overestimating its independence, and underestimating the tensions of civil society. Marx and Gramsci avoided his mistakes, but naïvely thought that once the classes were abolished the state could be dissolved into a loosely coordinated structure of the voluntary associations of socialized individuals. Many contemporary writers, including Walzer, idealize civil society without fully appreciating how deeply it is implicated with the economy and the state. Cohen and Arato's (1992) work provides a stimulating account of how the discourses on civil society and democracy should be integrated. While drawing on the rich insights of the tradition of discourse on civil society from Hobbes to Walzer, we also need to correct and go beyond them.

References

Cahoone, L. (2002) *Civil Society: The Conservative Meaning of Liberal Policies*, Oxford: Blackwell.

Cohen, J. and Arato, A. (1992) *Civil Society and Political Theory*, Cambridge MA: MIT Press.

Ehrenberg, J. (1999) *Civil Society: The Critical History of an Idea*, New York: New York University Press.

Ferguson, A. (1767) *An Essay on the History of Civil Society*, Cambridge: Cambridge University Press.

Gramsci, A. (1971) *Selections from Prison Notebooks*, edited and translated by Q. Hoare and G. Nowell Smith, London: Lawrence and Wishart.

Keene, J. (1998) *Civil Society: Old Images, New Visions*, Stanford: Stanford University Press.

Marx, K. and Engels, F. (1973) *Selected Works*, vol. 1, Moscow: Progress Publishers.

Putnam, R. (2000) *Bowling Alone: The Collapse and Revival of American Community*, New York: Simon and Schuster.

Taylor, C. (1975) *Hegel*, Cambridge: Cambridge University Press.

Walzer, M. (ed.) (1994) *Toward A Global Civil Society*, Providence RI: Berghahn Books.

3 The problem with civil society

Putting modern European history back into contemporary debate

Frank Trentmann

The revival of 'civil society' since the 1980s has been intimately linked to questions of democratic renewal. From communitarians rediscovering the 'social capital' provided by local associations (Putnam 1995) to radical pluralists championing associative democracy (Cohen and Rogers 1995), from critical theorists highlighting processes of deliberative reason (Cohen and Arato 1992; Habermas 1992) to advocates of cosmopolitan democracy (Held 1995), civil society has served as a bridgehead of democratic reform. Civil society has transmuted from a social theory into a political theory. The line of inquiry has been from the social to the political: what political outcomes do social norms and processes produce? In this sense, the revival of civil society as a ubiquitous category of current debate is strictly less a renaissance than a mutation, a reworking of its diverse social, cultural and political meanings in European history (Kaviraj and Khilnani 2001; Keane 1999; Trentmann 2000).

This chapter will reinsert a critical historical perspective into the contemporary infatuation with civil society. European history has served commentators more to legitimate current ambitions than as a terrain to study the workings and dilemmas of civil society in the past. This essay redresses this teleological orientation and its broadly secular, liberal–democratic reading. Instead, it will draw attention to three neglected or misunderstood aspects of civil society in the European past: the centrality of religion and toleration, the tension between association and democracy, and the virtual disappearance of the concept prior to the rise of totalitarian projects. A more critical, historical use of civil society may help clarify the expectations placed on it today and lead to a more balanced, pluralistic assessment of its global future.

Three connected problems plague recent celebrations of civil society: the selective appropriation of canonical authors, the gulf between interest in these authors and relative indifference to the broader cultural and sociopolitical workings of civil society, and the positing of a European tradition that either is or is not felt to be applicable to other settings. Of course, writers invoking civil society today position themselves next to different canonical authors and produce different intellectual family trees. Nonetheless, most writing is informed by a strikingly similar narrative, which can be crudely summarized as follows. The modern idea of civil society begins with a fusion of civil society and political society (Locke). The Scottish Enlightenment reveals it as commercial society (Smith). Kant identifies the properties of public reason. A generation later Hegel 'modernizes' the theory of civil society by bringing it into line with the realities of industrial society, separating civil society from state and family. Tocqueville reveals the democratic habits formed in local associations. Marx impoverishes the concept by reducing it to a sphere of bourgeois private interest. The rise of totalitarian ideologies virtually extinguishes the oxygen needed by civil society, although a few candles remain burning amongst Anglo-Saxon pluralists and Gramscian socialists.

There are several problematic assumptions here. This is a secular, broadly liberal narrative highlighting the expansion of elements of reason, self, and liberal government supposedly distinctive to modern Europe. Canonical authors are used as evidence of an unfolding civil society in Europe – inversely, their absence elsewhere has been used to debate its viability on non-European soil. Canonical texts appear ambiguously as both normative and descriptive sources. Few would claim that Locke's account of the transition from natural society to civil society described a historical process, yet Smith's or Hegel's writings are often viewed as grand accounts of real societal changes, as if they were recording the evolution of European civil society. Of course, Smith and Hegel were aware of social changes around them. Nonetheless, their texts were normative, projecting a dream of civil society into the future – Smith was discounting facts that, to him, were part of an unnatural state of affairs caused by interference with markets, while Hegel invoked corporations (institutions of declining significance) as crucial sources of *Sittlichkeit* (ethicality) in civil society (Poovey 1998: 246–7; Stedman Jones 2001).

The point here is not that philosophers should become historians, but that it is not advisable to use canonical authors as shortcuts to the nature of European civil society as a whole. What if there were no fit between the mentality, behaviour and institutions of social groups and the ideals of canonical authors? What if readers then read these texts differently from theorists now, or read other texts altogether?

God and civil society in Europe: diversity within a Christian framework

The following discussion will move from civil society as theory to civil society as an idea in action. Let us begin with a critical repositioning of some canonical texts, then ask about more popular uses and, finally, place the evolution of the idea next to the evolution of the institutions of civil society.

In the century and a half before the French Revolution (1789), the principal political use of the idea of civil society was in the battle against centralizing regimes, not for democracy. Montesquieu, Burke and others hoped civil society would preserve mixed regimes against the despotism of either absolute monarchy or democracy. Balance and diversity, with spaces for traditional elites (such as aristocratically constituted parliaments) was their ideal. Republicanism provided a second tradition. Ferguson's *Essay on the History of Civil Society* (1995 [1767]) was a paean to a masculine, martial culture of propertied citizens. Citizenship here rested on civic and military service for the well-being of the community, not on rights, suffrage or representation. And republican civil society required international rivalry – the reverse of the pacific tendencies sometimes associated with democratic civil societies today. Interestingly, continental Europeans had no problem with reading Ferguson in a frame of analysis even further removed from liberal associations: to Germans, *Staatsbürger* read 'subject' not active republican citizen (Oz-Salzberger 1995). Although by the late eighteenth century some writers, such as Paine, pushed civil society in a democratic direction, it is unwise to see this as the inevitable flowering of some liberal democratic shoot of the idea. After all, Hegel – so easily invoked as the modernizer of civil society – reserved constitutional spaces for professional corporations: closed and compulsory bodies.

The anticentralizing thrust of civil society was partly a response to the feared consolidation of monarchical power in the seventeenth century, but it was also framed by a Protestant vision of divine order. The two enemies of civil society, in this vision, were fanaticism and atheism. Both threatened to erase the space between the Earthly City and the City of God, the first by rejecting the legitimacy of institutions in civil society, the second by denying that civil society was divinely inspired. As the Reformation unleashed heretical movements, the binary opposition of civil society versus fanaticism hardened. The Aristotelian idea of civil society became fused with a Christian defence. Luther and Melanchthon supported the brutal attack on Anabaptists and rebelling peasants, seeing them as dangerous fanatics who wanted to break down the difference between civil society and the City of God. These arguments gave renewed legitimacy to civil society as an autonomous sphere based on natural law with its own institutions. This autonomy remained decidedly relative, however: civil society was divinely ordained and its integral function was to strengthen Christianity (Colas 1997).

The conceptual autonomy of civil society and the emphasis on its contractual nature as political society *vis-à-vis* the state of nature was being worked out by anchoring it firmly in a Christian framework, not by casting it off from its religious mooring. Locke's contribution was indicative of a broader mental current feeding into civil society in modern Europe. As Dunn (2001) has emphasized, the state of nature was the conceptual foundation for Locke's argument for civil society. Practical reason and Christian belief were inseparable – hence the fear of atheism which threatened to dissolve the functioning of practical reason, which, for Locke, included a fear of the avenging God and human obedience to His Law that was the Law of Nature. Now, it might be argued today that these were just Locke's personal beliefs and that it is possible to extract a secular theory from his writings. This is a historical misreading. The theocentric vision was woven into the fabric of Locke's civil society – it was not an add-on. Significantly, in his argument for the right of resistance, he presented the people making an 'Appeal to Heaven'.

The religious nature of arguments for civil society becomes even clearer when we shift our focus from canonical texts to common uses of the idea. In contrast to the modern genealogy of right, reason and toleration, Burke's influential *Reflections on the Revolution in France* (1987 [1790]) offered a widespread Whiggish version of civil society as the product of convention and balance, hierarchical order and religious establishment: 'religion is the basis of civil society and the source of all good and of all comfort' (p. 79). The state's legitimacy rested on its connection with the Church of England. Liberty depended on the religious cement between state and civil society. 'All persons possessing any portion of power', Burke emphasized, 'ought to be strongly and awfully impressed with an idea that they act in trust, and that they are to account for their conduct in that trust to the one great Master, Author, and Founder of society' (p. 81). This Whig view of civil society, with its accompanying fear of journalists and public opinion, is miles apart from the more sanitized Habermasian version of Kantian deliberative reason. Moreover, the Burkean strand was far more popular at this stage than that of his radical opponents (Clark 1985; Colley 1992).

The link between religion and civil society is, indeed, by far the most prominent theme of publications in English in the eighteenth and early nineteenth centuries, judging by the English Short Title Catalogue and the Bodleian index. A typical text would be *Civil Society and Government Vindicated from the Charge of Being Founded on, and Preserved by, Dishonest Arts*, a sermon preached at London's Guildhall by Robert Burrow (1723), chaplain to the lord mayor. Burrow argued against Mandeville's *Fable of the Bees* with its idea that the evolution of society and public interest proceeded from vice and self-interest. Instead, Burrow insisted, humans had turned to civil society for reasons of mutual love and social solidarity. Religion played an integral role in this evolution, for God was righteous and beneficent and taught men the necessary knowledge of Himself and His perfections, and this enabled humans to distinguish between good and evil. Civil society, unlike barbaric communities, was founded on mutual obligations between its members, including the magistrate. Civil society avoided anarchy and evil, but only through the divinely inspired ability to know about sin and virtue. Trust, a phenomenon figuring prominently in debates about civil society at the time, was essentially Christian. Throughout the eighteenth century, the discursive opposition of civil society with barbarism was employed to document how the former had advanced together with Christianity. Religion (not nature or reason) provided the respect for others necessary for civil society's harmonious functioning: if man stopped walking with fear of his Creator, he would simply betray his family and community (Douglas 1792).

Anglican texts such as these might not match the brilliance of certain enlightenment ideas. They did not need to. Popular demand and establishment backing ensured their dominance. It has been noted that Ferguson's *Essay* was one of the few titles to employ the term civil society. What has been ignored is the next series of texts which did so, the wave of loyalist writings in the 1790s sparked by fears of revolution. Take for instance Rev. Thomas Clarke's sermon on *The Benefits of Christianity Contrasted with the Pernicious Influence of Modern Philosophy upon Civil Society* (1796): from creation to the present, history proved 'that the civil and religious existence of Nations is inseparable, that the stroke which shocks the one pervades the other: sap Religion and you sap the State'. Likewise civil society depended on obedience to a sovereign ruler, without whom there would be 'Wars perpetual, dissentions eternal, robbery universal' (p. 14). In the 1790s, the renewed frequency of civil society as an argument against despotism and social anarchy was moulded by Christian loyalism into an argument against revolution and democracy. Civilization, trust and peaceful social relations required an order only monarchy and monopoly religious establishment could provide. Civil society here required fear (of God) and obedience (to King), not reason and rights. Far from being separated, Anglican loyalism kept alive a view of civil society as political and religious society.

Civil society, in short, was divinely bounded. And this boundedness imposed clear limits on toleration. The overwhelmingly Christian substance of civil society arguments in eighteenth-century Britain might be brushed aside as a deviation from a European trend. Yet, unless we wish to move towards an essentialist interpretation of civil society (of which current theorists are rightly cautious), we need to take diversity seriously. Most Britons had a religious understanding of civil society. Whether this understanding would pass the test of current theorists is irrelevant, since they held these views about civil society in their world, not in ours. If we wish to know what civil society in modern Europe was like, a good place to start is to ask what people meant by the term.

Much has been made of the learning experience of early modern Europeans in the transition from civil violence to a state of living with difference (Rawls 1993). Already in the sixteenth and seventeenth centuries, 'civility' began to spread as a new language and code of social behaviour encouraging self-fashioning and restraint, politeness and sociability (Burke *et al.* 2000). In the eighteenth century, after bloody civil wars and revolution, there was an expanding atmosphere of toleration that allowed Anglicans and Dissenters to live peacefully next to each other and argue in clubs and societies. Nonetheless, this was a tendency, not a comprehensive state of affairs: many contemporaries were left outside its virtuous circle. That circle drew a sharp line between Protestant civil society and its enemies. Civil society was also supporting Empire and slavery. Civility was part of an Anglicizing imperialism that attacked 'barbarous' Celtic and native Indian communities. Catholicism (associated with despotism) remained suspect, as William Wake, rector of St James's Westminster, made clear when discussing the destructive effects of popery on civil society (1700). Dissenters, Catholics and Jews continued to be excluded from the polity and from many professions until the mid-nineteenth century. Like the sun on a typical English day, toleration only pierced the atmosphere in parts of the British Isles, leaving plenty of room for sectarian conflict and violence, especially in Ireland.

This has consequences for the ideal-typical contrast in current writing between man in modern European civil society and man elsewhere. Gellner's image of 'modular man' (1994) as the prerequisite of civil society is here as misleading as it is brilliant – when civil society expanded in modern Britain, there were clear limits to the mixture of individualism and egalitarianism, to the fluidity that made modularity.

Civil society in nineteenth-century Europe: associational expansion, declining theory

What happened to the concept of civil society in the century after the French Revolution? Attention has focused on the reworking of *bürgerliche Gesellschaft* by Hegel and Marx. Underneath continued references to *bürgerliche Gesellschaft*, a conceptual shift occurred from earlier traditions to that of a class-based, capitalist society (Riedel 1972: 779ff.). Paradoxically, in Victorian Britain and the United States – societies seen today as illustrations of the linkage between democracy and associations – the concept of civil society fell into disuse at the very time when clubs and associations reached their popular peak. By 1830 one-quarter of male British workers were members of a friendly society, by 1880 three-quarters (Morris 1990). Associational life structured more and more of urban and rural life, from philanthropy to leisure. By the second half of the nineteenth century, however, reference to 'civil society' had become rare. Pulszky's *Theory of Law and Civil Society* (1887) is exceptional, as are the handful of references to Christianity and civil society (Smith Harris 1883).

It is possible to argue that popular radicals and pluralists kept exploring questions of civil society without using the term (Hirst 1994; Trentmann 2001). Nonetheless, for a cultural and intellectual history it is significant that the concept had virtually become extinct in English by the mid-nineteenth century. The decline of civil society preceded totalitarianism, rather than being caused by it.

This paradox relativizes further the connection between civil society and liberal democracy. Britain's transition to democracy (1832–1928) did not require a concept of civil society. France democratized long before granting the freedom of association (1901). Nor did associations reflect on their own practices by invoking 'civil society'. We should be careful before viewing the historical absence of the idea in non-European cultures as an inherent obstacle to democratic pluralism.

The recent revival of civil society (casting fascism and socialism as enemies) has distracted from the larger question of how a concept valued for its non-ideological qualities coped with ideologies in the nineteenth century – including liberalism. Arguably, the idea of civil society was undermined by liberalism as well as later by socialism, nationalism and fascism. Posing questions of representation, rights and national sovereignty was an active programme to democratize the state, which contrasted with the civil society strategy to prevent despotism and anarchy. Popular liberals rallying for democratic reform used the organic language of 'the people', not 'civil society'.

Therefore, it is misleading to see liberalism as taking over the ground previously occupied by civil society and expanding it. The civil society argument had been strongest when raised as an antidote to religious and political projects of uniformity or unaccountable central power. In Britain, once the threat of despotic rule and internal anarchy receded, and politics moved towards democratic reform, 'civil society' had much less to offer. Worse, in Italy and Germany, where anxieties of 'mass politics' were greater, many liberals saw the spread of popular associations and public communication as dangerous sources of societal fragmentation. For those liberals, the nation-state offered unity whereas civil society became synonymous with class conflict (Lyttelton 2000; Riedel 1972: 795ff.).

By uncoupling the idea of civil society from the dynamics of associational culture, it is possible to arrive at a more ambivalent assessment of the democratic contributions of associations than those painted in neo-Tocquevillian accounts (Putnam 1993, 1995). Some associations kept the spirit of civil society alive, but many more departed from its early modern concerns (trust and order versus anarchy; diversity and balance versus antidespotism) and instead pursued self-referential, exclusionary solidarities, offered by nation, empire, class or confession. Most Europeans were members of associations that were not strictly open and modular, nor that specialized in deliberative reason and toleration. Evangelical religion inspired most associations in nineteenth-century Britain, ranging from missionary movements to the Sabbatarians: their project was to impose a particular moral and social order, not to live with difference (Maughan 2000). British civil society was always also an imperial society. On the Continent, associational expansion was driven by nationalism and confessionalism. What emerged was less an open, overlapping network of associations nursing a modular mentality than a rough landscape of isolated associational subcultures for different confessional groups. As the Dutch and Belgian cases suggest, democratization did not necessarily have to suffer from civil society being 'pillarized'. Quite the opposite: confessional associations, by attacking secular liberalism, played an important role in mobilizing people and turning them into citizens (Ertman 2000).

Conclusion

Much current discussion about the global prospect of civil society operates with a simple dichotomy between civil society and religion, between modular modern man and traditional man, between democratic and non-democratic societies – a divide anchored in a liberal, secular reading of the European origins of civil society. This divide, this chapter has suggested, is historically flawed and politically dangerous. Through its connection with Empire, civil society was inevitably not just a peaceful or self-contained European phenomenon – to separate those who had civil society (Europe) from those who did not does not make analytical sense given the imprint of Empire (Comaroff and Comaroff 1999).

If history is any guide, the idea of civil society has always been confronted by enemies from within associational culture. In the second half of the nineteenth century the concept of civil society declined. The strength of the concept and the depth of associational culture are a poor predictor of democratic development. In nineteenth-century Britain, the concept disappeared just as liberal democratic reforms proceeded; in Germany, *bürgerliche Gesellschaft* remained in usage and associations proliferated but all too frequently in directions that fuelled nationalist passions and arrested democratic development. All this points to a much-needed levelling of the argumentative playing-field between past and present accounts of civil society, where the complex current state of non-European societies is all too frequently compared to a simplified abstract derived from a few European master texts. Instead of merely asking 'where did civil society come from?', we should also ask 'how did civil society work in action?', indeed, 'did European civil society work?'. A more rounded and critical consideration of the competing ideas and social dynamics of civil society in European history would assist a more balanced assessment of its global potential today, avoiding historically unjustifiable claims of European exceptionalism as well as recognizing the dilemmas and diversity of civil society in different times and places.

References

Burke, E. (1987 [1790]) *Reflections on the Revolution in France*, London: Pocock Hackett.

Burke, P., Harrison, B. and Slack, P. (eds) (2000) *Civil Histories, Essays Presented to Sir Keith Thomas*, Oxford: Oxford University Press.

Burrow, R. (1723) *Civil Society and Government Vindicated from the Charge of Being Founded on, and Preserved by, Dishonest Arts*, London.

Clark, J.C.D. (1985) *English Society 1688–1832. Ideology, Social Structure and Political Practice during the Ancient Regime*, Cambridge: Cambridge University Press.

Clarke, T. (1796) *The Benefits of Christianity Contrasted with the Pernicious Influence of Modern Philosophy upon Civil Society*, London.

Cohen, J. and Arato, A. (1992) *Civil Society and Political Theory*, Cambridge MA: MIT Press.

Cohen, J. and Rogers, J. (eds) (1995) *Associations and Democracy*, New York: Verso.

Colas, D. (1997) *Civil Society and Fanaticism: Conjoined Histories*, Stanford: Stanford University Press.

Colley, L. (1992) *Britons. Forging the Nation, 1707–1837*, New Haven: Yale University Press.

Comaroff, J.L. and Comaroff, J. (eds) (1999) *Civil Society and the Political Imagination in Africa*. Chicago: University of Chicago Press.

Douglas, J. (1792) *Discourses on the Influence of the Christian Religion in Civil Society*, London.

Dunn, J. (2001) 'The contemporary political significance of John Locke's conception of civil society', in S. Kaviraj and S. Khilnani (eds), *Civil Society: History and Possibilities*, Cambridge: Cambridge University Press.

Ertman, T. (2000) 'Liberalization, democratization, and the origins of a "pillarized" civil society in nineteenth-century Belgium and the Netherlands', in N. Bermeo and P. Nord (eds), *Civil Society Before Democracy*, Lanham MD: Rowman and Littlefield.

Ferguson, A. (1995 [1767]), *An Essay on the History of Civil Society*, edited by F. Oz-Salzberger, Cambridge: Cambridge University Press.

Gellner, E. (1994) *Conditions of Liberty: Civil Society and its Rivals*, London: Allen Lane, Penguin.

Habermas, J. (1992) *Zwischen Faktizität und Geltung* [Between Facts and Norms], Frankfurt am Main: Suhrkamp Verlag.

Held, D. (1995) *Democracy and the Global Order*, Stanford: Stanford University Press.

Hirst, P. (1994) *Associative Democracy*, Cambridge: Polity.

Kaviraj, S. and Khilnani, S. (eds) (2001) *Civil Society: History and Possibilities*, Cambridge: Cambridge University Press.

Keane, J. (1999) *Civil Society: Old Images, New Perspectives*, Oxford and Stanford: Polity Press.

Lyttelton, A. (2000) 'Liberalism and civil society in Italy: from hegemony to mediation', in N. Bermeo and P. Nord (eds), *Civil Society Before Democracy*, Lanham MD: Rowman and Littlefield.

Maughan, S. (2000) 'Civic culture, women's foreign missions, and the British imperial imagination, 1860–1914', in F. Trentmann (ed.), *Paradoxes of Civil Society: New Perspectives on the Evolution of Civil Society in Modern Britain and Germany*, Oxford and New York: Berghahn Books.

Morris, R.J. (1990) 'Clubs, societies and associations', in F.M.L. Thompson (ed.), *The Cambridge Social History of Britain, 1750–1950*, vol. III, Cambridge: Cambridge University Press.

Oz-Salzberger, F. (1995) *Translating the Enlightenment: Scottish Civic Discourse in Eighteenth-Century Germany*, Oxford: Clarendon.

Poovey, M. (1998) *A History of the Modern Fact: Problems of Knowledge in the Sciences of Wealth and Society*, Chicago: Chicago University Press.

Pulszky, A. (1887) *The Theory of Law and Civil Society*, London: T.F. Unwin.

Putnam, R. (1995) 'Bowling alone: America's declining social capital', *Journal of Democracy*, 6: 65–78.

——, with Leonardi, R. and Nanetti, R.Y. (1993) *Making Democracy Work: Civic Traditions in Modern Italy*, Princeton: Princeton University Press.

Rawls, J. (1993) *Political Liberalism*, New York: Columbia University Press.

Riedel, M. (1972) 'Gesellschaft, bürgerliche' [Society, civil], in O. Brunner, W. Conze and R. Koselleck (eds), *Geschichtliche Grundbegriffe* [Key Historical Concepts], Stuttgart: E. Klett.

Smith Harris, S. (1883) *The Relation of Christianity to Civil Society*, London.

Stedman Jones, G. (2001) 'Hegel and the economics of civil society', in S. Kaviraj and S. Khilnani (eds), *Civil Society: History and Possibilities*, Cambridge: Cambridge University Press.

Trentmann, F. (ed.) (2000) *Paradoxes of Civil Society: New Perspectives on the Evolution of Civil Society in Modern Britain and Germany*, Oxford and New York: Berghahn Books.

——(2001) 'Bread, milk, and democracy in modern Britain: consumption and citizenship in twentieth-century Britain', in M. Daunton and M. Hilton (eds), *The Politics of Consumption*, Oxford and New York: Berg Publishers.

Wake, W. (1700) *The False-Prophets Try'd by their Fruits*, London.

4 Civil society in multilingual polities

Neera Chandhoke

Civil society in contemporary theory has been entrusted with many significant tasks: forging a democratic discourse, countering authoritarian state power, providing a platform that is alternative to the power-driven market order, reconciling notions of individual interest and the social good. Underlying all these expectations of civil society is the fairly powerful assumption that the inhabitants of civil society can enter into a dialogue with each other, or that they speak a common language. By language, as I indicate later in this chapter, I mean not only the spoken word, but shared understanding (Chandhoke 2003).

However, if a society like that of India is marked by a plurality of languages, what, we may ask, are the processes by which this *mélange* of vocabularies is transformed into something that we recognize as the discourses of civil society? What procedures will allow for the articulation, the reconciliation, and perhaps the transcendence of rival perspectives in a just manner? How does a discursive community reconcile competing claims fairly? Correspondingly, are all languages represented in the sphere, or is civil society receptive to only one language? Does it speak in many tongues, or only in one? These it seems to me are serious issues for any theorist of civil society who is sensitive to the problem of multilingual societies.

And it is precisely here that we run into some trouble, because we can take it for granted that people will come to the discursive spaces of civil society equipped with their own beliefs of what a good society and a good polity should look like. We can hardly dismiss these beliefs as mere surmises or as fleeting considerations, because at least some of them are likely to be anchored in deep structures of cognition and convictions. And it is not unknown to anyone who has participated in the discussions of any community, whether in trade unions or faculty meetings, that these convictions will be not only different but also conflictual. People simply speak different, perhaps even incommensurable, languages.

This does not by any means indicate that languages can be put into neat compartments, or that the speakers of one language cannot understand other languages. They certainly can, provided of course that they are willing to cognitively invest in the process. Further, it is not unknown that languages borrow from each other and overlap with each other, creating in the process a wider linguistic community. But it may so happen that on some, perhaps crucial, issues two languages may just hold divergent conceptions of the world. By definition, therefore, these languages will not share allegiance to any common norm that can help arbitrate clashes between them.

This is troublesome because conversation in civil society is only possible when it, as a discursive community, possesses a referral. In other words, if one of the participants puts forth a proposition, say that x means y, other participants should be able to comprehend what the participant means when he or she suggests that x means y. This does not by any means indicate that they have to agree with the proposition. A second participant may believe that x means z, someone else may suggest that x means y to the power of two, and yet another person can insist that actually the proposition that x means y is nothing but a language game and that all meaning is random and contingent. Four different participants in the dialogical forum of civil society can interpret the same proposition differently. But this is not important. What is important is that the participants are able to readily understand the proposition on offer – that x means y – *before* they agree, disagree, subtract or add to it. For unless they can immediately understand what our first participant means when he or she puts forth this proposition, no dialogue can take place in civil society for people will simply speak different languages.

For language presupposes shared understanding. In other words, we can make sense of a proposition only when we relate it to certain assumptions, which are indicated but not expressed along with the narration of a sentence. Therefore, to speak a language is to inhabit the world of shared understandings, which of course are necessarily mediated through common historical experiences. If this is so, then what happens when two languages expressing different understandings encounter each other in the public sphere of civil society?

Certainly, as suggested above, many of these languages may reach out to each other through common historical experiences, and create in the process shared understandings that are not specific to any one community. This shared language may be that of the nation, which has been constructed through the freedom struggle, and through narratives and symbols of nationhood. People in a market economy speak the language of the commodity, just as road users understand the discourse of road rules, and music lovers comprehend the notation of classical music. People can speak shared languages of, say, cuisines and dress codes, of politics and of the media. Languages are not locked up in glass cases; they lend and borrow from each other to create overlapping linguistic communities. At other times, some people speaking languages that pertain to themselves alone – death rites for instance – do so within their own communities, while other people within a different community will have a different language for the same situation. They speak different languages in these contexts that are specific to them alone.

To stop at this would be to say that all languages live in peaceful coexistence in civil society, and that they reach out to other languages or retract at will. But this would be to overlook the fact that some languages acquire hegemony in the domain of civil society and others do not, simply because the former constitute, as well as are constituted by, different forms and modalities of power. Therefore, they are in a position either to subdue or to ignore other languages. Think of the power of the language of national unity, to which regional languages of self-determination are ruthlessly subordinated. Equally, envisage the power of the language of commodity that overwhelms other forms of economic transactions: that of the domain of moral economy, for instance. Think of legal and bureaucratic languages that, even as they penetrate civil society, are embedded in the power of the state. Both connected to as well as constitutive of power, dominant languages lay down standards governing which vocabularies are acceptable within the politico-linguistic domain and which are not. In the process, they also delineate norms that arbitrate between different languages in cases of conflict. In the example of the dominance of the language of national unity, the language of secession or self-determination is not recognized in the public domain, and even banned entry into the sphere – for the vocabularies of, the understandings of, as well as the norms of national unity have already constituted this domain.

There is an apocryphal story about a 'tribal' person faced with displacement in the Narmada valley in western India that may further illustrate what I am trying to say. I use the term 'tribal' in dual, though not unrelated, senses. Literally, the term indicates the inhabitants of the valley who have been subjected to massive displacement because of the building of a gigantic complex of dams in the area. The term tribal, however, can also be used as a metaphor for those inhabitants of civil society who have been marginalized from the politics of dominant languages. In other words, the term tribal can stand in for subaltern or marginal groups. And subalterns simply 'lack voice' inasmuch as they are unfamiliar with the terms of the dominant language.

I am by no means suggesting that the subaltern lack agential capacity when I say that they 'lack voice'. Nor am I indicating that they are incapable of self-representation. To 'lack voice', I suggest, is to lack linguistic and epistemic authority in the deliberative domain, which is arguably governed by a rule-bound set of languages, that of political modernity (Beverly 2000; Spivak 1988). To put it another way, the marginalized by definition do not participate in the construction of what counts as 'reasonable', or indeed what constitutes appropriate and legitimate knowledge in the domain of civil society. If they did contribute in the construction of such knowledge, they would not be marginal to the domain; they would not be subaltern.

Having said this, let me return to the story: a revenue official, surveying land holdings in the valley for the purposes of assessing the amount of compensation allowed to the displaced, asked a tribal about his land holdings. The tribal pointed towards an area of land and claimed proprietorship of that land. Expectedly, he was asked to show the relevant papers that establish land ownership – the *patta*. Equally expectedly, the tribal did not possess any such *patta*. 'How do you know in this case that the land is yours?' asked the revenue official. 'I know,' answered the tribal. 'But how? You have no papers, no legal ownership of the land.' 'The bones of my forefathers are buried along the boundaries of the land,' answered the tribal. 'No compensation,' ruled the revenue official as he walked away, condemning the tribal who had been cultivating the land under usufructuary rights to landlessness, joblessness and homelessness, without any hope of compensation, even as his land fell under the submergence zone of the gigantic Narmada valley project.

This story can be read in many ways. It can be read in terms of land ownership or lack of land ownership, in terms of bureaucratic indifference and apathy towards the victims of displacement, in terms of mindless and ahistorical interpretation of laws, and in terms of the multiple tragedies that are effected by big development projects. It certainly can be read in terms of the status or the lack thereof of the tribals in India. Let me read it in a different way – the collision between two languages and the victory of one at the expense of the other.

We realize that only the language of legal and political modernity constitutes the modern domain of the state and of civil society in India. Therefore, it is evident that different languages that express other understandings will have to be translated into the terms of the dominant language in order to be heeded. Recollect, however, that we cannot speak of strict and exact translation from one language to another, in abstraction from the power of the translator who controls the terms of translation. Translation, as countless literary critics have told us, is all about interpreting one language into the conceptual terrain of the language of the interpreter. Translations are matters for and of power unless of course the translator is equidistant from both languages. But this would mean that he or she is located in a third language, which does not resolve the problem for us. Problems of translations are thus one aspect of the wider conundrum when two unequally placed languages meet in the public sphere.

What happens if a language is incapable of being translated conceptually into the modern language of the public sphere because the meaning systems underlying the two languages are incommensurate? When our tribal has said 'this land is mine, for the bones of my ancestors are buried at the boundaries of the land', does this make sense to the practitioner of the dominant language, embedded as he is in a different structure of meaning, that of legal title to land? Will it be addressed, and heeded, or will there be no conversation, no give and take of reasons, and actually no hint of dialogue in such an event?

The two languages just happen to express different understandings and different social worlds. For the revenue officer, who speaks the language of Max Weber's bureaucratic efficiency, ownership of land holding can only be established when the claimant has undergone the entire gamut of tiresome rituals that saturate the legal profession. We are familiar with these rituals in some sense or the other – the filing of an affidavit, subjecting the land to survey, filling in of endless forms, assessment and payment of taxes and other such tasks. This really means that most of us must be conversant with the convoluted language and the philosophy of law. We should be familiar with alien and rather frightening institutions such as law courts, lawyers, judges, revenue officials, corrupt and eminently 'bribe-able' inspectors, reams of paperwork, shelling out on a never-ending stream of fees – stamp fees, lawyers' fees, lures and baits. Anyone who wants to establish ownership, and who is entitled to compensation when that land is submerged, must possess a working knowledge of the law and the vocabularies of legal modernity. But recollect that most of us, even those of us who call ourselves literate and who presumably are located in the conceptual universe of political modernity, hire lawyers and chartered accountants to do our work for us.

Our tribal person, on the other hand, speaks an entirely different language: that of tilling land that his ancestors had cultivated, those ancestors whose bones have been interred on the boundaries of that land. Understandings of usufructuary rights and proprietorship, boundaries, even cultivation of land mean something radically different to him from what they mean to people immersed in the modern language of politics. Therefore, his language may well be incomprehensible to the impatient and contemptuous revenue official who is located in a different language altogether. There can be no dialogue in such cases, for the two languages are just incommensurate.

First, the tribal interprets land holding differently from the revenue official. Second, the tribal ranks legal ownership of land in a manner divergent from the laws of the country. Third, our tribal speaks a language of land holding and ownership that does not make sense to the official of the state, grounded as the latter is in a different understanding altogether. In all three senses, we can conclude that the tribal and the revenue official as the representative of the state speak incommensurable languages. Left at that, we would have at the most seen that two participants speaking incommensurable languages 'talk past' each other and proceed on their own separate ways. We could therefore conclude, and our conclusion would carry some significance for the notion of civil society as a discursive community, that there can be no dialogue when two languages express different understandings. But this is not what we see, because another vital dimension has intervened and intruded into this deadlock, and resolved it in favour of the state official. The dimension is that of power. The tribal does not even have the right to exit from the exchange and go his own way, for he has no option but to accept the language of the official.

There is no dialogue not only because the two participants express different understandings, but because the language of the tribal has been neutralized from the start. Both the conceptual underpinnings and the power dimension of the language employed by the official have set the agenda for the discussion regarding compensation in exchange for the *patta*. The discussion – which could have been transformed into a dialogue, marked by the give and take of ideas, receptivity, and mutuality – proves in effect to be a non-starter. It degenerates into a monologue, for the language of the tribal remains unaddressed, unheeded and unattended, subordinated as it is to the more powerful language.

To put it differently, since the language of the *patta* has already set the boundaries of the discussion between the revenue official and the tribal, the terms of exchange have been preordained, preformed and prevalidated: the capacity of the other language to establish ownership of land has been cancelled from the initial moment. In effect, our tribal does not have a whit of a chance in his conversation with the revenue official to press his own point of view, buttress it with reasonable arguments, to persuade, to cajole, to talk through. The conversation has ended before it even began. All because one language, revealing the imprint of power in civil society, just does not acknowledge the other language as a free and equal partner in debate.

The power of language of course reflects and codifies material power. When our revenue collector exercises power through a verbal transaction it has to be heard and heeded. But recollect that he would not be so heard unless his verbal utterances represented a structure of codified power: that of legal rules, and that of the state. Underneath and around this verbal utterance, therefore, lies an entire web of legal, political and bureaucratic power, which in turn lends epistemic authority to ideas of legal titles of land. The verbal act of asking the tribal to show the *patta* is backed by a web of pre-understanding that validates legal ownership of land and invalidates any other way of conceptualizing the relationship of a tiller to his land. It is this web of understanding that allows an official to epistemically overcome those who may subscribe to a different relationship to land.

Recollect also in this connection that the idea that land ownership is based on a contract between the state and the private proprietor is a supremely modern one, connected to the production of discourses about the commodity. Contrast it to a premodern social order where land ownership is vested in a feudal chief who has the power to gift land to his loyal vassals. Conversely, if the vassal proves untrustworthy, he has the power to confiscate land he has earlier granted. Equally contrast modern ideas of land ownership to notions of usufructuary rights practised in premodern economies, where tilling land is considered more than enough to establish a relation with and ownership of land.

More importantly, the testimony of our tribal that 'this is my land for the bones of my forefathers are buried along it' is not unknown in history. In earlier societies this was a recognized way of laying claim to property. Harrison (2001: 399) puts it this way: 'places are not only founded but are also appropriated by burial of the dead ... The surest way to take possession of a place and secure it as one's own is to bury one's dead in it'. He goes on to quote Vico (p. 399) in *New Science*, who declared that: '[t]hus by the graves of their buried dead the giants showed dominion over their land ... With truth they could pronounce these heroic phrases: we are sons of this earth, we are born from these oaks' in support of his argument. Vico, suggests Harrison, called these people (our ancestors) the 'giants' because they were the sons of the earth who descended from buried ancestors whose place in the ground they could point to as their own.

In a society such as India, which is marked by plural and conflicting notions of land ownership because of the prevalence of different modes of production, all these differing and conflicting ideas of proprietorship necessarily mark the relationship between land and the proprietor. Therefore, when the revenue official representing the state asserts that only one form of land ownership is valid, he establishes both epistemic authority as well as validity over other ideas of land ownership. Power in this case has to do with the establishment of one system of meanings as simply more valid and justifiable than the others are.

Our tribal person has consequently lost out not only because he speaks a different language, or because his language of land ownership proves incommensurable with official languages, but also because he is powerless. He is powerless in two ways: in a basic sense he is powerless in material terms, but he is also powerless because his language is not reflected in, recognized by, or even understood in the modern public sphere. He and his language are both bypassed.

I am aware that I am juxtaposing two domains here: that of political society to which the revenue official belongs and civil society to which our tribal belongs. Someone can rightly object to this on the grounds that dialogue is the property of civil society and coercion is the property of political society. However, this hypothetical objection does not hold water: we cannot separate political society, that is the state, and civil society conceptually, even if we distinguish between them analytically. To separate them conceptually would be to fall into the liberal fallacy that the state occupies a different universe from that of civil society. The state in powerful ways constitutes civil society. Therefore, what the revenue official purportedly said to the tribal could easily have been said by a member of a voluntary agency, who – subcontracting for the government – was delineating the map of displacements and compensation.

Whoever does the epistemic overcoming, it is clear that speakers of subaltern languages simply lose out in the power games of linguistic politics, despite all stipulations of democratic dialogue in civil society. Why? Because the language of dialogue in civil society has, in the words of Foucault (1984: 109), been 'controlled, selected, organized and redistributed by a certain number of procedures whose role is to ward off its [society's] powers and dangers, to gain mastery over its chance events, to evade its ponderous, formidable materiality'? Because it has already set in place what Foucault calls 'procedures of exclusion' (p. 109)? And recollect that one of the things that has been excluded from dialogue is other ways of conceptualizing something as fundamental to a society like India as land proprietorship.

In effect, the more powerful language in civil society does not even have to practise savageness, to bludgeon, club or hammer the less powerful language into insensibility. The dialogical space of civil society has been already colonized, already saturated with power that privileges certain ideas of land proprietorship. It is already controlled because it has set in place the mechanics of monitoring. It has herewith institutionalized 'procedures of exclusion'. And it can do all this because the more powerful language, which reflects material power in society, has set the terms of the dialogue.

References

Beverly, J. (2000) *Subalternity and Representation: Arguments in Cultural Theory*, Durham: Duke University Press.

Chandhoke, N. (2003) *The Conceits of Civil Society*, Delhi: Oxford University Press.

Foucault, M. (1984) 'The order of discourse', in M. Shapiro (ed.), *Language and Politics*, Oxford: Basil Blackwell.

Harrison, R.P. (2001) 'Hic jacet', *Critical Inquiry*, 27(3) (spring): 393–407.

Spivak, G. (1988) 'Can the subaltern speak?', in C. Nelson and L. Grossberg (eds), *Marxism and the Interpretation of Culture*, Urbana: University of Illinois Press.

5 In the church of civil society

Chris Hann

Civil society is one of those terms where it seems especially important to distinguish *Begriffsgeschichte* from the concrete development of the phenomenon at issue. The concept was not in use for most of the nineteenth and twentieth centuries, though presumably the object it describes underwent certain changes in this period. I cannot pursue the long-term historical discrepancy in this brief contribution, but elsewhere I have described how the concept was rediscovered in the last years of the Cold War as a result of a curious coalition of East European 'dissidents' and left-leaning Westerners (Hann 2000). Here I want to suggest that in its revived career following the Cold War it is again helpful to distinguish between words and things, between the rhetoric of civil society and the actual course of social change. For reasons of space I shall restrict the discussion spatially as well as temporally, concentrating on those parts of postsocialist Eurasia where I have some personal fieldwork experience.

For intellectual company in these reflections I depend heavily on Ernest Gellner. At the end of his life (he died in November 1995) he was enthusiastic about the reinvention of the concept of civil society, regardless of its 'muddled' history, because it seemed to him the best term to encapsulate the most attractive features of the open, liberal and individualist society of which he approved (Gellner 1994). It is worth recalling that Gellner began his career with an attack on Oxford linguistic philosophy (1959). Though he was more interested in understanding the concrete development of 'things', linguistic idealism and 'speech act' theory exerted pervasive influences on his adopted discipline of social anthropology. Gellner was obliged to recognize that even Bronisław Malinowski, founder of the modern British empirical, fieldwork-based tradition, verged on a suspect idealist epistemology when exploring the magical power of certain Trobriand words (Gellner 1998). We are forced to recognize that words, including social science concepts, can indeed have material effects in society.

My first point is that the phrase 'civil society', whether in a local translation or left in English, where it may have an extra hint of mystery, has been taken up in a magical sense in many parts of postsocialist Eurasia. At first *społeczęstwo obywatelskie* (Polish) or *polgári társadalom* (Hungarian) appeared in the obscure, semi-clandestine publications of tiny groups of intellectuals. With the collapse of socialist regimes, the concept of civil society entered into the programmes of new political parties and into the mass media. It signified utopian conditions of democratic participation and tolerance, the antithesis of 'totalitarianism', but more precise definitions were seldom forthcoming. It suited new power holders to have a term of the 'motherhood and apple pie' ilk, from which no one could possibly dissent. A decade on, in countries such as Poland and Hungary where more or less stable political institutions have emerged, the term has already faded from the public sphere. However, in countries such as Russia the concept of *grazhdanskoe obchystwa* still has this magical function when it is uttered by politicians.

These magical performances have impacted on society in various ways. New groups of enthusiasts have emerged, primarily as a consequence of the adoption of one specific notion of civil society by governments, foreign foundations and aid organizations. Partly because the latter needed a quantitative measure for their own bureaucratic reasons, the health of a civil society came to mean (especially in the Anglo-Saxon world) the number of associations it had, more specifically the number of non-governmental organizations (NGOs). There are distinguished precedents in Western intellectual history for a focus on associations, notably in the work of Tocqueville. However, the emphasis on NGOs and the 'third sector' that was supposed to be an autonomous force beyond the spheres of state and market was both a simplification and a distortion of the two principal classical strands of civil society theorizing – that which refuses a state versus society dichotomy (Ferguson, for example) and that which identifies civil society with the atomistic world of the market (for example, Marx). In the dislocation of postsocialist transformation, the establishment of free associations became a priority of public policy. The channelling of public money through these new organizations led to many distortions. At its most harmless, this could lead to sports clubs that previously functioned under the control of the state or a trade union continuing for most practical purposes unchanged, but now classified as embodiments of civil society. At the other end of the spectrum, the proliferation of clubs and associations led in some circumstances to some very 'uncivil' consequences and even interethnic violence. For example, I have documented how in a city in southeast Poland a small group of Polish nationalists was able to abuse new media freedoms to pursue, in the name of civil society, an aggressive campaign against the local Ukrainian minority (Hann 1998).

The routing of a high proportion of aid funds through these NGO channels can make already weak states even weaker. Even governmental programmes to dispense aid and technical assistance inevitably become caught up in local political rivalries (Wedel 1998). The foreigners who appeared on the scene, not only as businesspeople but as the purveyors of democracy and civil society, could afford to pay higher salaries than local organizations, and so the receiving country's best university teachers and civil servants were easily persuaded to change sectors. These new elites often ended up changing countries as well, for following extended contracts and regular training periods abroad, they often became unemployable in their home countries (Mandel 2002; Sampson 2002). This has resulted in understandable envy towards those who succeed in the new foreign-funded NGO sector. The logic of the current situation leads the most talented to put all their energies into learning English, management studies and of course the jargon of civil society project management, rather than pursue established professions. The emphasis on free associations and organizations obliges donors and even governments to set about creating the missing 'non-governmental' bodies (known as DONGOs and GONGOs respectively, see Mandel 2002) that are essential if the flow of 'aid' is to continue.

Civil society has therefore brought changes in the living conditions of specific social groups, but the impact on the wider society has been modest. Many postsocialist citizens have experienced a decline in state provision – for example, in the value of pensions, or in education and health – without experiencing any compensating material benefits from an NGO. Some of the consequences have been unintended, and even the opposite of what was intended, notably the brain drain abroad. Of course not all projects have failed, and some NGOs, both foreign and domestic, have creditable records. But I suggest that the general thrust of civil society intervention has been misconceived. The intentions were usually laudable – few would object to the decentralized principles stressed by the British Foreign Office's 'Know-How Fund', for example – but even schemes such as this one were experienced as experiments in social engineering. The main difference from socialism was that the new interventions had a foreign slogan, foreign managers and foreign criteria of success regarding what makes a decent society. Current programmes of 'civil society export' often amount to the imposition of a specifically Anglo-Saxon notion of social cohesion. Yet most people (perhaps even many among the new Westernized elites) would presumably prefer to adapt their own ideals, typically based on kinship or religious or ethnic loyalties rather than on formal associations and individual agents. Civil society export can lead to the abortion of local processes of change, whether embryonic or already underway. These considerations bring us to the root of anthropological critiques of the recent international propagation of civil society.

One alternative is to expand the definition of civil society beyond the enlightenment heritage of liberal individualism (Hann 1996). This would allow us to recognize other ways of achieving accountability, participatory politics, tolerance of group differences, and other *desiderata* associated with a concept that has become inescapably normative. Ernest Gellner rejects this approach. In this context he is perhaps untypical of contemporary anthropologists: for example, when he characterizes tribal society as a 'tyranny of cousins' and rules out the possibility of an Islamic civil society (1994). It is true that some critical intellectuals in Muslim countries may agree with this position of Gellner's and prefer to emphasize the modern, Western associations of civil society, in the field of gender rights for example, when they challenge the traditions of their own societies (see Eickelman and Anderson 1999). Others have argued that the ethnocentric bias of scholars such as Gellner leads them to deny the real presence of civil society in Islamic societies, even when the classical Western criteria are applied (see Kamali 2001, following a model specified by Shmuel Eisenstadt). However, a more satisfying anthropological approach would be to pay closer attention to local patterns of sociality and to investigate how issues of political and moral accountability can be resolved in civil ways that differ from modern Western solutions. To date, the pioneers of such enquiries into cross-cultural ethical systems seem to be political theorists and philosophers (see Chambers and Kymlicka 2002).

Instead of entering into these debates, too many anthropologists have responded to the civil society vogue by accepting the Anglo-Saxon, neoliberal definition and restricting the focus of their fieldwork to the NGOs. Though sometimes able to offer valuable insights into the impact of new associational forms, such studies generally fail to pay sufficient attention to local patterns of sociality outside the organizations. Yet many of these either persist unaffected by the NGOs, or develop in new ways as a consequence of external interventions. Though often readily explicable in terms of funding conditions and logistics, it is disappointing when anthropologists – the only members of the academy equipped, through the methods of participant observation, to penetrate the complexities of local societies – end up spending much of their fieldwork speaking English to other foreigners engaged in civil society development projects.

For Gellner, socialist societies could never provide an attractive alternative to the standard liberal model. The difference, compared to Islamic societies, is that socialism, at least in Eastern Europe and Russia, emerged on the immediate periphery of the industrializing West, so that in principle the problems of 'translating' civil society should be greatly reduced. It is nonetheless depressing to have to note that a distinguished tradition of civil society theorizing in Germany has been swamped by the Anglo-Saxon vogue. The German concept of *bürgerliche Gesellschaft* has been largely replaced by the Anglicism *Zivilgesellschaft* (similarly in Hungary, where *polgári társadalom* has been supplanted in recent years by *civil társadalom*). At any rate, in the postsocialist countries, perhaps unlike other parts of the world, I detect no intellectual ferment around the concept of civil society. Many people have become cynical. A decade after the collapse of socialism, I found that no academics in Moscow took the notion of civil society seriously. It was simply a magical phrase that it was always desirable to include in any foreign grant application, just as a phrase about Russia's cultural or spiritual renaissance was obligatory for grant applications within the country. Things have reached the point where civil society seems to be a symptom of the diseases of non-democratic governance and intolerance, rather than a cure to these problems (Hann 2003). As in other parts of the world, in Russia the crudities and abuses of the foreign NGO sector lead people to react by reaffirming older loyalties. This seems to be one factor behind the resurgence of ethnonational sentiment, and also of continued nostalgia for socialism and the popularity of political platforms exploiting that heritage all over Eurasia. The discomforting implication of this anthropological relativizing of the concept of civil society is that huge numbers of postsocialist citizens, perhaps in many countries a majority, feel that they enjoyed a more civil society under the old regime than they do today – not, of course, in the sense that they had more free associations and more participatory forms of governance, but in the sense that their personal and social lives were more secure and their communities more firmly anchored in a moral framework, one that emphasized key values of mutual support and civility.

Let me give an example from Eastern Europe. There has been a wide measure of agreement that Roma groups have experienced new and intensified forms of social exclusion following the transformation of socialist economic planning and social security services. The new democratic conditions require that even such marginalized groups have adequate political representation, but ensuring effective Roma participation has proved highly problematic. Some attempts to improve matters have focused on strengthening Roma civil society, in the sense of funding new organizations and projects to promote Roma goals. For example, Daniela Tarnovschi is a sociologist who specializes in Roma civil society in Romania. According to her account (2003; for more information about Roma organizations and projects see the website of the Ethnocultural Diversity Resource Centre: www.edrc.ro), this civil society came into existence in 1926 with the establishment of the first formal organization to represent Roma interests. There was no Roma civil society in the socialist period, but it re-emerged at once in 1990 and the number of Roma associations expanded impressively after facilitating legislation was passed in 1996. It may be too soon to judge the impact of the large number of organizations and projects on the general conditions of Romania's Roma population, numbering some 5 per cent of the total population. My point is simply that an anthropological approach cannot limit itself to these new organizations, but would explore through fieldwork what other Roma think of the new elites who control these civil society interventions. To understand the problems of the Roma today it will certainly be necessary to analyse their situation under socialism, but perhaps also to consider alternative models of how to organize social and political participation. It is possible that older structures based on the office of the 'Gypsy King' can be incorporated into the new structures of formal associations; but it is also possible that many Roma will resist such incorporation. Thus, even if one insists on retaining the narrow definition of civil society, focusing on formal organizations, it will be necessary to undertake research outside these limits in order to understand the circumstances in which this new model of civil society spreads or fails to spread. This, it seems to me, should be the main purpose of anthropological work.

Despite mounting evidence that the promotion of an impoverished notion of civil society is not working, the magic of the concept still seems strong for large swaths of Anglo-Saxon academia. How do we explain this? I do not think it can be attributed solely to cynical instrumentalism, and in any case this begs the question of why the term civil society retains its magical power for so many donors and governments. Another of Gellner's favourite metaphors is useful here. He liked to refer to the partisans of 'closed' systems of thought, such as Marxism and psychoanalysis, as 'churches' (for example, Gellner 1965). I suggest that the partisans of civil society – a concept that, in his estimation, exemplified the open, liberal vision of society – are in danger of becoming another intellectual church. It is ironic, too, that one of the major temples should be the London School of Economics, home not only to Gellner but to Malinowski and Popper before him.

This new church of civil society is roughly comparable to the secular religion it has replaced across much of Eurasia, the Marxist–Leninist variety of socialism. Both are varieties of non-spiritual religion. Their visions of the good life are somewhat different, as are the techniques they employ, but both suffer from a common deficiency. By proclaiming that salvation is to be found here on this earth, through improvements in human institutional arrangements, neither is able to connect with the transcendental, with that sense of the sacred, which so many human beings appear to need. Ernest Gellner used to argue in the case of socialism that its promise of a better future in this world must have contributed to its delegitimation, once it became clear to everyone in the stagnation and corruption of the Brezhnev years that there was no longer any prospect of improvement whatsoever. My sense is that the salvation promises of civil society have an even shorter life span. Many enthusiasts of the 1980s and early 1990s have already lost faith. Outside academia the church is struggling, at least in the postsocialist world. The combination of a continuing flood of rhetoric but dwindling material transfers and mounting moral revulsion may be enough to send civil society back to the conceptual graveyard from which it was so recently exhumed.

References

Chambers, S. and Kymlicka, W. (eds) (2002) *Alternative Conceptions of Civil Society*, Princeton: Princeton University Press.

Eickelman, D.F. and Anderson, J.W. (eds) (1999) *New Media in the Muslim World: The Emerging Public Sphere*, Bloomington: Indiana University Press.

Gellner, E. (1959) *Words and Things: A Critical Account of Linguistic Philosophy and a Study in Ideology*, London: Gollancz.

——(1965) *Thought and Change*, London: Weidenfeld and Nicolson.

——(1994) *Conditions of Liberty: Civil Society and its Revivals*, London: Hamish Hamilton.

——(1998) *Language and Solitude: Malinowski, Wittgenstein and the Habsburg Dilemma*, Cambridge: Cambridge University Press.
Hann, C. (1996) 'Introduction: political anthropology and civil anthropology', in C. Hann and E. Dunn (eds), *Civil Society: Challenging Western Models*, London: Routledge.
——(1998) 'Postsocialist nationalism: rediscovering the past in South East Poland', *Slavic Review*, 57(4): 840–63.
——(2000) 'Zivilgesellschaft oder Citizenship? Skeptische Überlegungen eines Ethnologen', in M. Hildermeier, J. Kocka and C. Conrad (eds), *Europäische Zivilgesellschaft in Ost und West, Begriff, Geschichte, Chancen*, Frankfurt am Main: Campus.
——(2003) 'Civil society: the sickness, not the cure', *Social Evolution*, 2(2): 55–74.
Kamali, M. (2001) 'Civil society and Islam: a sociological perspective', *Archives européennes de sociologie*, 42(3): 457–82.
Mandel, R. (2002) 'Seeding civil society', in C.M. Hann (ed.), *Postsocialism: Ideals, Ideologies and Practices in Eurasia*, London: Routledge.
Sampson, S. (2002) 'Beyond transition: rethinking elite configurations in the Balkans', in C.M. Hann (ed.), *Postsocialism: Ideals, Ideologies and Practices in Eurasia*, London: Routledge.
Tarnovschi, D. (2003) 'Roma civil society in Romania', paper presented at the conference 'Intercultural Relations, Citizenship and Human Rights in the Context of Central and Eastern Europe', Coppet, Switzerland, 26–29 June 2003.
Wedel, J.R. (1998) *Collision and Collusion: The Strange Case of Western Aid to Eastern Europe 1989–1998*, New York: St Martin's Press.

Part III

Owning the concept

Latin America and Eastern Europe

6 Civil society in Latin America

Uncivil, liberal and participatory models

Leonardo Avritzer

The concept of civil society, emerging in the eighteenth and nineteenth centuries, could not initially make its way out of the West because the social processes it expressed belonged exclusively to the West. In Latin America, the early modern differentiation between the economy and the private sphere did not take place until the early twentieth century. In the context of nation-building, this resulted in a disproportionately large private sphere and the continual possibility that personal relations could be extended to the political realm. Franco (1974) shows how in postcolonial Brazil the public activities of free men took place in the private space of the big landowners. Guerra demonstrates a similar phenomenon in Mexico, where the large haciendas 'constituted more important centres than the small villages. For those who inhabited their centres as well as those who inhabited their peripheries ... they represented the centres for the exercise of worship, festivals, etc.' (Guerra 1988: 134). Thus, the kind of society built in Latin America during its three hundred years of colonization is a society with a strong private space that personalizes formal relations, establishing some sort of hierarchy between all free members of society. In this social structure there was no space for civil society for two reasons: first, because a holistic and hierarchical conception of society could not have led to a society of equals; second, because the fusion between the private and the state could not have led to any process of differentiation. Thus, the idea and concept of civil society remained alien to the Latin American political and social scenes.

The concept of civil society re-emerges in the late twentieth century with two strong differences from its nineteenth-century meaning: it reappears involving a tripartite meaning in which civil society is differentiated both from the market and the state, and it reappears as a concept that seeks to explain social processes taking place in the West, in Eastern Europe and in Latin America (Cohen and Arato 1992; Habermas 1996; Keane 1988). It has received different formulations in the literature, including the seminal life-world oriented treatment by Cohen and Arato (1992: 429), the neo-Gramscian differentiation between civil society, political society and the state (Bobbio 1988; Oxhorn 1995), and a neo-Tocquevillian or neo-Durkheimian tradition (Alexander 1998; Shils 1997).

Civil society in Latin America expressed the new tripartite conceptualization in its own particular way: it linked the emergence of the concept to the process of reconstitution of social ties by the poor (Alvarez *et al.* 1998; Oxhorn 1995) and the middle class (Olvera 2003; Peruzotti 2002; Stepan 1988) in a situation in which social actors were under the pressure of an authoritarian regime. Civil society was thus understood as a concept capable of demarcating the newly emerging actors from both the authoritarian state and the market, understood as the private economic interests associated with the authoritarian regime.

This article will focus on six Latin American countries, which can be considered as ideal-types for three different models of state and civil society: Argentina, Brazil, Chile, Colombia, Mexico and Peru. A first model was grounded in the experiences of the Southern Cone countries, in which the previous presence of an organized civil society and the complete outlawing of political society constituted the major explanatory device (Oxhorn 1995). A second model relates to Brazil and perhaps Mexico, where civil society was understood as a reaction to a process of economic modernization, and in which civil society actors express demands for a more radical form of citizenship and democracy. Lastly, there is the Andean model: Colombia never experienced a breakdown of democracy, and Peru did only briefly, but civil society there expresses a form of social organization related to the satisfaction of very basic needs, which resulted from the extreme weakness of the state (Peru) or even its disintegration (Colombia).

Civil society in Latin America: emergence of the concept

The emergence of civil society in Latin America can be attributed to four interrelated causes, occurring in different combinations and at different times in different parts of the region: the anti-societal authoritarianism in the Southern Cone, which reaped its own resistance (Argentina, Brazil, Chile); the technocratic process of economic modernization (Brazil and Mexico); the lack of accountability in the political process (Mexico); and the impact of economic liberalization on social ties (everywhere).

While there are clear differences between the trajectories in different countries, there are three areas of overlap. In all cases, there is an authoritarian regime involved in the formation of civil society. Colombia could be considered as an exception, but despite being democratic it tends to behave very similarly to authoritarian states. Yet, the way the authoritarian state targeted political society or social actors was linked to the specific historic processes of each country. In Brazil and Mexico, the possibility of maintaining some form of electoral competition throughout the authoritarian period led to a lower level of repression of political society. In Chile and Argentina, outlawing political society, particularly *peronistas* in Argentina and socialists and communists in Chile, was at the centre of authoritarian policy.

There is a second common element between all the cases, namely the emergence of neoliberal economic policies (Oxhorn and Ducatenzeiler 1998). However, the reaction to neoliberalism formed part of the organization of civil society in Chile and Mexico from the very beginning. In Peru and especially Brazil, neoliberalism emerged much later. It played a role not so much in the emergence of civil society as in its subsequent occupation of alternative spaces.

Thirdly, there has been a shift in associative patterns and a reconstitution of social ties in the whole region. In Brazil, there were few associations before authoritarianism, in Chile and Argentina there were associations but they were traditionally linked to political parties, and in Mexico there was a huge number of associations, but they were traditionally linked to the state. In all cases, there was a move to more autonomous forms of association, in many cases linked to new actors entering the political sphere (Oxhorn 1995).

Thus, in spite of differences between different countries, there is sufficient common ground in the emergence of civil society to consider it the same phenomenon. It is also clear why the new tripartite model was so relevant to Latin America: in all cases, while civil society was a reaction to an authoritarian regime it was also a response to a process of further differentiation of market and society that was brought about by neoliberal policies. Civil society survived the process of democratization, necessitating the identification of common ground concerning its role in the new Latin American democracies.

Civil society under democracy in Latin America

Democratization has come about in different ways: in Argentina the authoritarian regime collapsed, in Chile there was a negotiated settlement, Brazil formed an intermediate case, and Mexico differs from all the others because it concerned a case of deep-rooted party authoritarianism rather than military authoritarianism, and because its emancipation from the rule of the Partido Revolucionario Institucional (PRI: Institutional Revolutionary Party) is still fresh and, possibly, fragile.

While the transition to democracy in Argentina was completely different from that in Chile, the role of civil society in both countries is similar, concentrating mainly at the level of social accountability (Peruzotti 2002). Human rights movements and non-governmental organizations (NGOs) are the main actors, and their main activities are challenges to the state, the judiciary and the legislative branch concerning inefficiency and corruption, and efforts towards developing a civic culture in which officials are held to account. Civil society organizations target state institutions to make them more accountable to citizens, but they do not seek to redefine the boundaries between civil society, political society and the state.

In Peru and in the Andes more generally, civil society has created self-help structures to offset the impoverishment caused by neoliberal policies and the disintegration of the state. The hyperinflation at the end of Alan Garcia's government in Peru sharply reduced the state's tax-collection capability, and thus its role as a systemic actor. At the same time, the civil war caused 27,000 deaths and displaced 570,000 people. In this situation of conflict between civility and incivility the traditional form of political and social mediation vanished. Peruvian civil society was the result of society's need to produce the primary 'public goods' usually provided by the state: personal security and social security. Civil society in Peru encompassed more than 5,000 self-defence committees by 1994 as well as self-help groups including soup-kitchens (*comedores populares*), milk-providing groups (*comites de vaso de leche*) and mothers' clubs (*clubes de madres*). Developments in Colombia have been similar despite a previous liberal tradition. Plagued by civil war, Colombia has seen the rise of incivility and the attempt by civil society to create peace zones. The problem with such attempts in both Peru and Colombia is that the disintegration of traditional forms of mediation, particularly political society, created a problem for democratization despite strong social action in both countries. In these cases, civil society lacks the possibility of pacifying the political space, and thus it cannot connect with a tradition of rights and the rule of law.

In Brazil, civil society activity grew from a low base, because 'parties in Brazil have historically been inclined in the direction of the state ... limiting their search for representativity in civil society to electoral periods and to mechanisms seen as most effective in these moments: patronage, exchange of favours, personalism, etc.' (Dagnino 2002: 3). Civil society associations have since taken advantage of the redesign of the country's constitution in 1988 to propose many new forms of political participation either for individuals or for associations. Article 14 of the constitution guarantees a place for 'popular initiative' in the exercise of people's sovereignty. Article 29 on the organization of cities requires the 'cooperation of representative associations in the process of city planning'. Article 194 assures the 'democratic and decentralized character of the social security administration through the participation of representatives of labour, employees in the social security administration, retirees and the government'. Article 227 suggests the participation of NGOs in the assistance of children and teenagers, to be organized by the state. In these and other cases, subsequent legislation has implemented the constitution's promise of participation. In other cases, such as participatory budgeting, the emergence of participatory policies was a result of previously existing practices and negotiations between civil society (in this case represented by neighbourhood associations) and the state. These participatory policies, negotiated by civil society and now to some extent constitutionally guaranteed, have opened up new public spaces. According to Dagnino, 'the very existence of these spaces confronts ... the elitist conceptions of democracy as well as technocratic and authoritarian conceptions of the nature of decision-making inside the state' (Dagnino 2002: 21).

The role of civil society in Mexico, although its trajectory was unique, shares some traits with the Southern Cone experience and others with that of

Brazil. In the 1980s, in Mexico as elsewhere in the region, urban social movements struggled for the legalization of urban tenure, particularly after the 1985 earthquake, when government plans to remove the poor population to the outskirts of Mexico City were successfully opposed by newly formed neighbourhood associations (Avritzer 2002). This had mixed results, leading on the one hand to the emergence of forms of social action independent from the state, but on the other hand to a state attempt to incorporate social leadership (Zermeño *et al.*, 1990). In the 1990s, in response to generalized fraud in the 1988 elections, there was an attempt to constitute a civic movement for monitoring the elections. In December 1993, seven NGOs with different backgrounds, memberships and aims started to meet with the aim of promoting free elections. They initiated a comprehensive observation that involved taking polls, advocating electoral reform, and inquiring into cases of vote-buying and coercion. The movement led eventually to negotiations between civic associations, political parties and the PRI government on a comprehensive electoral change.

Unlike in the Southern Cone, the space for political society was not completely closed; moreover, the authoritarian regime party (PRI) occupied the centre of the political spectrum, flanked by opposition parties both on the right (Partido Acción Nacional (PAN): National Action Party) and on the left (Partido de la Revolución Democrática (PRD): Party of the Democratic Revolution). In Guadalajara, the explosion of a sewage pipe led to the realization in conservative circles that support for PRI had led to corruption, irresponsible behaviour and a general lack of accountability. An organization of a conservative women's group was formed to campaign for the PAN candidate, who won the governorship of Jalisco, but the women's group proposed a new standard of accountability, and was not coopted by conservative politicians or entrepreneurs (Olvera 2003). This situation shows a liberal dimension of democratization of a kind similar to those in the Argentinean and Chilean cases.

In Mexico City, the opposition PRD was able during the electoral campaign for governor to retrieve the tradition of citizen participation in decision-making on the distribution of public goods. The victory of PRD candidate Cardenas overcame old corporatist arrangements and opened new venues for citizen participation (Olvera 2003). A law was passed leading to the participation of 572,000 people in the election of 8,410 representatives to neighbourhood commissions, and introducing a more horizontal form of claiming material goods and negotiating their delivery with local authorities. Thus, in Mexico, there is also a second path of connection between civil and political society, which is participatory rather than liberal.

Models of civil society in Latin America in the twenty-first century

The above discussion points in the direction of three main models of civil society. The first I call the uncivil model, and it is characterized by three elements. The first of these is a weak state that cannot guarantee the rights constituting a precondition for the existence of civil society. Civil society in this situation constitutes itself without the guarantees that are part of the pacification of the political space. The second element is that the market economy appears mostly as an imposition of privatized social relations, within which a network of social ties is not able to expand. Thirdly, political society either does not exist (Peru), or it is so fractured that it sees civil society as a danger (Colombia). While features of the uncivil model exist today in all Latin American countries (for instance in the form of land conflicts in Brazil or the Zapatista uprising in Mexico), I would argue that the Andean region comes closest to it as an ideal-type because of the weak state structures and the damage caused by civil war and a fractured political society. The many forms of collective action that exist in the region are subordinated to the destructive dynamics of state politics. It should be clear that it is not only the state that can transform society from civil to uncivil – the market also has the ability to do this. The challenge of the Andean case is whether civil society can produce civility in spite of the state and the market.

The second model I would call a liberal civil society model. In the liberal case, the process of state construction had been relatively successful prior to the authoritarian period. These structures acquired the capacity to exercise mediation, and were reconstructed after the authoritarian period. Civil society is related to the reconstruction of a rights structure and to forms of collective action aiming to secure accountability and the rule of law. Thus, civil society cannot be reduced to political society, even if the level of collective action is usually low. It builds on a structure of rights that are not put at stake either by civil or by political actors. The actions of civil society in the democratized period did not challenge the available structure of political mediation. Civil society triggers social action only when the political system fails to fulfil its proper role within the liberal order. Again, this model might apply to many forms of civil society action in Latin America, but it appertains most closely to the Argentinean and Chilean case.

The third model of civil society organization in Latin America I will call the public participatory model. In this model the constitution of civil society took place within the framework of an already consolidated process of state construction. However, civil society challenged a central aspect of the process of mediation between political society and the state not only by introducing alternative practices at the societal level but also by institutionalizing these practices at both the constitutional and the legal levels. This model clearly relates most closely to the case of Brazil, while it is too early to be certain whether Mexico will evolve in the direction of the participatory or the liberal model.

This typology not only helps us to understand the different manifestations of civil society in Latin America, it also helps us to see which kinds of roles civil society can fulfil in the near future. In the case of 'uncivil civil societies', their role should be to contribute to the civilization of the political process, which should involve the reduction of levels of violence and the attempt to link civil society construction to the pacification of political disputes and the acknowledgement of rights. In the liberal case, civil society should seek to fill the gaps left open in the process of political mediation, which is incomplete, by pushing the present limits of participation. In the participatory situation, it should extend participation to other sectors and construct effective forms of political mediation. In all situations, there is the risk of falling back into the uncivil conditions that still persist throughout Latin American society. Yet in all cases there is also the potential to move to a more civil, liberal and participatory society.

References

Alexander, J. (ed.) (1998) *Real Civil Societies: The Dilemma of Institutionalisation*, London: Sage Publications.

Alvarez, S.E., Dagnino, E. and Escobar, A. (1998) *Culture of Politics; Politics of Cultures: Re-visioning Latin American Social Movements*, Boulder CO: Westview Press.

Avritzer, L. (2002) *Democracy and the Public Sphere in Latin America*, Princeton: Princeton University Press.

Bobbio, N. (1988), 'Gramsci and the concept of civil society', in J. Keane (ed.), *Civil Society and the State: New European Perspectives*, London: Verso.

Cohen, J. and Arato, A. (1992) *Civil Society and Political Theory*, Cambridge MA: MIT Press.

Dagnino, E. (ed.) (2002) *Sociedad, esfera pública y Democratizacion en America Latina: Brasil* [Society, Public Sphere and Democratization in Latin America: Brazil], Belo Horizonte: Universidade Estadual de Campinas and Fondo de Cultura Económica.

Franco, M.a.d.C. (1974) *Homens Livres na Ordem Escravocrata*, São Paolo: Atica.

Guerra, X.F. (1988) *Mexico: del antigo regimen a la revoluccion* [Mexico from the ancien regime to the revolution], Mexico: Fondo de cultura.

Habermas, J. (1996), *Between Facts and Norms: Contributions to a Discourse Theory of Law and Democracy* (German original 1992), Cambridge: Polity Press.

Keane, J. (ed.) (1988) *Civil Society and the State*, London: Macmillan.

Olvera, A. (ed.) (2003) *Sociedad civil, esfera pública y democratizacion en America Latina: México* [Society, Public Sphere and Democratization in Latin America: Mexico], Mexico City: Universidad Veracruzana and Fondo de Cultura Económica.

Oxhorn, P. (1995) *Organizing Civil Society: The Popular Sectors and the Struggle for Democracy in Chile*, Philadelphia: Pennsylvania State University Press.

Oxhorn, P. and Ducatenzeiler, G. (eds) (1998) *What Kind of Democracy? What Kind of Market? : Latin America in the Age of Neoliberalism*, University Park PA: Pennsylvania State University Press.

Peruzotti, E. (2002) 'Emergencia, desarollo y reconstruccion de la sociedad civil Argentina' [Emergency, development and reconstruction of civil society in Argentina], in A. Panfichi (ed.), *Sociedad civil y governanca democratica* [Civil society and democratic governance], Mexico: Fondo de cultura.

Shils, E. (1997) *The Virtue of Civility: Selected Essays on Liberalism, Tradition, and Civil society*, Indianapolis: Liberty Fund.
Stepan, A. (1988) *Rethinking Military Politics*, Princeton: Princeton University Press.
Zermeño, S., Granados, G., and Cuevas Diáz, J. (eds) (1990) *Movimientos sociales en México durante la década de los 80* [Social movements in Mexico during the 1980s] México, DF: Universidad Nacional Autónoma de México, Centro de Investigaciones Interdisciplinarias en Humanidades.

7 Collective action or public participation?

Civil society and the public sphere in post-transition Latin America

Jenny Pearce

The concept of civil society reached Latin America in the course of the 1980s in two guises. The first was through its appeal as a normative ideal to social actors living under repressive and military governments. The second, which appeared somewhat later, was as a concept of liberal governance for those concerned with postdictatorship institution building. During fragile transition processes, civil society remained conceptually unelaborated; 'civil society' against the 'state' appealed to all who sought to end authoritarian rule at a time when the fragility of the process required some unity of purpose. Sociologist and later Brazilian President, Fernando Henrique Cardoso points out how in Brazil 'everything which was an organized fragment which escaped the immediate control of the authoritarian order was being designated *civil society*. Not rigorously, but effectively, the whole opposition ... was being described as if it were the movement of Civil Society' (Cardoso 1989: 319).

As democratization progressed in the 1990s and revealed its limitations to those seeking more rapid and fundamental social and political transformations, the conceptual differences began to widen. For social actors, civil society was their agency for such transformations; for liberals, it included extending public participation but in ways that were compatible with governance. What is the relationship between social activism and formal democracy? Is there any way of reconciling the differences between those on the periphery of the formal system and those who step inside in order to ensure that the sphere of civil society is a legitimate and relevant space for democracy's critics as well as democracy's builders? And can this be done before disenchantment sets in amongst critics and the ideal of an autonomous sphere of public deliberation and free associationalism is weakened by the disaffection of its most vibrant participants, leaving the space open for authoritarian and populist appeals to an atomized population?

Democracy and civil society in post-transition Latin America

Latin America's state institutions evolved to serve narrow political and economic interests. They preserved cultures of their own where the electorate was seen more as a clientele for the power struggles of politicians than as citizens with rights. The struggle to reform Latin America's state institutions and make them capable of enhancing democracy has been one of the most difficult tasks in the years that followed Latin America's transition from authoritarian and military rule. Some scholars have emphasized the problem of constitutional form and discussed the relative advantages of parliamentary and presidential political systems for Latin America (Linz and Stepan 1994; Mainwaring and Shugart 1997). Others turned to civil society as a means to build accountability mechanisms between state institutions and society and deepen the quality of post-transition democracy. In particular, those in the business of building post-transition democracy, such as external donors, began to see civil society as an instrument for institutional reform and democratization.

The Inter-American Development Bank (IDB) and other financial institutions turned their attention to Latin America's weak state institutions in the early 1990s, and a great deal of money was invested in judicial and administrative reform. Economic liberalization, it was argued, would require profound public-sector reform. It was acknowledged that this would challenge entrenched political interests, and civil society came to be seen as an essential ally in this process (Howell and Pearce 2001). At first civil society was little understood as a concept. It was equated with the non-governmental organizations (NGOs), which in Latin America had grown to support grass-roots social mobilizing during the Cold War, and was highly politicized. In the wake of the Cold War, the NGO became a vehicle for new forms of service delivery that could bypass the state. Gradually, however, the concept of civil society was broadened to include a wide range of organizations working for democracy and human rights and against corruption. The associational sphere of Latin America was 'mapped' and quantified, and became the focus of external efforts to boost the quality of democracy in Latin America. 'Civil society strengthening' programmes proliferated in the region and encouraged NGOs to become increasingly donor oriented (Howell and Pearce 2001).

Tensions emerged between some NGOs and the social organizations with which they had once been connected. Many NGOs became more professionalized. They came to identify themselves with the 'democracy building' project (Pearce 1997a). The language of the external support programmes referred to building a 'Third Sector', which amongst the politicized Latin American social organizations had a technical resonance that was meaningless to their experience and the challenges they faced. The distance grew between social-movement actors and grass-roots organizations that expected democracy to deliver not only a reformed state and greater political participation but also distributive justice in the economic field. Partnership between the state and civil society meant little to these activists who believed that the state still represented the interests of a minority which feared the autonomous and often oppositional character of civil society. They came to view those NGOs who collaborated with the state, not just in service delivery but also in advocacy roles, as coopted.

Authors of the Third Sector approach captured something of this growing divide. They saw Latin America as a duality in which 'in a sense, two separate non-profit sectors exist ... one of them composed of more traditional charitable organizations and other agencies linked to the social and economic elite and the other associated with the relatively newer forms of grass-roots organizations and so-called nongovernmental organizations (NGOs) that support them'. Amongst the ways of overcoming the duality, the authors recommend capacity building: 'Latin America', they argue, 'is ripe for a major non-profit sector capacity building campaign to bring the less formal part of the region's civil society sector more fully into a position to operate on a par with the more traditional part, and with partners in government and the business sector' (Salamon and Anheier 1999: 17).

Grass-roots activists, however, saw their strength in their location on the periphery, in their representation of the excluded and impoverished majorities, and in their mobilizing capacity. These 'less formal' parts of civil society were not ready to accept that governments or multilateral financial institutions were sincerely interested in their participation, a participation that would challenge and provoke. Leonardo Avritzer carried out a survey of voluntary associations in Brazil in the late 1990s and found that the nature of their claims remained primarily collective and transformatory rather than self-interested and material. In a survey of 311 respondents from 159 voluntary associations in Belo Horizonte and São Paulo, over 36 per cent put working for some form of social change as their main motivation for participation (Avritzer 1998).

A radical framework for conceptualizing civil society had begun to emerge in the 1980s and 1990s, though unevenly. The framework that Latin America's radical thinkers drew upon derived from Antonio Gramsci. Gramsci's work encouraged a significant sector of the Latin American left to re-evaluate the character and importance of civil society (Pearce 1997b), which had previously been understood in classical Marxist terms as the class structure of capitalism. The organized left had traditionally marshalled and channelled the energies of social movements as part of a variety of bids for state power, and those movements had often struggled with the left and the authoritarian state for autonomy and space to develop. However, Gramsci suggested that civil society was an autonomous arena between economy and state, where the hegemonic ideology of capitalism could be challenged as well as reproduced. Social movements gained value in their own right. They were resisting cultural and social as well as economic forms of domination and repression. In some countries party and social activists began to move apart; the Workers' Party of Brazil was an important exception but nevertheless there were tensions between the two worlds. Many political parties of the left had been weakened by repression and by the collapse of articulating ideologies, and were poorly equipped to adapt to post-transition politics. The new societal politics of the social movements gained credibility and momentum, however, building on their role in the struggle against authoritarian rule.

The idea of a public space independent of the state and market, and free from manipulation by political parties and leaders, was a new idea for Latin America. But Gramscian influence led many to interpret civil society as equivalent to the protagonism of social movements. It was not a pluralist arena of negative liberty, housing a heterogeneous assortment of interests that liberals valued in itself as a protection against the encroachments of state power or to ensure that no particular interests could dominate over others. Many social movements of Latin America spoke of themselves as civil society, the new force for emancipation in the region. This was not about the building of a civil society arena of public participation within a market-driven economy that external donors had in mind. Nor did they wish merely to collaborate with governments that used the language of democracy to mask the unequal wealth and power that still characterized the region. Participation was considered a value in itself, a means by which the poor and marginalized could critically challenge from their peripheries. It was not about building a democratic infrastructure that could guarantee the integrity of the civil society arena as an end in itself. Civil society meant direct democracy and the importance of the general good over particular interests, even the pluralities of civil society. This was a view more akin to the classical republicanism of Rousseau than the modern republicanism of Montesquieu (Leiva and Pagden 2001).

The division between those wishing to deepen and strengthen democracy, the 'builders', and those critical of its failure to deliver the expectations of the poor majority, the 'critics', became more apparent and more consequential in the course of the 1990s. Yet the division was much more polarized in the minds of activists than in reality. Collaboration and cooperation between many non-governmental and intergovernmental builders was less due to whether or not they believed in the status quo and the neoliberal economic agenda it had adopted, than in a shared commitment to civilian government and the rule of law, citizens' rights and human rights, and an end to corruption and venality. While there were opportunistic NGOs, there were many who were consciously prioritizing this agenda as the most urgent for Latin America at this phase in its history – the struggle against neoliberal economic policies should continue but within this new framework. Many NGOs and members of other associations and organizations did not wish to remain on the periphery, but claimed their legitimate place in emerging public spaces, including those provided by governments and external donors, where they could influence government policy and make it accountable. External donors might have different motivations in that economic liberalization was for them the flip side of political liberalization, but they were at least now prepared to support the latter. The danger of cooption was nevertheless real, but in the polarizing climate the question of how to avoid cooption by developing a shared understanding and agenda between radical NGOs and social movement activists was rarely discussed.

In a series of regional workshops that I ran in July and August 2002 in Managua, Caracas and Asunción on the subject of civil society and democracy for Catholic social activists of the Social Pastoral of the Latin American Bishops' Conference (CELAM), the extent of their distance from the liberal idea of civil society and the public sphere, as well as the disaffection from the democratic transition amongst people very close to the real world of the poor in Latin America, was very evident. There were conceptual confusions around the meaning of civil society in all regions, stemming from a sense that governments and multilateral institutions had selected only a part of civil society to strengthen, excluding the more critical elements. For instance in the Managua workshop, which brought people together from Central America and Mexico, participants challenged the title of the workshops and wanted to exclude civil society altogether so that the focus became 'social movements and democracy'. In Caracas, which was a workshop for activists from the Andean region as a whole but where participants were mostly from Venezuela, the concept of 'civil society' had been appropriated by the opposition to President Hugo Chavez. This opposition was associated mostly with the wealthy elites, and the social activists, even those who were anti-Chavez, had to be convinced that the concept had any general relevance. In the Southern Cone countries represented in the workshop in Asunción, civil society was still acceptable and relevant but only in so far as it represented the agency of the social activists, not as a pluralist sphere of public deliberation. In all three workshops, there was great fear of incorporation and cooption, and an over-riding concern with addressing the structural causes of inequality before accepting that the transition to democracy was authentic; there was a pervasive view that an authentic democratic order had also to be a socially and economically just order; and it was felt that democracy also had to include active participation and what was termed 'citizenship co-responsibility', the idea that the citizen should be considered an active participant in the political decision-making process. Radical republicanism rather than modern liberalism attracted the activists because it recognized them as active participants in the polity, a polity whose aim was to protect the common good not the particular interests of the few. The democratic transition to a liberal form of governance had been unconvincing to them; it neither valued the participation of the poorest nor did it offer sincere solutions to their predicament.

By the beginning of the new millennium there was more evidence that the disaffection of these activists was echoed in the wider society, although for a range of reasons. The Latin American opinion poll *Latinobarómetro* was recording the most serious disaffection with state institutions since it began its polls in 1996. Only the Church commanded a very high level of respect (72 per cent). Public support for the judiciary, the police, the national congress and political parties ranged between 32 per cent and 19 per cent ('An Alarm Call' 2001). There was a dramatic drop in the share of respondents who clearly preferred democracy as a system of government from an average of 61 per cent of citizens in 1996 to 48 per cent in 2001, while the percentage of those who felt that the form of government made no difference rose from 16 per cent to 21 per cent; 50 per cent of respondents agreed with the statement that it would not matter to them if the military assumed power (Mark Payne *et al.* 2002: 29).

Yet events such as the Porto Alegre Social Forum in January 2003 brought some 100,000 social activists together, over 80,000 of them (by some calculations) from Latin America, to show that, if faith in post-transition democracy institutions and governance was waning, the Latin American tradition of popular mobilizing and contentious politics remained very much alive (Albert 2003) . What might be the relationship between this form of politics and democracy building? Does perhaps the concept of civil society encapsulate both?

Civil society and democracy under stress

The Inter-American Development Bank (IDB) published a study of the process of politics and reform in Latin America in 2002 in which they expressed some pessimism for the future:

> The experience of the past two decades along with historical trends over time, suggests that the democratic wave that has swept through Latin America could be reversed. While no countries in the region have abandoned elections or permanently shut down democratic institutions, in several instances extra-constitutional manoeuvres have been used to retain, usurp or augment power. Given the tremendous challenges posed by economic volatility, high levels of poverty and inequality, and organized crime and violence, democracy remains under stress in many countries.
>
> (Mark Payne *et al.* 2002: 25)

There is no doubt that post-transition democracy building in Latin America is fragile at the beginning of the new millennium. However, while one way of seeing the tensions between democracy builders and democracy critics is that they will contribute to greater fragility, another is to see them as the seeds of longer-term change. The tension itself does not alter the significantly new attitudes towards the meaning of civil society and the public sphere that have emerged through the practice of both builders and critics. For instance, the struggle for human rights and the rule of law that has been shared by both critics and builders has been of deep importance to the possibility of freedom of association; the right of associations to debate not only how to make existing institutions work better but to question who they do, and do not, serve has been established in a more or less solid way in many countries; the right of associations to challenge the distributional deficits of society and for the most excluded to speak out safely has begun to be recognized; serious challenges to deeply embedded gender and ethnic inequalities have emerged; and significant inroads into the time-honoured brokerage mechanisms between state and society have taken place, albeit unevenly. It is true that none of these advances is irreversible as yet, but they nevertheless mark some significant advances over the past.

In the context of Latin America, with its high levels of social and economic inequality and exclusion, it is unlikely that the public sphere will develop without a strong component of collective action for change. Many of the changes outlined have come about as a result of the action of social movements; others with the help of the advocacy work of NGOs and voluntary groups. The contentious nature of social movements is what defines them and what continues to be their most abiding characteristic, even when some gain greater capacity in advocacy and using the legal system to press for change (Tarrow 1996: 5). Social movements lack the stable resources – money, organization, access to the state – that other forms of public engagement enjoy. At the same time they express deeply felt lived experiences that, if contained, can express themselves in less constructive ways than social action. The element of contention distinguishes what social movements bring to the civil society idea. It has contributed to the reinvention and reinvigoration of a concept that lay virtually dormant for decades, arguably since the late eighteenth century (Howell and Pearce 2001). It is about how powerless or power-poor people have taken on the powerful to extend rights, to access economic opportunities and to change the values that drive societal development and those which exclude them.

Collective action in Latin America has arguably contributed more than a greater commitment to individual rights and the deepening of a liberal language and consciousness in the politics of the region. Latin American scholars have begun to identify specific ways in which social movements in the region could be contributing to structural changes in how the public space is understood. The Brazilian scholar Leonardo Avritzer has argued that in Latin America since the 1980s new social actors have transformed the role of the public expression of political ideas and the meaning of a public and democratic identity in the region. Avritzer does not see such transformation as uniquely the role of social movements: he argues that voluntary associations of all kinds have become the standard ways of organizing and occupying the public sphere (Avritzer 2002: 81). A three-volume study by Latin American scholars has now begun to look at the evolution of civil society and the public space in all regions of Latin America (Dagnino 2002; Olvera 2003; Panfichi 2002).

The new value given to the public sphere and civil society by Latin American intellectuals is a reflection itself of changes in progress and a new confidence in the possibility that the public sphere has become a means for transforming political language and practices. The totalizing project that characterized collective action in the 1960s and 1970s has given way, it is argued, to more focused public political engagement. This does not necessarily translate into the liberal civil society model *per se*, but perhaps would be another Latin American political hybrid. Wiarda (2003) might be right when he suggests that the outcome of sociological and economic change in Latin America will not be a North American model of civil society and the public sphere. Associational life may not settle into the pressure or interest group model of civic engagement, but something more participatory, active and political, something more akin to Nancy Frazer's idea of 'strong publics' (Frazer 1994).

In this approach movements create new spaces of public deliberation alongside the parliamentary and congressional spaces of representative politics. Social movements retain their essential quality of contestation and their critical democratic values but they move in from the periphery and engage with representative and institutionalized bodies in constructive ways, on their own terms, and with the objective of achieving substantive change in the daily lives of people rather than through some totalizing and future-oriented societal vision. In so doing, they nevertheless develop criteria for assessing when protest action becomes a morally justifiable option for seeking change. Similarly, they develop criteria for choosing their allies amongst the more professionalized NGOs and voluntary associations who work within the public political space but who, like them, wish to see more profound changes in the socioeconomic order of the region. The latter would also learn to respect the importance of the ongoing public engagement of the less formal civil society groups whose activism ensures that democratization is not just a negotiation between elites (O'Donnell and Schmitter 1986).

Conclusion

Could a 'strong publics' vision of Latin American civil society reverse the polarizing tendencies between social movement activists and non-governmental and other groups who opt to work within the spaces for public participation opened up from above (by governments) and from the outside (by external donors)? Distrust remains pervasive within and between all these actors in the democratization process in Latin America, and civil society is no longer the unifying concept it was. Despite some positive trends that point towards a certain amount of transformation in the Latin American public sphere, there are many dangers. Economic shocks, stagnant growth, and the rise of social crime and violence could all foster the growth of the authoritarian and populist impulses that remain strong throughout the region. In this context, the search for some common ground and mutual respect between democracy's 'builders' and its 'critics' becomes more urgent.

References

Albert, M. (2003) *World Social Forum: Where to Now? www.forumsocialmundial.org.br.*

'An Alarm Call for Latin America's Democrats' (2001), *The Economist*, 26 July.

Avritzer, L. (1998) 'Social Equity and Participatory Politics: Reflections about the Non-Organized Sectors', Paper presented to the Latin American Studies Association, Twenty-First International Congress, Chicago, Illinois, 24–26 September, mimeo.

——(2002) *Democracy and the Public Sphere in Latin America*, Princeton: Princeton University Press.

Cardoso, F. (1989) 'Associated dependent development and democratic theory', in A. Stepan (ed.), *Democratizing Brazil*, New York and Oxford: Oxford University Press.

Dagnino, E. (ed.) (2002) *Sociedad, esfera pública y democratizacion en America Latina: Brasil* [Society, Public Sphere and Democratization in Latin America: Brazil], Belo Horizonte: Universidade Estadual de Campinas and Fondo de Cultura Económica.

Frazer, N. (1994) 'Rethinking the public sphere', in C. Calhoun (ed.), *Habermas and the Public Sphere,* Cambridge MA: MIT Press.

Howell, J. and Pearce, J. (2001) *Civil Society and Development: A Critical Exploration*, Boulder CO: Lynne Rienner.

Leiva, L. and Pagden, A. (2001) 'The fate of the modern republics of Latin America', in S. Kaviraj and S. Khilnani (eds), *Civil Society: History and Possibilities*, Cambridge: Cambridge University Press.

Linz, J. and Stepan, A. (1994) 'Presidential or parliamentary democracy: does it make a difference?', in J. Linz and A. Valenzuela (eds), *The Failure of Presidential Democracy*, Baltimore: Johns Hopkins University Press.

Mainwaring, S. and Shugart, M. (eds) (1997) *Presidentialism and Democracy in Latin America*, Cambridge: Cambridge University Press.

Mark Payne, J. *et al.* (2002) *Democracies in Development: Politics and Reform in Latin America*, Washington DC: IDB and International Institute for Democracy and Electoral Assistance.

O'Donnell, G. and Schmitter, P. (1986) *Transitions from Authoritarian Rule*, Vol. 4 *Tentative Conclusions about Uncertain Democracies*, Baltimore: Johns Hopkins University Press.

Olvera, A. (ed.) (2003) *Sociedad civil, esfera pública y democratizacion en America Latina: México* [Society, Public Sphere and Democratization in Latin America: Mexico], Mexico City: Universidad Veracruzana and Fondo de Cultura Económica.

Panfichi, A. (ed.) (2002) *Sociedad civil, esfera pública y democratizacion en America Latina: Andes y Cono Sur* [Society, Public Sphere and Democratization in Latin America: Andes and Southern Cone], Lima: Universidad Catolica de Peru and Fondo de Cultura Económica.

Pearce, J. (1997a) 'Between cooption and irrelevance? Latin American NGOs in the 1990s', in M. Edwards and D. Hulme (eds), *Too Close for Comfort*, Basingstoke: Macmillan.

——(1997b) 'Civil society, the market and democracy in Latin America', *Democratization*, 4(2): 57–83.

Salamon, L., and Anheier, H. (1999) *The Emerging Sector Revisited: A Summary*, Baltimore: Johns Hopkins University Press.

Tarrow, S. (1996) *Power in Movement*, Cambridge: Cambridge University Press.

Wiarda, H. (2003) *Civil Society: The American Model and Third World Development*, Boulder CO: Westview Press.

8 Civil society in Eastern Europe

Growth without engagement

Jerzy Celichowski

Civil society in Eastern Europe finds it hard to avoid comparisons with the period of 1989–90, when the concept provided a framework for massive mobilization around the fall of Soviet socialism (I prefer this term to the commonly used 'communism', as the East European states neither called themselves communist, nor were in essence such) raising hopes, also beyond the region, for a new form of politics. The prominence achieved during this period is long gone but the concept seems to have taken root in Eastern Europe for good, developing along different paths in response to the different social and political environments . This differentiation means that it is more appropriate to speak of 'civil societies' than 'a civil society' of Eastern Europe.

Most simply civil society has been defined as the space between the state, the market and the family (for example, Gellner 1994; White 1994). A number of authors, however, have proposed narrower definitions such as groups that 'follow the general liberal democratic principles' (Howard 2003: 41), or groups that, among others, 'agree to act within pre-established rules of "civil" or legal nature' (Schmitter 1995: 4–5). In these cases a strong normative element is present, reflecting an underlying belief that civil society is a 'good' thing. However, as some authors have argued (Carters 1999–2000; Kopecký and Mudde 2003), this is both intellectually inconsistent and factually incorrect. For this reason I will adopt the first-mentioned general definition, which is the only one that I believe allows a full understanding of the paths of development of civil societies in Eastern Europe.

My main focus will be on the Czech Republic, Hungary, Poland and Slovakia (Central Europe), as this is where the concept of civil society (re)emerged in the 1970s, which warrants closer attention to them. However, I will make references also to other East European countries, which for the purposes of this article I will understand as those non-USSR European countries that were ruled by communist parties after World War Two.

Before 1989

The idea of civil society was conceptualized by Central European intellectuals in the 1970s and the 1980s. For Václav Havel the post-totalitarian system required 'living within a lie', hence the proper response was 'living within the truth', or revolt against any form of manipulation (Havel 1990: 48–66). György Konrád went even further in his dislike for the state, rejecting all forms of political involvement through his concept of antipolitics (Tempest 1997: 134). Adam Michnik represented views closest to the classical concept of civil society. In his concept a self-restraining 'new evolutionism' society, with workers as a main driving force, organizes to demand concessions from the state (Michnik 1985: 144). All these three approaches share a negative view of the state, which should be protested against (living the truth), escaped (antipolitics) or fought against (new evolutionism), and this attitude influenced strongly the understanding of civil society in Eastern Europe.

With the exception of Poland, which saw a massive social self-organization during the 1980s, these ideas did not find a broad following until 1989–90. For instance, the number of the signatories of Charter 77, a major Czechoslovak dissident group, was less than two thousand (Glenn 2001: 63).

This dissident perspective came to dominate the discourse of civil societies in Eastern Europe, leading to a situation where other civil society manifestations, which frequently did not call themselves 'civil society', have been overlooked in research. Churches played a role, for instance, the most prominent of them being the Polish Catholic Church. In addition to providing the well-known support extended to dissident groups, the Church was a civil society actor in its own right hosting a range of informal groups that performed the same functions as non-governmental organizations (NGOs) today, for instance working with the disabled. Less known is the Slovak secret church, which maintained between 1943 and 1989 a parallel sphere of religious activities including publications, petitions, pilgrimages and finally street demonstrations with a grass-roots support exceeding that of dissident groups (Doellinger 2002). Sometimes official organizations, for instance the scouting association in Poland, provided space for semi-independent activities, though this was an exception rather than a rule. The massive mobilization of 1989–90 relied to a large extent on individuals who developed their civic attitudes through participation in these sorts of activities.

1989–90

The period around the fall of Soviet socialism in 1989–90 was the heyday of civil societies in Eastern Europe. They were both leading actors in the changes and provided the vocabulary for an emerging alternative to communist rule. The adjective 'civic' appears in both the name of Civic Forum, the umbrella of Czech opposition, and of civic committees, which conducted the election campaign in Poland on behalf of the Solidarity camp in 1989.

These spectacular successes gave new impetus to earlier speculations that civil societies in Eastern Europe and the new social movements in the West could become a new organizing principle of democracy (Keane 1988; see also Wainwright, this volume). Havel, the main proponent of this idea, asked rhetorically: 'are not these informed, non-bureaucratic, dynamic and open communities that comprise "parallel polis" a kind of rudimentary prefiguration or symbolic model of those more meaningful "post-democratic" political structures that might become the foundation of a better society?' (Havel 1991: 213). The catapulting of several dissidents into key political positions gave this idea an aura of reality.

After 1990: different paths of development

These expectations were to be quickly ruined by splits of the victorious opposition previously united under the umbrella of the civil society concept. Czech Civic Forum and Slovak Public Against Violence were transformed into classical political parties; Poland's 'war at the top' led to the dissolution of the civic committees.

Even though they included former dissidents, the newly elected governments often showed arrogance towards societies, evoking memories of the recent past. The most spectacular case of such behaviour took place in Hungary in 1991 where, faced by spontaneous taxi road-blockades against petrol price rises, the government toyed with the idea of sending in the army against the protesters. It helped revive the us–them dichotomy and diminished hopes for a new arrangement between the rulers and the ruled.

At the same time differences in the development paths between various countries began to surface. Some pursued democratization, others turned towards authoritarianism, and yet others saw wars. Civil societies developed everywhere within the space available, adjusting themselves to these different environments. In the paragraphs that follow I will present a few examples of the models that have emerged so far.

Thanks to a favourable political, legal and fiscal environment, civil societies in Central Europe are relatively sophisticated. Establishing independent organizations has been legal in Hungary and Poland since the late 1980s. Tax privileges granted to foundations in the early 1990s were so advantageous that foundation status came to be frequently abused, which resulted in a tightening of regulations in 1992 (Siegel and Yancey 1992: 30–2). Efforts have been made to depoliticize the question of state funding to civil society. For instance, Hungarian and Slovak civil sectors have benefited from so-called 1 per cent laws, which allow tax payers to indicate a non-governmental organization to receive one per cent of their tax. The biggest problem at the moment seems to be the decreasing flow of foreign donor funds caused by the EU accession of these countries.

The most significant manifestations of 'non-governmental nationalism' (Bieber 2003) have emerged in the Balkans, particularly in Serbia, where the nationalist movement operated through NGOs. The Yugoslav Helsinki Group, set up in 1987, proclaimed in its founding memorandum that those 'who preach the use of violence, or are in favour of national, racial, religious or ideological intolerance' will be excluded from membership, but a significant number of the signatories later engaged in the propagation of hate speech and promotion of nationalism (Bieber 2003: 23), setting a trend among non-governmental groups in Serbia. Croatia had a similar range of nationalistic groups, which included the prominent movement of war veterans (Fisher 2003). Both countries, however, also saw successful campaigns with significant civil society participation that led to the removal of their authoritarian regimes.

The province of Kosovo lost its autonomy in 1989, which led in consequence to the dismissal of a large number of Albanians employed in public administration, the education system and the media. Inspired by the Central European example the Albanians responded with non-violent resistance and the reconstruction of the public sphere outside the state structures, achieving impressive results. For instance, in 1995 the education system encompassed 5,291 preschool pupils, about 312,000 elementary school pupils, 59,920 secondary school pupils, as well as 20 faculties and colleges with about 12,200 students. Funds to run this system (some $20–25m annually) were raised by voluntary contributions of 3 per cent of the earnings of the Kosovars and Albanians living in the West (Maliqi 1998: 114–15). However, the system worked imperfectly and contributions soon began to slip. The end of Serbian control of the province in 1999 led to the dissolution of the system.

In Belarus, a hostile environment has been detrimental to the development of a civil society. In 1999 activities of unregistered NGOs became punishable by law, and the compulsory re-registration in the same year resulted in an almost 50 per cent decrease in the number of NGOs (Zagoumennov 2001: 8). Financing NGO operations is difficult as they enjoy no tax privileges and are obliged to pay a 40 per cent tax on foreign assistance received. In 1997 the local Soros Foundation, a major provider of assistance to civil society, was forced to close down. In these conditions civil society organizations are neither numerous nor strong. As the regime does not show signs of relenting some have begun to talk of civil society as 'the new dissidents keeping alive the vision of democracy' (Ottoway and Carters 2000: 310).

Foreign aid and civil society's role in democratization

After 1989 civil societies in Eastern Europe attracted interest not only from theorists looking for 'postdemocratic' politics but also from 'transitologists'. The claim they made is that civil societies can contribute to the transition from authoritarian to democratic regimes through their role in monitoring the state, stimulating participation in public affairs, creating space for the development of democratic attributes such as moderation, compromise or respect for opposing views, providing channels for articulation of interests, and establishing links across society (Diamond 1994: 7–9).

The implications of these views have been significant, as foreign donors providing assistance to the East European transitions included civil societies as one of the targets of aid under the category 'democracy assistance'. For practical purposes, the understanding of civil society was, at least initially, limited to advocacy NGOs focusing on 'what aid providers considered to be sociopolitical issues touching the public interest – including election monitoring, civic education, parliamentary transparency, human rights, anticorruption, the environment, women's rights, and indigenous people's rights' (Carters 1999: 210). Importantly, assistance has often reflected the donor country's domestic liberal agenda: support would rarely go to anti-abortion or pro-death-penalty groups, or a business association seeking to relax environmental laws (Carters 1999: 212). The combination of the promotion of particular issues with the focus on one kind of NGO meant that large swaths of the civil societies benefited little from foreign aid.

Civil society support, primarily technical assistance and training, reached about 1 per cent of the total $100bn provided as aid to Eastern Europe during the 1990s (Quigley 2000: 192). Foreign assistance, coming not only as a part of official aid but also at a grass-roots level, can be credited with the success of transplanting the hitherto unknown idea of NGOs. It was also crucial in promoting previously marginal issues such as women's rights or the environment.

Critics have argued that instead of fostering grass-roots activism the aid has created a class of NGO professionals much more attentive to donors' wishes than to the opinions of their fellow citizens (Carters 1999). Some even think that the aggressive promotion of foreign models may have actually delayed the emergence of indigenous groups and movements (McMahon 2001). The focus on NGOs may be indirectly responsible for pathologies in the third sector. For example, corruption among some Macedonian NGOs has to do with the fact that it is easier to register an NGO than a company, and that getting a grant requires relatively little effort. As a result an NGO job can be simply an easy way of earning a comfortable life (Dimitrov 2003).

Taking stock

How have East European civil societies fared so far? This question can be answered in three ways: by looking at the number of associations and their members, by analysing participation in them, or by analysing expectations attached to them.

Current civil societies started growing from a rather low level. Their predecessors included a few small independent groups and communist-controlled associations boasting a massive, though usually quasi-obligatory, membership. Official associations need to be mentioned as they later underwent 'renewal' and claimed to have become 'independent' and as such a part of a civil society.

Change against this initial situation can be measured by looking at the overall number of these organizations. The figures have been rising, particularly in the early1990s (Karatnycky *et al.* 1997; 2002), though there are certainly exceptions such as the fall of the number of NGOs in Tudjman's Croatia in the mid-1990s. This approach has three disadvantages. First, it takes into consideration only 'births' of organizations but not their 'deaths', leading to overblown figures. Second, it does not say anything about the membership of a given organization or its character. Some NGOs consist of just a few members, but in this approach they are given equal weighting to groups with massive membership; similarly, the approach includes NGOs that are just covers for explicitly political or economic activities, such as donor-driven NGOs (DONGOs), money-making organizations (MONGOs) and so on. Third, officially registered NGOs may not exhaust the organizational forms of civil society. Groups may prefer to avoid formal registration in order not to draw attention to themselves or may simply choose informality as their core value.

A second approach does not look at the number of the NGOs but at the number of their members. Based on World Values Surveys, East European civil societies are weak: the average number of organizational memberships per person is 0.91, while respective figures for postauthoritarian countries and old democracies are 1.82 and 2.39 (Howard 2003: 62).Worse than that, membership rates have shown a decrease (Howard 2003: 72). The main problem with this approach is that it treats residual membership in a formerly official organization such as a trade union in the same way as a membership in a new grass-roots group, something that may have been particularly important in the early 1990s. It also fails to detect participation in informal groups.

The World Values Survey data also provide information on the likelihood of engagement in typical civil society activities such as signing petitions, participating in boycotts, demonstrations, strikes or occupations of buildings. East European civil societies score worse than the old democracies (data from Glasius, Kaldor and Anheier 2002: 365–6). Compared to the postauthoritarian countries they score minimally better only on strike participation. Looking at the data from 1990–93 and 2000 one can observe a decrease in support for these activities, with the exception of a minimal growth in the propensity to join a boycott.

Earlier dissident visions have not been fulfilled. This is not necessarily to be mourned: while the antistate feelings underlying dissident thinking may have been useful in the fight against Soviet socialism, they are not conducive to civic engagement under democracy, except for protest movements. Similarly, the hopes for new postdemocratic politics seem to belong irretrievably to 1989–90, the period of extraordinary politics. In the years that followed some civil society groups and activists who turned to traditional party politics often displayed an aptitude for dirty political games or promoting 'uncivil' values.

It is difficult to estimate whether civil societies have fulfilled the hopes attached to them by the transitologists, one reason being the difficulty in separating their influence from other factors. This said, there is no doubt about their role in the get-out-the-vote campaigns before elections, removing authoritarian regimes in Romania (1996), Slovakia (1998), Croatia (2000) and Serbia (2000), even though a similar mobilization attempt in Belarus (2001) was not successful. However, one cannot interpret this as definite proof of the definitely prodemocratic and pluralistic potential of civil societies: these regimes themselves had heavily relied on nationalistic manifestations of civil society.

In one sense, civil societies have met expectations connected with them. The desire of so many East Europeans to 'return to Europe' usually translated into remoulding their countries according to the Western model, of which a civil society is an indispensable part. If these countries are more 'European' now than before, as the EU enlargement process indicates, civil societies have had their share in this success.

Conclusion

In spite of their impressive growth East European civil societies are still weak with regard to their ability to engage citizens. They have failed to bring about a qualitative change in the way politics is conducted, as hoped for by Havel and others, or to exercise a strong influence on the region's transition towards democracy. Robust civil societies are desired but hard to build, like other elements of the Western model East Europeans aspire to, and the process of constructing them is not going to be fast or easy. As Ralph Dahrendorf has said: 'The trouble is this: It takes six months to create new political institutions; to write a constitution and electoral laws. It may take six years to create a half-viable economy. It will probably take 60 years to create a civil society. Autonomous institutions are the hardest thing to bring about' (Dahrendorf 1990: 42).

References

Bieber, F. (2003) 'The other civil society in Serbia: non-governmental Nationalism – the case of the Serbian resistance movement', in P. Kopecký and C. Mudde (eds), *Uncivil Society?: Contentious Politics in Post-communist Europe*, London and New York: Routledge.

Carters, T. (1999) *Aiding Democracy Abroad: The Learning Curve*, Washington DC: Carnegie Endowment for International Peace.

——(1999–2000) 'Think again: civil society', *Foreign Policy*, winter: 18–29.

Dahrendorf, R. (1990) 'Has the East joined the West?', *New Perspectives Quarterly*, 7(2) (spring): 41–3.

Diamond, L. (1994) 'Toward democratic consolidation', *Journal of Democracy*, 5(3): 4–17.

Dimitrov, P. (2003) 'Corruption rife among Macedonia's NGOs', *Transitions Online*, Available from http://wire.tol.cz/look/wire/article.tpl?IdLanguage=1&IdPublication=10&NrIssue=740&NrSection=1&NrArticle=10337 (accessed 27 November 2003).

Doellinger, D. (2002) 'Prayers, pilgrimages and petitions: the secret church and the growth of civil society in Slovakia', *Nationalities Papers*, 30(2): 215–41.

Fisher, S. (2003) 'Contentious politics in Croatia: the war veterans' movement', in P. Kopecký and C. Mudde (eds), (2003) *Uncivil Society?: Contentious Politics in Post-Communist Europe*, London and New York: Routledge.

Gellner, E. (1994) *Conditions of Liberty: Civil Society and Its Rivals*, London: Hamish Hamilton.

Glasius, M., Kaldor, M. and Anheier, H. (eds) (2002) *Global Civil Society Yearbook 2002*, Oxford: Oxford University Press.

Glenn, J.K. III (2001) *Framing Democracy: Civil Society and Civic Movements in Eastern Europe*, Stanford: Stanford University Press.

Havel, V. (1990) 'The power of the powerless', in W. M. Bronton and A. Rinzler (eds), *Without Face or Lies. Voices from the Revolution of Central Europe in 1989–90*, San Francisco: Mercury House.

——(1991) *Open Letters*, London: Faber & Faber.

Howard, M.M. (2003) *The Weakness of Civil Society in Post-Communist Europe*, Cambridge: Cambridge University Press.

Karatnycky, A.K., Motyl, A. and Shor, B. (eds) (1997) *Nations in Transit 1997: Civil Society, Democracy and Markets in East Central Europe and the Newly Independent States*, New Brunswick and London: Transaction Publishers.

Karatnycky, A.K., Motyl, A. and Schnetzer, A. (eds) (2002) *Nations in Transit 2000–2001: Civil Society, Democracy and Markets in East Central Europe and Newly Independent States*, New Brunswick and London: Transaction Publishers.

Keane, J. (ed.) (1988) *Civil Society and the State: New European Perspectives*, London, New York: Verso.

Kopecký, P. and Mudde, C. (eds) (2003) *Uncivil Society?: Contentious Politics in Post-Communist Europe*, London and New York: Routledge.

McMahon, P.C. (2001) 'Building civil societies in East Central Europe: the effect of American non-governmental organizations on women's groups', *Democratization*, 8(2): 45–69.

Maliqi, S. (1998) *Kosova: Separate Worlds*, Peja: MM.

Michnik, A. (1985) *Letters from Prison and Other Essays*, Berkeley, Los Angeles, London: University of California Press.

Ottoway, M. and Carothers, T. (eds) (2000) *Funding Virtue: Civil Society Aid and Democracy Promotion*, Washington DC: Carnegie Endowment for International Peace.

Quigley, K.F.F. (2000) 'Lofty goals, modest results: assisting civil society in Eastern Europe', in M. Ottoway and T. Carothers (eds) (2000) *Funding Virtue: Civil Society Aid and Democracy Promotion*, Washington DC: Carnegie Endowment for International Peace.

Schmitter, Ph. (1995) 'Some reflections about the concept of civil society (in general) and its role in the liberalization and democratization of Europe in the nineteenth century (in particular)', paper presented at the conference 'Civil Society before Democracy', Princeton University, 6–7 October.

Siegel, D. and Yancey, J. (1992) *The Rebirth of Civil Society: The Development of the Nonprofit Sector in East Central Europe and the Role of Western Assistance*, New York: The Rockefellers Brothers Fund.

Tempest, C. (1997) 'Myths from Eastern Europe and the legend of the West', in R.

Fine and S. Rai (eds), *Civil Society: Democratic Perspectives*, London and Portland OR: Frank Cass.

White, G. (1994) 'Civil society, democratization and development (I): clearing the analytical ground', *Democratization*, 1(3).

Zagoumennov, Y. (2001) 'Belarus civil society: in need of a dialogue', *Civicus Index on Civil Society Occasional Paper Series*, 1(3).

Part IV

Western Europe and the United States

Rediscovering the concept

9 Civil society in the United States of America

Prototype or exception? An essay on cultural self-understanding

Helmut Anheier

While the concept of civil society as such is not common currency in the USA, there is nonetheless a deep-seated cultural understanding that civil society finds its clearest expression in this country. Indeed, a strong political and cultural current running through US history and contemporary society sees the USA as an ongoing experiment in civility, community-building, democracy and self-governance. Not only the country as a whole, but also cities such as New York, Miami or Los Angeles in particular regard themselves as the 'social laboratories' of modern urban life: they are among the most diverse in the world in ethnic, religious and social terms, with large portions of immigrant populations, small local government, and high levels of individualism and community organization.

Cultural self-understanding

A strong expression of this cultural self-understanding is that the USA, despite all its imperfections and injustices, is nonetheless regarded as the embodiment of human political progress. Sometimes, this ideological current assumes near-mythical dimensions, perhaps because it is so closely linked to, and rests on, major documents, events and symbols of US political history. In countless political speeches and in popular culture as well, frequent references are made to highly symbolic events and documents. The following are among the most prominent of such cultural–political icons.

- The Declaration of Independence of 4 July 1776 establishes legal equality and unalienable rights (life, liberty, pursuit of happiness), and that 'to secure these rights governments are instituted ... , deriving their just power from the consent of the governed'.
- The US Constitution begins with the forceful sentence 'We, the people of the United States, in order to form a more perfect union ... '.
- The Bill of Rights (First Amendment) limits the power of government *vis-à-vis* society and declares that 'Congress shall make no law

respecting an establishment of religion, or prohibiting the free exercise thereof'.

- In the *Federalist Papers* (Volume 39), Madison speaks of the 'great political experiment' and the 'capacity of mankind for self-government'; in Volumes 10 and 15, he argues that, in a republic equipped with adequate checks and balances, special interests (economic, political, religious etc.) should be encouraged to compete on equal terms and to lobby governments.
- President Lincoln's Gettysburg Address includes the emphatic wish 'that government of the people, by the people, and for the people, shall not perish from the earth'.
- Martin Luther King's 'I have a dream' speech speaks about his vision of the USA as a 'table of brotherhood' and invokes strong biblical images – a not at all uncommon reference in US political discourse.
- President Reagan led the (still continuing) roll-back of the Federal Government by encouraging Americans 'to take back from government what was once ours', referring back to the Declaration of Independence and reconfirming that the USA is first a society of and for individuals and their communities, and only secondarily a national political entity defined by power.

Together, these cultural icons suggest a culturally and politically compelling portrait of the USA as a self-organizing and self-governing civil society of citizens. Indeed, the US political tradition reflected in these cultural icons understands government in a broad sense: not only government by a 'state', but also social governance as an expression of formal political liberty, participation, and communal and individual obligations. Governance, the constitution of society, and the rights and obligations of citizens are interlinked and part of the US political canon. What are the historical roots of the cultural self-understanding fuelled by these and other icons, inviting the popular notion among Americans from all walks of life that the USA is a distinct, exceptional society, different from others, in particular its closest relative Europe, but also from Asia, and Latin America? In the rest of this section we identify some of the major factors involved, which are summarized in stylized form in Table 1, together with what are suggested as implied features of societies outside the USA, in particular the 'state-oriented' societies of Europe, Canada and Australia. Of course, the distinctions in Table 1 serve to emphasize what are in reality no more than tendencies, but primarily function as the political beliefs of mainstream US society.

Civil society as associationalism

As a society, the development of the United States – and its emergent civil society – is rooted in a profound and successful reaction against eighteenth-century European absolutism, the power of state–church relations, and the rigidities of what the 'Founding Fathers', in the true spirit of the Enlightenment, saw as the dying political and social order of the 'old world'. In its place, the USA sought to develop a complex political system of direct and indirect democracy based on checks and balances, it also put constraints on government, instituted clear separation of power at federal and state levels, allowed for a distinct mobility-based economic class structure that departed from the symbols of hereditary ranks, and encouraged a religious system based on voluntarism with strict separation of church and state.

Table 1 US civil society in comparative perspective

Factors encouraging civil society as associationalism in the USA	*Factors discouraging civil society as associationalism elsewhere*
Religious diversity with emphasis on local congregations rather than institutional hierarchy	Long history and legacy of dominant state religion with hierarchical institutional structures
Local elites do not rely on control of government for power; alternative spheres of influence exist	Weak local elites; few alternative power stratums
Concentrations of wealth and political power overlap but are neither identical nor dependent on each other	National political and economic elite networks overlap significantly
Ethnic, linguistic and cultural heterogeneity as 'default value'	Ethnic, linguistic and cultural homogeneity as 'default value'
Decentralized government, weak federal government with strong division of power at centre and primacy of rule of law	Centralized government and state apparatus; limited capacity for local taxation and policy-making
Bridging capital, higher interpersonal trust	High bonding capital, lower interpersonal trust
'Diversity in unity' creates social innovation	Homogeneity and political control stifles innovation

In the course of the USA's existence to date, over 225 years, many prominent observers have tried to come to terms with what G. K. Chesterton (1922) long ago identified as the 'American Creed', and what social scientists such as Voss (1993) and Lipset (1996) call 'American exceptionalism'. The term suggests a profound departure of the USA from its European origins, and a qualitative difference in the development of the USA from British, French or German society. According to Lipset (1996: 19), US society – and its civil society – rests on the basic ideological factors of classical liberalism:

- *Liberty* This is the freedom from arbitrary interference in one's pursuits, either by individuals or by government, as stipulated in the Bill of Rights and the 13th, 14th and 15th Amendments to the US Constitution.
- *Egalitarianism* A formal legal principle, along with *individualism*, that originated with the ideas of Adam Smith and Jeremy Bentham, and which was identified by Alexis de Tocqueville as a fundamental element of American society (1969). It includes a value system whereby the individual is of supreme value, and all are morally equal. Individualism opposes authority without consent and views government as an institution whose power should be largely limited to maintaining law and order.
- *Populism* A seemingly non-ideological movement that combines elements of the political left and the right, opposes corporate power and large financial interests, and favours 'home-grown', 'hands-on' local solutions. It was strongest in the late nineteenth century, and arose from agrarian reform movements in the South and Midwest, but continues to surface in popular political movements such as the antitax sentiment in California or antifederal actions in states such as Alabama.
- *Laissez-faire policies* These favour a minimum of governmental action in economic affairs beyond the minimum necessary for upholding property rights and the maintenance of peace. It was adopted as a basic principle of economic policy throughout the USA; *laissez-faire* assumes that individuals pursuing their own preferences primarily also contribute to society as a whole.

Thus, in a very profound sense, the US Constitution is a product of classical liberalism, as is US civil society itself, both historically and in the modern day. Only in the USA, and not in Europe nor in countries such as Canada or Australia, did these factors join forces to shape society and polity as clearly and in such an unchallenged way. These factors are at the root of US civil society from the nineteenth century onward, and are also central for the development of the modern non-profit sector in the twentieth century.

It is, however, the complex mix of these five factors that accounts for many of the seemingly contradictory patterns of American society, and which over the decades has filled many pages of social analysis (for example, Bellah 1985; Farley 1995): egalitarian social relations *and* large inequalities in living standards across the population; deep-seated preferences for meritocracy *and* persistent ethnic and religious discrimination, to name but two. The British author H. G. Wells – writing from a Fabian, socialist perspective – put it succinctly when he observed that 'essentially America is a middle class ... and so its essential problems are the problems of a modern individualistic society, stark and clear' (1906: 72, 76); yet in contrast to Britain, in looking for political solutions US middle-class ideology was neither Tory (conservative) nor Labour (socialist), it was, as Wells concluded, simply 'anti-state', and frequently populist, putting what is seen as the 'wish of the people' above the administrative skills and governance experience of 'politicians'.

In today's parlance, the USA developed a prototype of a *liberal model* of civil society and state–society relations, where a low level of government spending (social welfare, health, education, culture) is associated with a relatively large non-profit sector that is engaged in both actual service provision and advocacy. This outcome, as Salamon and Anheier (1998) argue, is most likely where broad middle-class elements are clearly in the ascendance, and where opposition, whether from traditional landed elites or strong working-class movements, has either never existed or has been effectively held at bay. This leads to significant ideological and political hostility to the extension of government in scale and scope, and a decided preference for local, voluntary approaches instead – irrespective of effectiveness and equity considerations.

However, despite or perhaps because of these contradictory elements, US society has proven more resilient against some of the despotic, autocratic or dynastic ills that have befallen many other countries. In fact, the sometimes arduous and even violent path of US history (displacement of indigenous populations; slavery and civil war; ethnic discrimination; extreme 'moralist' policy measures such as Prohibition in the 1920s; McCarthyism in the 1950s; race riots in the 1960s; militia movements and domestic terrorism in the 1990s) has shown a remarkable capacity of 'self-correction' or 'self-mobilization', typically through the electoral process and its system of checks and balances, or, failing that, through the mobilizing power of numerous social movements that have shaped the political and social development of the country. Prominent examples are the progressive movement, the civil rights movement, the environmental movements, and the women's movement.

Much of this capacity for self-organization and self-correction is seen in the social power of associationalism, or what amounts to a perspective that features *local* civil society, as a community of individuals who through their actions support a network of political, philanthropic and voluntary associations in pursuit of specific interests. Early reference to this capacity for self-organization was made in Tocqueville's travelogue from the 1830s, in such famous passages as:

> Americans of all ages, all stations of life, and all types of dispositions are forever forming associations ... In every case, at the head of any new undertaking, where in France you would find the government or in England some territorial magnate, in the United States you are sure to find an association
>
> (Tocqueville 1969: 513)

After all, as Lipset (1996) reminds us, the USA is the only Western country where government and voluntary associations did *not* have to deal with preexisting, inert social formations and barriers to mobility, be they autocratic states (Germany for example), a centralized administration (France) or a rigid, quasi-aristocratic class system carried over from feudalism (England). Writing in the mid-twentieth century, A. Schlesinger spoke of the 'lusty progeny of voluntary associations' that he saw largely as a product of the religious voluntarism of the antebellum period, thereby keeping alive the Tocquevillian spirit of associationalism as a characteristic feature of American life:

> Traditionally, Americans have distrusted collective organizations as embodied in government while insisting upon their own untrammelled right to form voluntary associations. This conception of a state of minimal powers actually made it easier for private citizens to organize for undertakings too large for a single person
>
> (Schlesinger 1944: 24)

The implicit comparison with Europe is also present in a variant of associationalism, namely, the communitarian tradition, which was rooted in some form of moral community of virtuous citizens (Etzioni 1996). Communitarianism is a social philosophy that views community as a voluntary grouping of individuals who come together to identify common goals and agree to rules governing the communal order. The community is created in part by recognizing common policies, or laws, that are set to meet legitimate needs rather than having been arbitrarily imposed from 'above' and 'outside' the groups. Members of such communities – neighbourhood, city or nation – accept both legal and moral responsibilities to achieve common goals and greater collective well-being.

Communitarianism is a variant of the USA as a society of self-organizing communities. Frequent reference is made to another European thinker, this time Max Weber (1935), who emphasized the close link between the Protestant (Puritan) ethic of capitalism, moral communities and economic development. Religious congregations, and the voluntary associations they formed, provided the bonds that held early American society together, and complemented the five principles of American liberalism in political ideology, social structure and economic behaviour.

Following Weber's reasoning Ladd (1994) suggested that the political and the religious ethos reinforced each other most clearly in the case of Puritanism, since the local, independent Protestant congregations – in contrast to centralized, hierarchical Catholicism – fostered individualism and egalitarianism, populist values could take root that were procommunity but antistate, and that favoured local over central decision-making. As Bellah (1985) argues, American Protestant tradition again and again spawned movements for social change and social reform, most notably in the Progressive Era between 1893 and 1917, and the civil rights movement in the 1950s and 1960s.

State–society relations

Of course, there is more to US society than associationalism and the non-profit sector, and analysts such as Skocpol *et al.* (2000), Hall (1999) and others have challenged the voluntaristic, communitarian view of US social history. According to Tocqueville's view of Jacksonian America, the inclusionary capacity of voluntary associations, the formal egalitarianism they espoused, and the prevention of tyrannical majority rule through the 'art of association' facilitated both democratic and social development. Yet they were not, as Skocpol *et al.* (2000) have shown, locally isolated developments. In fact, many associations formed federated structures and assumed national presence. What is more, Hall (1999) argues that the late twentieth-century distinction between public, for-profit and non-profit sectors did not apply to the US institutional landscape until the Great Depression. Civil and public governance intermingled and many hybrid organizational forms existed. This was the true institutional innovation of the USA: a self-confident civil society works with, and not for, government, which it controls and is not subservient to. In Hannah Arendt's insight, 'the true objective of the American Constitution was not to limit but to create more power, actually to establish and they duly constitute an entirely new power center' (Arendt 1963: 152).

The interplay between national polity and federated structures of civil society continued into the nineteenth and early twentieth centuries. In addition, alternative spheres of power developed: for example, the importance of the Masonic movement and other 'secret societies' and fraternities such as the Elks, the Rotarians or alumni associations of many kinds. Large-scale institutional innovations brought the rise of philanthropic foundations, universities and think-tanks as independent centres of wealth, knowledge and power. By the mid-twentieth century, the density and diversity of civil society was such that, in the aggregate, it served to diffuse social conflicts by the very complexity of the institutional structure created. The civil rights, women's or environmental movements could develop in the context of a rich and varied infrastructure of civil society institutions.

The interplay also created the pattern of 'third party government', whereby the federal government and state governments use a complex system of financial grants and incentives to affect policies of many kinds – be they health-care delivery, social services, education or culture. Government reimburses or otherwise finances services delivered by the non-profit or business sector. However, this system is largely invisible to the average citizen, perhaps because of the complexity created by several layers of public administration and finance, but also because the actual, everyday experience is not with 'the state' but with an institution of civil society.

The late twentieth century saw a revival of Tocquevillian perspectives of a 'strong and vibrant civil society characterized by a social infrastructure of dense networks of face-to-face relationships that cross-cut existing social cleavages such as race, ethnicity, class, sexual orientation, and gender that will underpin strong and responsive democratic government' (Edwards, Foley and Diani 2001: 17). Norms of reciprocity, citizenship and trust are embodied in networks of civic associations. Sirianni and Friedland (2001) argue that these interpersonal and interassociational networks are a key source of social, cultural and political innovation in the USA, linking the future of US democracy to their constant 'renewal', just as Putnam (2000) links them to the survival of community and others such as Fukuyama (1995) to economic prosperity.

Thus, through associationalism and third-party government, civil society is neither the abstract, contextual phenomenon that is more characteristic of European debates, where it becomes a countervailing force holding markets and government in check (Gellner 1994), nor is it akin to the political perspective that views civil society as the true locus of democratic community outside power relations (Habermas 1962). The vibrancy of the USA is ultimately the vibrancy of its civil society, which is good for society and the economy. For neo-Tocquevillians, civil society is not only a bulwark against the state or a vehicle for democracy (as in the Central European dialogue of 1989, for example), it is much more than that: a general principle of societal constitution. Not surprisingly, political efforts to revitalize civil society either assume a voluntaristic tone that emphasizes social participation and mutual, interpersonal trust (in other words, social capital: see Putnam 2000; Wuthnow 2002), or appeal to moralist, even religious, sentiments of civic virtue (such as AmericanValues.org).

Concluding thoughts

In summary, two implications follow from the notion of civil society in the USA. First, in a curious sense, US civil society is being both taken for granted and frequently misunderstood. For better or worse, it is possible to think of German, Frenchn even British societies as being very different from what they are today – thanks to the European project that will see 25 countries through a profound political, economic and social transformation beyond the confines of the nation state and the enduring influence of national institutions. The USA, however, has no such new project, or, put differently, has itself been one for over two hundred years. Indeed, it is challenging to think that in the middle of the twenty-first century the USA could be a fundamentally different society from what it is at the beginning of this millennium. Of course, the USA has been one of the most mobile and increasingly diverse of societies, and one that has changed significantly and in many ways over the course of the twentieth century – but in contrast to Europe and other parts of the world, it has done so with basically the same creed of American exceptionalism that, now in its third century, the British writer Chesterton identified in the 1920s.

Second, the tensions inherent on the one hand in the notion of American exceptionalism, and on the other in the expansionist tendencies of US political and popular culture, including open market policies, have long found their expression in two contradictory policy positions. One position favours isolationism, and selective relationships with any country outside a narrowly defined sphere of influence – a stance that finds its historical roots in an understanding that views the USA as a rejection of the political systems of Europe, and certainly most other parts the world.

The other position advocates an active engagement with a world that can only benefit from American civilization, openness and largesse – a political current that reaches back to the period of domestic colonization in the nineteenth century, Wilson's policies in the 1920s, the Marshall Plan and the creation of the UN in the late 1940s, or the support of Europe in the Cold War of the latter part of the twentieth century. Caught between these tensions are ill-fated foreign policies such as Cuba, Vietnam, Somalia, and much of US Middle Eastern foreign policy since the early 1990s.

A longstanding characteristic of US foreign policy has been some uncertainty of how, if at all, it could relate to the wider world as a polity. This uncertainty is closely linked to the very notion of a society that distrusts the nation state as the ultimate seat of power. This distrust and a sense of human rights that exist above and beyond any claims of state power made the USA a liberating force in many parts of the world. At the same time, the unfailing belief in the superiority of its values and institutions has on many occasions caused the USA to ride roughshod over the values and institutions of other nations.

References

AmericanValues.org, www.AmericanValues.org. Website of the Council on Civil Society; cosponsored by the Institute for American Values and the University of Chicago Divinity School (accessed 26 November 2003).

Arendt, H. (1963) *On Revolution*, New York: Macmillan.

Bellah, R.N. (1985) *Habits of the Heart*, Berkeley: University of California Press.

Chesterton, G.K. (1922) *What I Saw in America*, New York: Dodd, Mead & Co.

Edwards, B., Foley, M.W. and Diani, M. (2001) *Beyond Tocqueville: Civil Society and the Social Capital Debate in Comparative Perspective*, Hanover: University Press of New England.

Etzioni, A. (1996) *The New Golden Rule*, New York: Basic Books.

Farley, R. (ed.) (1995) *The State of the Union. America in the 1990s*, New York: Russell Sage Foundation. Two volumes.

Fukuyama, F. (1995) *Trust: Social Virtues and the Creation of Prosperity*, New York: Simon and Schuster.

Gellner, E. (1994) *Conditions of Liberty: Civil Society and its Rivals*, New York: St Martin's Press.

Habermas, J. (1962) *Strukturwandel der Öffentlichkeit: Untersuchungen zu einer Kategorie der bürgerlichen Gesellschaft* [The Structural Transformation of the

Public Sphere: An Inquiry into a Category of Civil Society], Neuwied: Luchterhand.

Hall, P. (1999) 'Vital signs: organizational population trends and civil engagement in New Haven, Connecticut', in T. Skocpol and M. P. Fiorina (eds), *Civic Engagement in American Democracy*, Washington DC: Brookings Institution Press.

Ladd, E.C. (1994) *The American Ideology: An Exploration of the Origin, Meaning, and Role of American Political Ideas*, Storrs CT: Roper Center for Public Opinion Research.

Lipset, S.M. (1996) *American Exceptionalism: A Double-Edged Sword*, New York: Norton.

Putnam, R. (2000) *Bowling Alone*, New York: Simon and Schuster.

Salamon, L. and Anheier, H. (1998) 'Social origins of civil society: explaining the nonprofit sector cross-nationally', *Voluntas*, 9(3): 213–47.

Schlesinger, A. (1944) 'Biography of a nation of joiners', *American Historical Review*, 50 (October): 1–25.

Sirianni, C. and Friedland, L. (2001) *Civic Innovation in America: Community Empowerment, Public Policy, and the Movement for Civic Renewal*, Berkeley: University of California Press.

Skocpol, T., Ganz, M. and Munson, Z. (2000) 'A nation of organizers: the institutional origins of civic voluntarism in the United States', *American Political Science Review*, 94(3): 527–49.

Tocqueville, A. de (1969), *Democracy in America*, New York: Harper and Row [1835–40].

Voss, K. (1993) *The Making of American Exceptionalism: The Knights of Labor and Class Formation in the Nineteenth Century*, Ithaca NY: Cornell University Press.

Weber, M. (1935) *The Protestant Ethic and the Spirit of Capitalism*, New York: Scribner's [1905].

Wells, H.G. (1906) *The Future in America*, New York: Harper & Brothers.

Wuthnow, R. (2002) 'Bridging the privileged and the marginalized', in R. Putnam (ed), *Democracies in Flux*, Oxford: Oxford University Press.

10 In Paris, the global place is no longer Saint Germain des Prés

Civil society and the French debate

Bernard Dreano

> If we can enter the twenty-first century with strong popular organizations it will be a more honourable achievement for our own century. I believe that we will thus find warmer acceptance in the twenty-first century. The future may then, perhaps, pardon some of the crimes committed in our time.
>
> (Kemal 1993)

The concept of 'civil society' – considered as a political space where 'citizens' are self-organized independently from the state, the clanic/family structures and the profitable economy – has always been a matter of controversy in France. This is still the case today, even among the activists of the 'antiglobalization' movement – or, as they call themselves in France, the *altermondialistes* – found in trade unions, non-governmental organizations (NGOs), and left-wing political parties. Many of these activists are cautious of a concept that seems to be imported, and which is used in the vocabulary of the World Bank.

A new movement such as the Association for the Taxation of Financial Transactions for the Aid of Citizens (ATTAC) is a good place to witness this debate. ATTAC is a powerful network against international financial institutions, which is promoting demands like the Tobin Tax. ATTAC itself could be described as an organized form of modern civil society. This association was established at the end of June 1998 as a 'campaign' by a number of leftist magazines' editorial boards, trade unions and associations, including for instance the main associations for the unemployed in France. It was also open to individual membership and, to the surprise of the founders, tens of thousands of individual activists joined the movement. As Pierre Rousset explains, 'ATTAC is a very pluralistic association, united around the issue of taxation and control of capital by a common democratic will. It considers that economic choices have to be made by the citizens, and not by the "experts" and the "powers that be"' (Rousset 1998). In ATTAC you meet people coming from the different historical streams of the French left.

As early as December 1998 ATTAC-France started to initiate an international network, which five years later had spread to fifty countries, from Germany to the Ivory Coast, from Italy to Chile, Hungary and Japan (*Sand in the Wheels*). The success of ATTAC in France was the result of a process initiated several years before, exemplified by the mobilization for the countersummit when the international leaders known as 'G7' met in the French town of Lyon in 1996 (the 'Other Voices of the Planet' campaign; the 'Summit of the Seven Civic Resistances', and so on) and the successful anti-MAI (Multilateral Agreement on Investment) campaign in 1998. ATTAC is a typical product of this new 'global civil society': it is both local and international, rooted in the new social movement, organized more as a network than a traditional centralized body, and it counts among its membership sophisticated experts, rank-and-file activists and non-politicized citizens. And yet, even in such a group, many participants would be reluctant to accept being described as 'civil society'. This is probably the consequence of a long-standing tradition of French political philosophy.

The centralist legacy and the emergence of a 'self-organization' tradition

The concept of civil society has a long history, since the *koinônia politike* of Aristotle or the *societas civilis* of St Augustine. It re-emerged along with political liberalism in the eighteenth century, especially among British philosophers (Locke, Hume, Ferguson), even though the idea was also familiar to French philosophers from Montesquieu to Rousseau. In the nineteenth century Alexis de Tocqueville advocated the idea of a civil society building itself against the despotism of the modern state. Tocqueville is often considered as the founder of modern 'right-wing' liberalism in France, and his ideological influence became stronger in the second half of the twentieth century than during his own lifetime, in particular through the influential political philosopher Raymond Aron in the 1950s and 60s.

In reaction, leftist intellectuals remained cautious towards such a 'bourgeois liberal' concept, referring rather to the idea of 'general will' developed by Rousseau and his republican and socialist heirs in the tradition of Jacobinism – I am referring not to the historical radical faction during the French Revolution, but rather to their political legacy, the republican or Bonapartist centralism in the nineteenth and twentieth centuries, influencing modern political parties, both left wing (socialist, communist, radical) and right wing (Gaullist). For the French, freedom was to come through the building of the common state (la République) rather than from the construction of society against, or independently of, the state. This Jacobin heritage has impregnated French Marxists, who ignored for decades the 'libertarian' face of Marx and, later, Gramsci's civil society approach.

It must also be emphasized that the French ruling classes equally adhered to the idea of the centrality of the state implemented by Napoleon. And the 1791 Le Chapellier law banning 'corporations' – supposed to fit with the

Rousseauist idea of preventing any intermediary between the citizen and the state – was used by these ruling classes to ban trade unions up to 1884.

And yet, traditions other than Jacobinism existed within the French left that were less statist and more open to the idea of the self-organization of citizens: the *libertaire* (anarchist) wing of the socialist movement, which, significantly, founded the main trade union (CGT) at the beginning of the twentieth century; and the Christian left, sometimes called the 'second left', which played an important role in the 1960s and 70s, also significantly within the second biggest trade union (CFDT).

The re-emergence of the concept of civil society in political thinking took place through a complex process at the end of the twentieth century: not through philosophical theories but through civic activism in a very pluralistic process in Central Europe, Latin America and also in Western Europe (notably France in the period after 1968, even though the term 'civil society' was not used there). The notion of self-management (*autogestion*), for example, was not simply a programme of workers' control in factories, but a vision of self-organized citizens' autonomy. The women's movement also developed similar perspectives, as did the autonomist movements in several regions such as Brittany and Corsica, the pedagogical movement, the new ecologist movement ... it was a sort of synthesis of the revolutionary anarchist and *libertaire* traditions with the reformist 'second left'. It had a strong influence on several post-68 French Marxist-revolutionary groups, driving them far from their original neobolshevism. But politically it failed at the end of the 1970s and during the 1980s: the left-wing socialist party PSU and several other small political parties disappeared, and the CFDT trade union deserted the self-management cause. And François Mitterrand, the socialist leader who won the presidential election in 1981, had very little sympathy for the 'self-management' way of thinking.

However, as a positive legacy of that period, broad coalitions were formed around symbolic struggles such as those of the workers of Lip, a wristwatch factory, and the peasants of Larzac, the latter being particularly fruitful. The Larzac plateau, in the south of France, had been selected by the authorities as the site of the biggest military training camp in Europe. For over a decade (1970–81), the non-violent resistance of the local peasants was both imaginative and resolute. They were able to organize a broad movement – tens of thousands came to Larzac regularly to support their cause – which was finally successful. The plateau became a symbol both of peace and of a new agriculture. At the beginning of the twenty-first century the 'new alliance' seems even stronger and broader, although less political in terms of party politics. Very significantly, José Bové comes from the Larzac solidarity movement, like other leaders of the new activism. A less well-known but nonetheless significant example is Gilles Lemaire, the national secretary of the Greens, the environmental party, also a former member of the Larzac solidarity movement.

However, when the term 'civil society' later became fashionable, it was less among leftist activists than among journalists and traditional politicians. Some government members (both conservatives and social democrats) are regularly defined as 'coming from civil society', simply because they are not officially affiliated to a traditional political party.

Nevertheless, during the 1990s, social movements came back into the foreground, and this renewal of civic activism was labelled 'civil society from below' by François Houtart of the Belgian Tricontinental Centre (CETRI). The traditional 'third-worldist' associations devoted to development in poor countries have grown into modern NGOs, even if their development is less impressive in France than in the rest of northern Europe; the same phenomenon is visible in environmentalist groups such as Greenpeace and Friends of the Earth. Humanitarian emergency movements such as Médecins sans Frontières and Médecins du Monde became very visible in the 1980s and the 'French doctors' became popular figures.

Other new movements outside the NGO sphere also became major political and social actors in the 1990s: the 'sans' galaxy ('without': without rights, without housing, without jobs, etc.), including movements of the unemployed (for example AC! – Action contre le chômage), the homeless (DAL – Droit au logement), the 'sans papiers' (illegal immigrants), asylum-seekers, new feminist groups, and new cultural groups. Traditional trade unionism was also partly affected by this new spirit of self-organization, with the success of the farmers' union Confédération Paysanne – its leader José Bové becoming a star of the world antiglobalists – with the growth of a new form of unionism (the SUD coalition), and even including some changes within a traditional trade union such as the CGT. These various forms of organizations and movements do interact, even though their ideological backgrounds, their strengths and their structures are very different from one to another.

This new social activism is politically left-oriented, from radical left to social democracy, but is not well represented in the traditional political parties. And this was probably one of the keys to the defeat of Lionel Jospin, the socialist candidate, in the first run of the presidential elections in 2002. A very significant number of left-wing voters abstained or voted for small presidential candidates rather than Jospin: the Trotskyite Besancenot, the green Mamère and the 'radical' Taubira were considered as linked with the new activism and between them got 12 per cent of the vote. The same phenomenon of social activism is not visible in the right-wing hemisphere of French political society. It is strange to note the weakness of the 'mass organizations' of Le Pen's extreme-right party, Front National, compared to his enormous influence in the 2002 general elections (18 per cent of the vote). But some form of new self-organization can also be noted in spheres far from the left, in religious movements for example: Islamists, charismatic Catholics (including huge youth meetings organized by the Pope), evangelists, and radical Jews.

The *altermondialiste* movement – to use the French name – is the melting pot of this new left-oriented civil society, even if its members are still discussing whether it is convenient to use that concept. Compared to the no-global movement in Italy, the French *altermondialistes* are older (even if there are new youth groups such as Vamos, Aaarg and No Pasaran) and seem less organized. Paradoxically their influence on the mainstream political scene is stronger. The French media coverage of the Porto Alegre World Social Forum in 2002 and 2003 was as good as it was because of the participation in the Forum of prominent French political leaders, including members of the government: not only the left-wing Jospin government in 2002 but also the right-wing Raffarin government in 2003! President Jacques Chirac did not hesitate to say, during the violent anti-G8 demonstration in Genoa in 2001, that 'it was well-advised to listen to the demonstrators', and he keeps in direct contact with major NGOs such as ATTAC. Different factions of the Socialist Party paid tribute to *altermondialistes* in their congress platforms in spring 2003. In spite of all that, the more radical tendency of the left such as the Greens, the communists – especially the *refondateur* wing within the party – and the modernist Trotskyists of the Ligue Communiste Révolutionnaire (LCR) have a real influence in the movement. From Jacques Chirac to the young anarchists, everybody thinks that the *altermondialistes* are representative of an important stream within French society, that they are a formalized expression of 'civil society'.

The recovery of the right to speak: civil society in francophone Africa

So how do these activists of civil society – whether they like the word or not – imagine their relation with the international movement? Do they consider the existence of a 'world civil society'? French political philosophy has always been very universalist. It thus seems easier for these French *altermondialistes* to imagine themselves as part of a global movement than to really analyse their effect on their own country. More seriously, Gustave Massiah (2002), one of the leaders of the French movement, explains that the strength of the new citizens' movement, both at national and global levels, is its capacity for convergence: 'the convergence of the resistance, which means one can speak of a world-wide civic mobilization ... Such a mobilization gives confidence to those movements that take initiatives and make proposals' and, he adds, 'one can read the convergence in the practices and in the forms of mobilization. It is strong in each country, in each great region, and at the international level.'

Yet convergence is not the only keyword of this new spirit within civil society: the other keyword could be, in Gustave Massiah's eyes, responsibility: 'Responsibility, because the tendency is to progress from resistance to propositions, to develop the movement's capacity of expertise, thus giving breath to the idea that a new world is possible.' Gustave Massiah is one of the vice-presidents of ATTAC, president of CRID (Centre d'information et de recherche sur le développement, a gathering of 40 international solidarity organizations from different ideological backgrounds: Catholic, independent Marxist, third-worldist, environmental, etc.), and a long-time member of CEDETIM, a think-tank of the international solidarity movement founded in the 1960s, just after the independence of Algeria.

Paris is still a place where world activists meet. Or at least some of them. Of course there are now a lot of other similar places, from Porto Alegre to Mumbai, from Chiapas to London. And, of course, even in Paris things are not as they used to be – they are no longer centred around Saint Germain des Prés, the Café de Flore, and the ghost of Jean Paul Sartre. The second European Social Forum (ESF), which took place in November 2003, gathered tens of thousands of people in the Paris region, but the epicentre of this civic earthquake was not in Saint Germain or the Sorbonne but in the outskirts of the city: in Saint Denis, a working-class suburb.

In Saint Denis, it is impossible to look at European civil society only from a Eurocentric point of view. People from around the world have long inhabited and shaped this place. Some of the major debates taking place during the preparation for the Forum were on global topics, such as the Israeli–Palestinian conflict and its effect on Western society, which are particularly relevant to French society, especially in places such as Saint Denis where tens of thousands of Muslims and oriental Jews are living side by side. There were controversies about secularism and religious behaviour. A clash of civilizations? Not really, rather a particular moment in a universal debate, with, probably, less difference between members of the Présence Musulmane (the radical Muslim association), the Catholic relief organization CCFD, the secularist Ligue des Droits de l'Homme, and the far-left-oriented trade union SUD than between all of them together and the vision of the world defended by Tony Blair, not to mention George W. Bush!

Also involved in the European Social Forum, the Congolese Patrice Yengo has recently gathered the studies of several Africans regarding the emergence of a new civil society in that continent. It seems that French-speaking African intellectuals do not share the reluctance of their Parisian counterparts to adopt the concept of civil society. For Yengo (2003), the most important phenomenon in the development of an African civil society is the 'recovery of the right to speak', which is not primarily conquered through the development of an independent press but through the self-organization of society, which Ernest Marie Mbonda (2003) from Cameroon describes as 'the fifth power': after the three powers of constitutional democracy (legislative, executive, judiciary), and the fourth power (media), comes the fifth, 'the empowerment of civil society'.

In North Africa other civic and human rights activists share a similar analysis, like the founders of the 'Espace Associatif' in Morocco, who organize social, human rights and cultural initiatives, or those who launched the Moroccan Social Forum in Casablanca at the end of 2002. Of course, in Arabic countries such as Morocco, Algeria or Tunisia, the main form of independent social movements is dominated not by these secular and progressive-minded peoples but, unfortunately, by the Islamic fundamentalists. Nevertheless, undoubtedly, new forms of organized civil society are also blossoming there.

An actually existing civil society

The organizers of the second European Social Forum, following the first forum held in Florence in November 2002, are the groups discussed above: members of ATTAC, CRID, the trade unions, the 'sans', and so on. They are trying to build a collective answer to major questions: What will be the influence of civil society on the process of European integration? Can an integrated Europe be a counterweight to US domination? Is it possible to imagine a European social model as an alternative to ultraliberalism?

It will, certainly, take more than two European forums to answer these questions. But Saint Denis seems to be a much more global place than Saint Germain, not only because Patrice Yengo and friends or the activists of the Moroccan Espace Associatif were present at the forum but, primarily, because this is the kind of place many people of the world now live in. Seen from Saint Denis society seems more chaotic than from the theoretical point of view of the Ecole Polytechnique or the Ecole Nationale d'Administration (the High Schools that groom state elites), or from the Sorbonne. In such places civil society may still be considered as an 'unclear' and 'unscientific' concept. While global civil society may still be an illusion, there is undoubtedly something happening inside societies that is a global phenomenon. It is not a static formation of social structures, but as Samir Amin and François Houtart (2002), founders of the World Forum of Alternatives, describe it, a movement, 'created by the transformation of social relations, characterized by the inequality of the existing powers. In other words, by social struggles.' An 'actually existing' civil society is on its way somewhere in the housing estates of Saint Denis, as elsewhere.

References

Amin, S. and Houtart, F. (2002) *Mondialization des résistances, l'état des luttes 2002*. [Globalization of the resistances: the state of struggles, 2002], Paris: L'Harmattan.

Kemal, Y. (1993) 'Sivil Örgütlenme' [Civic Organization], in Helsinki Citizens' Assembly, *Avrupa Nevede Bityor? Where Does Europe End?*, Istanbul: Helsinki Citizens' Assembly.

Massiah, G. (2002) 'Le mouvement citoyen mondial' [The global citizens' movement], Paris: Cedetim. Available online at www.cedetim.org (accessed October 2003).

Mbonda, E.M. (2003) 'Le Cinquième Pouvoir en Afrique, la société civile et le droit de résister' [The fifth power in Africa: civil society and the right to resist], in P. Yengo (ed.), *Résistance et dissidences, l'Afrique (centrale) des droits de l'homme*

[Resistance and dissidents, the (central) Africa of human rights], Rupture-Solidarité No. 4, Paris: Karthala.

Rousset, P. (1998) Speech at the ATTAC international meeting in Paris, December.

Sand in the wheels, ATTAC Weekly newsletter – http://attac.org/attacinfoen/attacnews173.zip or http://attac.org/attacinfoen/attacnews173.pdf (accessed 12 March 2004).

Yengo, P. (ed.) (2003) *Résistance et dissidences, l'Afrique (centrale) des droits de l'homme* [Resistance and dissidents, the (central) Africa of human rights], Rupture-Solidarité No. 4, Paris: Karthala.

11 Western Europe

Democratic civil society versus neoliberalism

Hilary Wainwright

The legacy of '68

The exuberance of youth, the exhilaration of witnessing new sources of social power and the signs of the old order in moral, if not political, decay – all these things led the students and workers protesting in 1968 to believe they were making history. I would agree: along with the equally important, if less dramatic, feminist, green and peace movements of the 1970s, the students' and workers' movements did make history, but not in the way that they thought.

The character of the innovations brought about by these movements was thrown briefly into relief through dialogue with the civil movements that contributed to the final collapse of the Soviet bloc's hollow regimes. But even as such dialogues developed, the libertarian language of these new movements was being hijacked, first by a reborn neoliberal right and then by a social democratic variant of the same creed. In all this twisting and turning 'civil society' was both a seriously contested concept and a glibly abused phrase.

I write as a '68er' but with no fixed, iconic interpretation of that moment, and as someone who has been an active participant in many social movements since, including those that sought dialogue with the civic activists building democratic challenges to the regimes of the Soviet bloc.

In Western Europe in the late 1960s – most notably in France – students' and workers' movements did not use the concept of 'civil society' to theorize their perspectives. The dominant theorizations of the heady 'événements' of those years were the revolutionary or radically democratic traditions suppressed by the onward march of the party state: Trotsky's theory of dual power and permanent revolution; Mao's original theory of cultural revolution (before it became a party dictat); anarchist and syndicalist theories of workers' councils and workers' self-management.

The explosions of protest in the late 1960s were about many things, but what came to a head in the protests against the Vietnam war was total disillusionment with both sides of the Cold War. The ruthless imperialism of the USA-led West bore no relation to the democratic proclamations of Western parliamentary politicians, while the self-interested realpolitik of the Soviet Union and Maoist China emptied talk of 'solidarity and equality' of any meaning. The search was on, therefore, for genuinely alternative ways to reach the democratic and socialist goals that had been so discredited in the postwar years. It is not surprising that in Western Europe this search initially led to a retrieval of the defeated socialist, syndicalist and Marxist traditions associated with the early pursuit of these goals. In most West European countries socialist and communist parties had considerable weight (in contrast to the USA, where homegrown traditions of community politics and participatory democracy were the more powerful influence). What these traditions of Trotskyism, syndicalism and cultural-revolution Maoism had in common, reinforcing the sentiments of the movements that turned to them, was a strong belief in more vigorous forms of democracy than the representative parliamentary forms. An underlying reason for this invention of direct forms of democracy was the weakness or absence of representative democracy – indeed any kind of democracy – in the societies where these theories took shape. In late twentieth-century Western European countries, where parliamentary democracy had become a pale shadow of the aspirations of those who had struggled for it, it is understandable that those who desired radical social change looked to theorists of struggle who had sought to 'leap over' the phase of electoral democracy (Blackburn and Cockburn 1969; Cohn-Bendit and Cohn-Bendit 1968; Rowbotham 2000).

The theoretical traditions influential in the first flush of Western social movements following the Cold War paid scant attention to civil society. This was in part because of a dearth of experience of civil society in the predemocratic societies that inspired these traditions. (I will come later to Gramsci, the influential Marxist thinker who did focus serious attention on civil society.) Though Trotsky's writings on 'everyday life' began to take civil society seriously, traditions formed in his name did not develop this further. An explanation of the lack of discussion of civil society in these early radical movements, influenced as they were by the more creative traditions within Marxism, was that within most Marxist traditions (Gramsci included), civil society is a 'sphere' of society rather than a source of agency for change. Yet the West European movements of the late 1960s and early 1970s were above all self-confident of their capacities to bring about change.

Indeed, such was the self-confidence of these movements in their first years that they presumed the power they had awakened – on the streets, in the factories, in the universities – would somehow overwhelm the increasingly hollow institutions of parliamentary democracy, as if rushing in to fill a vacuum. There did not seem to be a problem in drawing on theorists of change who wrote in societies where the universal franchise had not been won; the assumption was that the mass of people could be relatively easily mobilized for change. The complexity and durability of the social and cultural institutions of the daily lives of the majority of people was not seriously considered.

But as the 1960s moved into the 1970s, the capitalist order began to regroup and recoup – shaken but not broken. There were moments of anxiety in the corridors of power: in 1973, a revolution in Portugal's armed forces triggered occupations on estates and factories across the country; in 1974 a British Tory government was effectively brought down by industrial action and replaced by a Labour government backed by a new radicalized Labour Party. But in neither case could the forces for radical change win sufficiently sustained popular support to maintain the momentum for change against the pressures of business, the permanent state apparatus and the US military and industrial establishment.

The influence of Gramsci

This dilemma – namely, the militancy of radicalized sections of the population promising a wholly different kind of society but unable to win the support of the majority and translate this promise into political power – preoccupied the Italian intellectual Antonio Gramsci (1971) in Turin from 1912 onwards. At this time in Italy workers were occupying the factories, forming workers' councils, reaching out to women in the communities and to intellectuals like Gramsci, but the established order was able to rely on the loyalty of the majority of people and to marginalize the radicals as a large, but ultimately powerless, minority. To understand this process and develop strategies to overcome it, Gramsci puzzled about the processes shaping people's attitudes to radical change in societies where the governments ruled through assent rather than by force. This led him to focus on the struggle for cultural hegemony. This is his relevance: he saw consent in fascist society, but he understood liberal democracies as based on a far more elaborate form of consent. Crucial to this cultural struggle were the influences and institutions shaping civil society; in other words, the institutions of everyday life. In Italy this meant the Catholic Church, particularly. In this context the left's struggle for hegemony was against – or sometimes seeking to gain influence within – the Catholic Church (Cohen and Arato 1992: 142–59).

The stress on cultural dominance within civil society as a necessary condition for gaining political power became influential throughout Western Europe as people looked for strategies to overcome the limitations of militant street protests, occupations and the like. It is worth noting here the assumptions about civil society that underlay this belief in the importance of cultural dominance. I am simplifying, but the assumption in Gramsci's arguments was that civil society was a sphere gently to be conquered by a party that would have roots in that society. The initiative would be with the party, not with civil society – which would be the object, not part of the subject. Thus the Italian Communist Party (PCI), deeply influenced by Gramsci's thinking, broadened its scope well beyond the activities of most communist or socialist parties at that time. The PCI organized festivals, holidays, theatre, and youth and old people's activities, as well as placing great emphasis on alliances with progressive opinion-forming cultural figures such as film directors, artists and editors. There was a permanent tension around the question of the autonomy of these different cultural initiatives, versus their subordination to the party (Ginsborg 1990).

Untheorized innovation in social movements

Gramsci's ideas on civil society were influential, especially with activists and within projects associated with those sections of the Communist tradition who were rethinking their politics, while remaining committed to radical transformation. But his ideas did not provide adequate tools for understanding the innovations of these movements, especially the feminist movement and the radical trade union movement.

In the women's movement, for example, direct attempts were being made to bring about change in the conditions of women's daily lives – through creating community nurseries, centres for battered wives, health groups focused on the specific health needs of women, and so on – and these initiatives, led by women active in the feminist movement, involved a distinctive approach, not yet theorized, to bringing about social change (Rowbotham 1989). Instead of (or as well as) demanding that a political party adopt and implement their policies, women came together, pooled their resources of time and money, and made changes directly, immediately. They had an urgent vested interest since their own personal lives and needs were changing, transformed by the new awareness and self-confidence many women gained in the feminist movement. Effectively, these women mobilized a form of social and cultural power. In many cases they achieved political changes and then won public resources to sustain these changes, even achieving the passing of legislation that gave these new institutions lasting legitimacy. However, the women's movement did not then become part of the state, but struggled to create or retain a new relationship between the state and civil society, though the term and concept 'civil society' was at that time not generally current. Within these new relationships politicians and civil servants managing public resources and implementing legislation were accountable not only via representatives, elected through the franchise, but also directly: to the people using and providing public services. The initiatives instigated by the women's movement (and also those of radical trade union organizations: Beynon and Wainwright 1979; Cooley 1987; Wainwright and Elliott 1982) were in relationship with, but independent from, the state. A question arises: how are we to understand this innovation theoretically?

Feminists were always inventing as they went along; innovation developed in practice. We rarely theorized our practice beforehand, partly because we were beleaguered and under pressure, struggling to survive. These particular initiatives – women's centres, community-controlled nurseries, well-women clinics, for example – cannot be understood simply as part of the women's movement, because where they were successful their roots went deeper and produced lasting institutions. But neither can they be understood as simply 'part of the state' or 'part of the market'. If the concept of civil society means 'public social relationships independent of the state, and not subsumable by the market', then these initiatives were part of it. Yet they were not only part of 'a sphere'; they were also consciously bringing about change. The people who went on to sustain what had been started, however – as distinct from the minority of initiators – did not, on the whole, begin with wider visions of social transformation. Rather, to meet needs in their own daily lives, they were struggling to demonstrate how an aspect of society both ought to be and could be. In the process, they created ripples of change, especially in the welfare state's relationship to the people it was meant to serve. This growing self-conscious awareness of innovation and change was an important source of energy for maintaining the original momentum of these initiatives, turning them into lasting institutions. In other words, here was civil society as a source of agency for social change. This experience in all its variety of forms shaped a new kind of left: it was never coherent enough to define so is best summed up in terms of the most powerful influences on it, as 'the social-movement left' (Eley 2002).

The struggle for civil society in Eastern Europe

Meanwhile, at a level that seemed far away from the preoccupations of the daily lives of women, in the struggle against the party states of Eastern and Central Europe and Russia, movements were using language and concepts that were strange at first but were in fact describing familiar phenomena. The totalitarianism of the regimes of Central and Eastern Europe was such that it was inconceivable for dissenters to follow the route of conventional democratic politics, lobbying a political party to take up a policy or demand. For years dissent had been expressed only in private, in the enclosed sphere of intimate relationships, but the momentary breathing space allowed by the Helsinki accords in the late 1970s , the climax of détente from above, led the bravest dissidents to make their personal dissent public. They stopped 'living a lie' as Václav Havel put it (Havel 1985). As détente from above gave way to the nuclear sabre-rattling of Thatcher and Reagan, the dissenters worked to create détente from below. As others in this book describe, a new kind of international relations developed: a 'people to people' diplomacy, with peace activists in the West working in active solidarity with rebels in the East, making democratic rights integral to the campaign to rid the world of nuclear missiles (Kaldor 2003: 50–77; see also Kaldor, this volume).

For the democrats in the East, in Poland and Czechoslovakia for example, the personal became unavoidably political. As Lech Wałęsa, the Polish shipyard worker and founder of Solidarity, remarked after the authorities had disciplined him for jokes at their expense, 'to laugh is to be political'. In Czechoslovakia, jazz clubs, underground theatres and other kinds of associations beyond the family were under suspicion. Dissidents found that to preserve their personal integrity, end their unintended complicity with the regime and stand up for what they believed, they had to fight for the right to a public association that was independent of the state and yet not part of the market. In those early days they were clear that they did not want simply to flip over into a society dominated by the commercial relationships and values of the market. Civil society became something to create and to fight for. And like the movements in the West, especially the women's movement, this politicization of the personal was a result of individuals' refusal to continue reproducing the conditions of their oppression on a daily basis. Such refusal could not be sustained without creating new ways of living.

In East and West, revolt linked the personal to the political. The new social and political relationships had an urgency that stemmed from closeness to the needs of people's daily lives. In both places 'the political' was 'the public' and was about social transformation, but was contemptuous of what officially constituted politics. In Hungary they called it 'antipolitics' and throughout Central and Eastern Europe they talked quite explicitly about 'democratic civil society'. In the West, already existing civil society became an agent for democratic change. In the East the language of many of the 'antipolitics' dissidents was explicit in its reference to the creation of a democratic civil society as an aim. The Western social-movement left took civil society for granted; in the East it had to be struggled for. Moreover, since in the East civil society was understood as a fundamental condition for democracy, democracy within civil society became an important issue. The West was less self-conscious about relationships beyond the family, independent of the state and distinct from the market. However, we increasingly insisted on autonomy from both the state and political parties for our initiatives, as well as independence from private businesses and the market; we understood such autonomy as a condition for negotiations and relationships with these political institutions (Burke, Thompson and Wainwright 1991). For me, this is when the notion of civil society, not simply as a 'sphere' of social life but as a source of agency for social transformation in its own right, became important.

How the moment was lost

The potential of civil society as an agent of democratic change – for transforming the state and the market – was never adequately explored, however. The spaces for democratic civil society, East and West, were rapidly closed, even as precarious East–West dialogues were beginning. Understanding has therefore never been developed of the wider political and economic conditions on which civil society depends, and these will necessarily vary historically and geographically. However, it is clear from the more institutionalized Western examples – such as Bologna in Northern Italy (Martin 1993) and London in the early 1980s (Carvel 1984; Mackintosh and Wainwright 1987) – that for democratic civil society to be the basis of lasting social and political improvements it needs the framework of an elected government which is committed to the redistribution of wealth and economic power, and which believes in sharing power with democratic initiatives beyond the state to achieve these aims. All chances of such a basis existing in the East, and all moves in that direction in the West, were ruthlessly and knowingly destroyed by a triumphalist right. The self-confidence of this right is typified by Norman Tebbit – Mrs Thatcher's right-hand man – declaring war on the Greater London Council: he said 'This is the modern kind of socialism and we will defeat it' (Wolf 2003).

It was possible in the East that through a steady democratic deepening of Gorbachev's perestroika and glasnost, an opening up of the old central state apparatus in favour of democratic civil initiatives and control could have occurred. Instead, the neoliberal governments of the USA and the UK, in particular, treated the collapse of the Soviet empire as a licence to deregulate the market, and destroy all forms of public intervention without restraint. Business interests – with strong governmental backing – were far, far stronger than the precarious movements for democracy, peace and social justice.

The first phase of this onslaught on any kind of public regulation and provision justified itself by the neoliberal Hayekian equation of freedom with the market, and any kind of public intervention with incipient dictatorship. The ability of the social-movement left in the West to stand up to this well-honed ideology was poor. Philosophically, those on the Western left, influenced by the social movements of the 1960s and 1970s, had not developed a theory of agency distinct from the discredited notions of the party and the state. The philosophical tools were there in the mounting critiques both of positivism and methodological individualism, but they had not yet been used to provide the foundations of a new democratic political practice (Wainwright 1994). This left had not established its identity sufficiently to convey any coherent alternative to the flawed reliance on the state to deliver social justice. In particular, it had not had the time or experience to develop forms of regulation, public intervention and provision of public services that could replace the disasters of the command economy. The shortcomings of a command economy were much exaggerated in the Western media, which dwelled upon its inflexibility. The onslaught from the right slowed down this process of rethinking, putting the disparate forces of the social-movement left on the defensive.

Civil society in the third-way version

This meant that by the time of the defeat of Thatcher and Reagan and the widespread recognition that the market was not all it was cracked up to be, there was no sufficiently developed alternative to lead democratic politics in a new direction – a genuine 'third way'. We faced instead, in Britain in particular, a politics that used the language of democratic civil society but whose practice continued to weaken the conditions for its realization.

example of the gap between rhetoric and realities is New Labour's s in the most deprived areas of England. These have involved only minimum redistribution of wealth or political change at a local, let alone national, level. The government's Social Exclusion Unit, however, did genuinely stimulate initiatives for democracy from within civil society, successfully evoking the concept of 'community' in its call for local alliances to compete to become part of the 'New Deal for Communities'. Coalitions – 'partnerships' in the lingo – from 38 estates were chosen to receive a commitment to £50 million to be spent over a ten-year period in a way that should be 'community led'. The whole process was controlled and monitored by central government. Far from democratizing local government, however, this appeal to 'community' bypassed elected local government, which meant bypassing a hive of Old Labour and leftists that the New Labour government could not comprehend or control (Wainwright 2003). In this thinking, 'community participation' and 'political democracy' were in two different compartments. However, actual people committed to the regeneration of their neighbourhoods and, given some initial space and rights to decide, tended not to accept these limits. In several cases they made demands on local councils and the government that highlighted connections between neighbourhood participation and the strengthening of local democracy. Genuine democratic power in 'the community' – that is, power based on a process that includes everyone and does not pitch one community against another – requires a mentality in government that recognizes the limits of its own role, the importance of democratic power springing from a non-state public sphere, and the ways in which government can help to strengthen this power.

Civil society experiments in reinvigorating democracy

There are more modest experiments in this direction elsewhere in Western Europe. In Italy, for example, the Gramscian acknowledgement of the political importance of civil society is being taken in more democratic directions than Antonio ever envisaged. The radical leaderships of several municipal authorities are opening up decision-making about the future of their towns and cities to the people. For instance, in the medieval seaside town of Grottamare, where I write this essay, there was a popular campaign against a highly commercial attempt to turn the harbour into a marina and complex of swimming pools and large hotels, making the town a centre for 'global tourism' and relegating its medieval centre to a curiosity. The campaign was successful and its leadership – a 'participation and democracy' coalition, made up of people both in parties and not – won the municipal elections. Immediately after their election they convened open public meetings for every citizen in every neighbourhood, leading to the creation of self-organized neighbourhood committees that became an independent check on the municipality's ability to enact its promises. Thus began a process of shared decision-making about the content of a new urban plan which, in the words of the first radical mayor, Massimo Rossi, 'started with the needs of the people'. Rossi displays the origins of his political thinking with a picture in the mayoral office of an unusually cheery Che Guevara. And the internationalism of the 1960s is probably one of the currents that makes these radically democratic experiments global in their connections. Grottamare, and municipalities like it, are connecting up with Brazil, Uruguay and other countries of the South in search of an alternative path of development.

What they all have in common is a commitment to creating, alongside electoral democracy, new forms of decision-making. Some see these as rooted in 'civil society', some refer to a 'new non-state public sphere', others to 'the empowerment of citizens'. All think of themselves as involved in a 'bottom-up globalization' challenging the global market. Like the 68ers that some of them are, they are challenging modern imperialism through a mobiliatzion of the people and reclaiming the values of the short-lived movements in Eastern Europe at the end of the Cold War. They are doing so by reinforcing, rather than destroying, electoral democracy. They are beginning a new phase in the history of relations between the state and civil society.

References

Beynon, H. and Wainwright, H. (1979) *The Workers' report on Vickers: the Vickers Shop Stewards' Combined Committee Report on Work, Wages, Rationalisation, Closure and Rank-and-file Organisation in a Multinational Company*, London: Pluto Press.

Blackburn, R. and Cockburn, A. (1969) *Student Power: Problems, Diagnosis, Action,* Harmondsworth: Penguin.

Burke, P., Thompson, M. and Wainwright, H. (eds) (1991) *After the Wall: Democracy and Movement Politics in the New Europe*, Amsterdam: Transnational Institute.

Carvel, J. (1984) *Citizen Ken*, London: Chatto and Windus.

Cohen, J. and Arato, A. (1992) *Civil Society and Political Theory*, Cambridge MA: MIT Press.

Cohn-Bendit, D. and Cohn-Bendit, G. (1968) *Obsolete Communism: The Left-wing Alternative*, London: Deutsch.

Cooley, M. *Architect or Bee?: The Human Price of Technology*, London: Hogarth.

Eley, G. (2002) *Forging Democracy: The History of the Left in Europe, 1850–2000*, Oxford: Oxford University Press.

Ginsborg, P. (1990) *A History of Contemporary Italy: Society and Politics, 1943–1988*, London: Penguin.

Gramsci, A. (1971) *Selections from the Prison Notebooks of Antonio Gramsci,* eds Q. Hoare and G. Howell Smith, London: Lawrence and Wishart.

Havel, V. (1985) 'The power of the powerless', in V. Havel *et al.*, *The Power of the Powerless: Citizens Against the State in Central-Eastern Europe*, London: Hutchinson.

Kaldor, M. (2003) *Global Civil Society: An Answer to War*, Cambridge: Polity Press.

Mackintosh, M. and Wainwright, H. (1987) *A Taste of Power: The Politics of Local Economics*, London: Verso.

Martin, B. (1993) *In the Public Interest?: Privatization and Public Sector Reform*, London: Zed Books, Public Services International.

Rowbotham, S. (1989) *The Past is Before Us: Feminism in Action since the 1960s*, London: Pandora.

——(2000) *Promise of a Dream: Remembering the Sixties*, London: Allen Lane.

Wainwright, H. (1994) *Arguments for a New Left: Answering the Free-market Right*, Oxford: Blackwell.

——(2003) *Reclaim the State: Experiments in Popular Democracy*, London: Verso.

—— and Elliott, D. (1982) *The Lucas Plan: A New Trade Unionism in the Making*, London: Allison and Busby.

Wolf, M. (2003) 'The future need not be as bleak as Davos man fears', *Financial Times*, 29 January.

Part V

Asia

Rooted or imported?

12 'Old' and 'new' civil societies in Bangladesh

David Lewis

The term 'civil society', sometimes translated into Bengali as *shushil shamaj* which literally means 'gentle society', is increasingly prominent in public debate in Bangladesh. Articles regularly appear in the newspapers debating the possible importance, meanings and roles of civil society. The government now speaks, from time to time, of a need for consultations 'with non-governmental organizations (NGOs) and civil society' and a Government/ NGO Consultative Council was established in the mid-1990s as a committee to build better relationships between government and NGOs. Behind the scenes, the international development agencies have pushed the idea of civil society as part of 'good governance' agendas. This chapter briefly discusses the concept of civil society in relation to Bangladeshi politics and development, taking a historical perspective in order to distinguish both 'old' and 'new' civil society forms and processes.

There has been relatively little research on civil society in Bangladesh, either as an idea or an empirical reality, though ethnographic work, theoretical analysis or historical study. While the recent rise of the concept is linked to Western development fashions, to which Bangladesh is particularly vulnerable due to its dependent position in the international aid system, it is also an idea with multiple local meanings and histories that are both politically contested and continually transformed. For example, many within Bangladesh's NGO community have enthusiastically embraced the concept of civil society as part of their own quests for organizational identity and legitimacy. Some NGO leaders also speak of constructing alliances between different groups within civil society, from grass-roots associations to women's and trade union movements, in order to mobilize citizens in support of political or social objectives. The concept of civil society may therefore have the potential to illuminate important aspects of Bangladesh's social and political processes, both past and present.

The NGO sector is a relevant starting point because Bangladesh's high-profile NGOs have their roots in a long tradition in Bengal of community organization and voluntary action. Self-help village-level organizations, such as the *Palli Mangal Samitis* (Village Welfare Societies) became common from the 1930s onwards, encouraged by local administrators in a combination of local good works and the building of local patronage relationships. Private voluntary work was undertaken by citizens in support of schools or mosques, or relief provision in times of natural disaster. Religious charity played a role in the form of the Islamic duty of *zakat*, the payment of one fortieth of one's income to the poor, or the Hindu tradition of providing food to *sadhus* and *faqeers* (Zaidi 1970). Christian missionary work brought voluntary education and health initiatives, as well as early forms of the community development approaches that now characterize many contemporary NGOs.

The war with Pakistan, which led to Independence in 1971, and the subsequent devastating cyclone disaster were both formative in the evolution of the modern NGO sector. International relief efforts linked local activists and entrepreneurs with the ideas, organizations and resources of the 'aid industry'. A new generation of development NGOs was born, building further on traditions of charity and self-help, as well as on Freirean conscientization. These NGOs provided services such as credit delivery and community health care, built local organizations of the landless, and some became involved in policy advocacy. A set of new vertical relationships emerged between people and NGO service providers (Hasan 1993; Lewis 1993).

The growth of the NGO sector was a response to state failure, but it has also arguably contributed to areas of state weakness. Increasingly challenged by political opposition, Sheikh Mujibur Rahman's attempt to create a one-party state in 1975 led to the reintroduction of military-bureaucratic rule until 1990. Government rural development work relied on trickle-down economics for the poor, an extension of clientelistic local government and half-hearted attempts to build village cooperatives. The state remained weak in terms of its capacities to provide social welfare, maintain an independent judiciary or collect taxes. NGOs became attractive to activists inspired by progressive political or developmental agendas, but who did not wish to enter formal political institutions. While highly successful, many NGOs also became drawn into extensive service delivery work, often 'substituting' for absent or inadequate government provision in health, education and rural development. The state has meanwhile increasingly 'discarded' its responsibilities for service provision and citizen accountability through the 'franchising out' of certain key state functions to NGOs and the private sector, which now cater – inadequately – to citizens as 'consumers' (Wood 1997). At the same time, mainstream democratic political institutions are undermined by a politics of confrontation. Interest groups in the form of political parties and associated groups frequently call for stoppages (*hartals*) and pursue political action outside formal political institutions. The political opposition has since 1991 routinely boycotted parliament, creating a façade of political institutions through which little meaningful democratic process is visible.

The NGO sector for many years remained isolated from wider society. The activities of many development NGOs – despite the growing international reputation of some – were met with scepticism by activists, the middle classes and the media, all of which saw NGOs as self-interested and over-accountable to foreign donors. The mass movement that emerged against the Khaleda Zia regime in the mid-1990s showed that some NGOs, through the Association of Development Agencies in Bangladesh (ADAB), were prepared to play a more proactive role in national politics. In the election of 1996 ADAB coordinated a Democracy Awareness Education Programme through which 15,000 trainers ran awareness-raising workshops across the whole country, contributing to an impressive voter turnout of 74 per cent (Ashman 1997). Gono Shahajjo Sangstha (GSS) promoted its landless group members as candidates in local union *parishad* elections and was met with violent resistance by local landlords (Hashemi 1995). Partly as a result of this more 'political' role, public awareness of NGOs has increased, but the price has been that some organizations have become identified in the public mind with particular political parties. Also, aid critics are suspicious of *shushil shamaj* as just another example of the ways in which powerful local clients of the aid machine can penetrate social and political life.

The well-documented development NGO sector in Bangladesh has contributed to a dominant view of a vibrant civil society. The emphasis on NGOs, however, can obscure a range of other important civil society processes, movements and activities. An important strand of 'old' civil society was the organized resistance in the cultural sphere in East Pakistan in the form of the 'language movement' in the 1950s, which asserted the Bengali language against the Urdu imposed by the West Pakistan leadership. It took the form of a nationalist civil society rooted in the democratic struggle for autonomy and eventually independence (Rahman 1999) but was later absorbed into the post-1971 Bangladesh state apparatus and effectively coopted. As Jalal (1995: 90) shows, after the liberation of Bangladesh, Mujib used the Awami League's party organization at least in part to 'establish state control over society'. Jahangir (1986: 44) describes the ways in which the Awami League government by 1975 secured the 'suspension or destruction of rival trade unions, student and youth fronts' and the control of 'pressure groups and potentially alternative points of organized political power'. This eventually led to the cooption of this old civil society into official organizations and party-affiliated groups. A militarization of 'civil' society subsequently occurred under General Zia Rahman with military priorities taking precedence over the 'social' (Jahangir 1986). Resistance to this narrowing of public space then contributed to the emergence of 'newer' organizations of civil society such as NGOs, pressure groups and umbrella organizations concerned with poverty, civil rights, gender and democracy.

Boundaries between state and civil society have therefore constantly shifted. Such blurring is apparent in the ways in which elements of 'old' civil society were absorbed into the post-1971 state, and in the ways in which many NGOs remain linked to government and other institutions through family ties, contracting relationships and an often overlapping dependence on foreign donors. But there is far more to civil society in Bangladesh than the histories and activities of development NGOs and their supporters. The frequent claims that are made about the vibrancy of civil society in Bangladesh also merit closer inspection. As in other parts of the world, the tendency to equate NGOs with 'civil society' is problematic because it leads to a marginalization of other types of organization and forms of action (Howell and Pearce 2001). A second problem is that NGO-focused analyses of civil society in Bangladesh are often ahistorical (Hashemi and Hasan 1999). Finally, it is generally unwise to assume – as liberal accounts of civil society tend to do – a simple dichotomy between civil society and the state, between kinship communities and civil society, or between vertical and horizontal ties (Chandhoke 2002).

Indeed, the emphasis on NGOs only serves to obscure the long history of state–society struggles in the country. What Hashemi and Hasan (1999: 130) call 'traditional' civil society organizations – students, lawyers, journalists, cultural activists, and so on –

> ... have historically played a monumental role in the struggle for Bengali nationalism, for building a secular society and for democratic rights. In fact the movement against the military dictatorships of Ayub Khan and HM Ershad, and even the war of independence, were often led by civil society organizations rather than narrow political parties.

The role of these 'old' pre-NGO civil society organizations changed from a relatively diverse range of citizen groups and interests to a gradually narrower, organized political movement under the Awami League party.

These histories serve to remind us that relationships in contemporary civil society reflect wider social tensions. For example, the work of NGOs in rural areas has occasionally brought cases of violent conflict between local religious groups and NGO field staff and clients. These cases have sometimes been used as evidence that NGO programmes which challenge local gender norms – female literacy and education, awareness raising in relation to women's rights – are proving influential. In 1994 female NGO field workers were assaulted in Manikganj and Sitakanda, and more recently in Brahmanbaria BRAC (Bangladesh Rural Advancement Committee) schools and staff were attacked (Rahman 1999). For some, this is evidence of clashes between the forces of local religious conservatism and NGOs as purveyors of Western modernity. Others have sought to explain such incidents as part of ongoing disputes over patron–client relations or land-related conflicts in which NGOs are merely convenient scapegoat targets, perhaps by threatening established interests by positioning themselves as 'new patrons' (Devine 1998).

Religious organizations may also be considered a part of civil society, and such cases are examples of the intrasocietal conflicts we would expect to find within Gramscian theories of civil society (Davis and McGregor 2000). Religious organizations such as development NGOs may also see themselves as acting in pursuit of the public good in response to local problems. For example, during 2001 in the Gopibagh area of Dhaka's Mirpur district, the leader of one mosque helped organize a community initiative designed to resist the problem of organized crime – believed to be linked upwards to political parties – experienced by local traders and residents in the neighbouring streets. Once whistles were issued to local shop keepers and wooden clubs provided to the congregation of the mosque, the activities of local touts and extortionists were believed to have been successfully reduced. A number of those accused were pursued and then beaten to death by a group of angry citizens carrying out a form of 'instant justice' (M.S. Siddiqi, personal communication).

Conflicts within civil society also reflect elite struggles for power. In the 1980s, the efforts of one NGO to campaign for an essential drugs policy, which would limit the importation of costly branded medical products primarily for use by urban elites and produce a list of widely used medicines that could be produced more cheaply locally, was resisted the Bangladesh Medical Association, the professional association of a medical establishment that stood to lose financially from any tampering with its lucrative relationship with international pharmaceutical companies (Chowdhury 1995). In the NGO community, too, there have been regular allegations of misbehaviour, in relation to mismanagement, corruption and scandal. Such cases serve to remind us of the dangers of the liberal vision of a too-benign view of civil society and the existence of what Keane has termed 'uncivil society', though such judgements about actions taken by organized groups in pursuit of their own or a community's interests very much depend on the values and beliefs of the observer.

Civil society cannot be seen as set apart from wider social and political hierarchies. Earlier analyses of the rural power structure by NGOs (for example, BRAC's 1978 study of 'The Net') emphasized patron–client relations as a key problem, justifying the need for NGOs to challenge rural informal money-lending institutions through providing an alternative source of low-cost loans. On the other hand, Devine (1998) and others have emphasized the roles of NGOs themselves as resource providers and, therefore, as potential patrons. In addition to opening up new political spaces, some NGOs may have also come to occupy more familiar older ones as they – rather than government or traditional moneylenders – become important in distributing resources and mediating with other power structures on behalf of 'the poor'. Karim (2001) finds evidence that some NGOs have used their economic power as lenders to exercise political influence by delivering votes to political parties.

The internal structures of NGOs may also help reproduce such hierarchies. Some advocates of civil society have claimed organizations are microcosms of democratic governance and egalitarian practice, which can contribute to wider norms of reciprocity and trust. Patron–client relations are transferred from wider social relations and reproduced within NGO structures despite the appearance of these structures as rational bureaucratic systems (Wood 1997). There is also a practical role for kinship and patronage networks in the recruitment of staff by NGO leaders in order to ensure loyalty and reduce risk within an often hostile wider institutional environment. Many organizations, particularly those with a local, less professionalized or formal character, find it difficult to free themselves from the ties of kinship loyalties in their structure and management (Béteille 2000).

As we have seen, there is more than one tradition of civil society in Bangladesh. The crucial turning point for bringing the 'old' and 'new' streams of civil society closer together, and into a more mainstream position in relation to the general public, was the 'people power' protests that brought down the military regime in 1990 and returned Bangladesh to a democratic system. Development NGOs were publicly seen to play a political role alongside the rest of civil society concerned with challenging the 'military' with the 'civil', even if they did join the movement relatively late. Today, at the beginning of the twenty-first century, there are tentative new links between old and new civil society in the form of alliances that stretch between left-leaning NGOs, trade unions, women's organizations and sections of the press, such as the *Oikabaddo Nagorik Andolan* (United Civil Society Movement) in which Proshika and a range of other civil society actors mobilized more than half a million people in February 2001 with a comprehensive set of demands to government on democratization, human rights and poverty reduction.

Whether the state – and perhaps ultimately the donors – have 'captured' NGOs and civil society in Bangladesh, or whether society – and not all of it 'civil' – has 'captured' the state (as White 1999 suggests), is a question that requires a more detailed analysis than is possible here, and one which also depends on distinguishing more carefully both the strong and weak characteristics that can coexist simultaneously in different levels and dimensions within the Bangladesh state, and the ways in which power is exercised within and between different institutional sectors. This chapter has attempted to explore the political, historical and cultural limits of such conceptions of civil society. Newer analytical accounts of civil society in Bangladesh are becoming more sophisticated in providing a critique of the imported 'donor model' of civil society, which tends to obscure issues of patronage, conflict and power and which tends to privilege the 'new' civil society represented by the country's high-profile NGO sector.

If civil society is in part an outcome of the operation of democratic institutions, it may be that much so-called 'civil society' in Bangladesh is really nothing of the kind. A more inclusive, locally adapted idea of civil society might acknowledge the role of vertical social relations, the blurring of boundaries in Bangladesh between civil society and household and kin networks, as well as with the state and the market, and ongoing relations of conflict and contestation between citizens and state. Within such a view, civil society becomes an entry point for the analysis of important social, economic and political themes, such as the changing expectations on the part of citizens towards the state, the changing influence of transnational actors on social and economic realities, and the nature of patronage systems, which continue to structure important aspects of political and economic life.

Note

This is a shortened version of a more detailed analysis to be published in *Contributions to Indian Sociology* in 2004 as 'On the difficulty of studying "civil society": reflections on NGOs, state and democracy in Bangladesh'. The support of the Nuffield Foundation is gratefully acknowledged for fieldwork which contributed to this chapter.

References

Ashman, D. (1997) 'The democracy awareness education program of the Association of Development Agencies in Bangladesh (ADAB)', *Discourse: A Journal of Policy Studies*, Dhaka: Institute for Development Policy Analysis and Advocacy (IDPAA), Proshika.

Béteille, A. (2000) 'Civil society and the good society', XIIth Zakir Husain Memorial Lecture, 22 February, New Delhi: Zakir Husain College.

Chandhoke, N. (2002) 'The limits of global civil society', in M. Glasius, M. Kaldor and H. Anheier (eds), *Global Civil Society 2002*, Oxford: Oxford University Press.

Chowdhury, Z. (1995) *The Politics of Essential Drugs: The Makings of a Successful Health Strategy*, London: Zed Books.

Davis, P. and McGregor, J. (2000) 'Civil society, international donors and poverty in Bangladesh', *Commonwealth and Comparative Politics*, 38(1): 47–64.

Devine, J. (1998) 'Empowerment and the spiritual economy of NGOs in Bangladesh', Paper to European Network of Bangladesh Studies, Fifth Workshop, University of Bath, 16–18 April.

Hasan, S. (1993) 'Voluntarism and rural development in Bangladesh', *Asian Journal of Public Administration*, 15(1): 82–101.

Hashemi, S.M. (1995) 'NGO accountability in Bangladesh: NGOs, state and donors', in M. Edwards and D. Hulme (eds), *NGO Performance and Accountability: Beyond the Magic Bullet*, London: Earthscan.

—— and Hasan, M. (1999) 'Building NGO legitimacy in Bangladesh: the contested domain', in D. Lewis (ed.), *International Perspectives on Voluntary Action: Reshaping the Third Sector*, London: Earthscan.

Howell, J. and Pearce, J. (2001) *Civil Society and Development: A Critical Exploration*, London: Lynne Rienner.

Jahangir, B.K. (1986) *Problematics of Nationalism in Bangladesh*, Dhaka: Centre for Social Studies.

Jalal, A. (1995) *Democracy and Authoritarianism in South Asia: A Comparative and Historical Perspective*, Cambridge: Cambridge University Press.

Karim, L. (2001) 'Politics of the poor?: NGOs and grassroots political mobilisation in Bangladesh', *Political and Legal Anthropology Review*, 24(1): 92–107.

Lewis, D. (1993) 'Bangladesh overview', in J. Farrington and D. Lewis with S. Kumar and A. Miclat-Teves (eds), *NGOs and the State in Asia*, London: Routledge.

Rahman, A. (1999) 'NGOs and civil society in Bangladesh', *Journal of Social Studies*, 84: 23–45.

White, S.C. (1999) 'NGOs, civil society, and the state in Bangladesh: the politics of representing the poor', *Development and Change,* 30(3): 307–26.

Wood, G.D. (1997) 'States without citizens: the problem of the franchise state', in D. Hulme and M. Edwards (eds), *Too Close for Comfort: NGOs, States and Donors*, London: Macmillan.

Zaidi, S.M.H. (1970) *The Village Culture in Transition: A Study of East Pakistan Rural Society*, Honolulu: East West Centre Press.

13 Seizing spaces, challenging marginalization and claiming voice

New trends in civil society in China

Jude Howell

Introduction

It is easy to dismiss without much ado the idea of civil society under an authoritarian regime such as China, or to suggest that the concept of civil society is so deeply entrenched in Western political thought and historical experience that it can have no place in analyses of Asian or African societies. On the first count, such a glib dismissal would fail to reveal or explain the gradual opening up of spaces for more autonomous organizing and expression in reform since the 1980s, despite the fact that the Chinese polity remains essentially authoritarian, albeit somewhat liberalized. The second dismissal would be to give way to a cultural and historical essentialism that impedes the investigation of multiple forms of organizing in pursuit of shared values, norms and meanings. The concepts of civil society, state, society and economy are never fixed and static; indeed, it is their fluidity, their complex layers of meaning, and the politics of their appropriation or otherwise that make them interesting. As abstract ideal-types that do not pretend to correspond neatly to reality, they offer vital analytic tools for critical enquiry into processes of social and political change.

This chapter argues that civil society, in the sense of a relatively independent sphere of non-coerced association for shared interests, has developed over twenty years of reform in China since the early 1980s, albeit in fits and starts. Of particular interest is the emergence from the mid-1990s onwards of a new layer of organizations concerned with the plight of marginalized groups in society, such as female migrant workers and those living with HIV/AIDS. It is argued that such a development reflects the deepening processes of social differentiation and class formation that the rapid introduction of market forces has spearheaded. But it also owes its roots to the changing relations between the party/state, and the economy and society. This chapter starts by tracing the rise of relatively autonomous forms of association from 1978 onwards. It then focuses on the specific features of independent organizing around marginalized issues from the mid-1990s onwards. Finally, it considers the implications of these new spaces, voices and practices for the future development of civil society in China (for a fuller account, see Howell 2003).

Evolution of civil society in the reform period (1978–2003)

Concerned that the development of China's technological and productive forces lagged noticeably behind its East Asian counterparts, in the early 1980s the new reformist leaders of the Chinese Communist Party in their drive for 'modernization' began to liberalize the spaces for more open discussion, intellectual debate and independent association. This stimulated the emergence of new forms of association, particularly those in the fields of academe, science and technology. As the private sector gradually expanded over the decade, traders, businesspeople and entrepreneurs began to establish associations so as to share market information, enhance access to supplies, and represent their interests. There was no unified system or standard set of practices for registering such 'social organizations' *(shehui tuanti)* or monitoring their growth (for further details on the historical development of the regulatory framework see White *et al.* 1996: 99–103).

The development of more independent forms of organizing reached a peak in 1989, when the spread of the democracy movement unleashed a tide of spontaneous protest and gave birth to a plethora of declared independent associations, especially autonomous students' and workers' organizations. The tragic events of 4 June brought this first phase of independent organizing to an abrupt and bloody halt. In October 1989 the Standing Committee of the State Council issued a new set of regulations for the registration of social organizations that required, *inter alia*, social organizations to affiliate to a supervisory body, which was responsible for supervising the day-to-day affairs of the social organizations beneath it. Whilst associations perceived as threatening to political stability and the power of the Chinese Communist Party – such as prodemocratic groups, independent trade unions and autonomous student associations – were prohibited, other organizations continued to register. This two-pronged approach reflected an awareness amongst top party leaders not only that total prohibition of any forms of independent association would be counterproductive to its broader goals of technological and economic modernization, but also that new forms of horizontal association were important for stabilizing society and for expressing new needs and interests in the context of rapid social transformation. Furthermore, with plans afoot to speed up the pace of state enterprise reform, a complete overhaul of the institutional fabric of urban social welfare and social security was needed. Social organizations could potentially play a key role in absorbing surplus employment and in providing vital social services that were previously supplied by state enterprises.

Though the growth of registered social organizations stumbled along at a snail's pace in the early 1990s, preparations for hosting the Fourth

International Conference on Women in Beijing in 1995 had a catalytic effect on the development of more autonomous women's organizations in China (Howell 1997). From the point of view of the party/state, it would have been ironic if China did not have a contingent of women's NGOs to present at the parallel NGO Forum. In the light of this the party/state actively encouraged research on women's issues and promoted the formation of women's associations, particularly female professional, academic and entrepreneurs' associations. There was a spate of articles and books on women's issues and gender analysis (Li 1993; Liu 1995; Tan 1995). Women's studies groups and informal salons proliferated across major cities in China (see Hsiung *et al.* 2001). Though some of these new women's organizations were founded from above, a considerable number also seized the opportunity to raise taboo issues such as domestic violence, to experiment with new ideas such as counselling, and to represent the voices of marginal groups such as single mothers and female divorcees. The proliferation of more autonomous women's organizations during this period was not without tension. The All-China Women's Federation responded with ambiguity to these new groups, sometimes collaborating with them, sometimes dominating them, sometimes refusing to court them. Nevertheless, the controversial hosting of this grand event in Beijing served to open up the spaces of autonomous organizing at a time when the political climate had retreated into authoritarian conservatism.

From the mid-1990s the number of non-registered and registered social organizations began to rise again. However, in November 1998 the Ministry of Civil Affairs revised the regulations for the registration of social organizations, laying down more detailed and stringent requirements than before, and thereby making it more difficult for small organizations to contemplate seeking official recognition. In order to register, for instance, a social organization needed to have at least 50 individual or 30 institutional members, and national-level organizations were to have a minimum of RMB 100,000 for their activities, and a fixed location.

Between 1998 and the end of 1999, the number of registered social organizations fell from 162,887 to 136,841, well below the 181,060 organizations registered in late 1989, either because the process of review had revealed apparent misdemeanours, or because they could not meet the conditions for registration. Overall the new regulations inhibited rather than promoted the further growth of registered social organizations.

However, since the late 1990s there has been a new wave of organizing that is distinguished by the novelty of its organizational forms and its focus of attention. The stringent requirements of the 1998 regulations have on the one hand inclined some new organizations towards registration as a non-profit enterprise under the Industry and Commerce Bureau, a less arduous process than registering under the Ministry of Civil Affairs. On the other hand, they have encouraged others to bypass the process of registration by establishing themselves as second-, third- or fourth-level associations, or as centres under research institutes and universities, or as loose networks, or as projects under larger institutions. Furthermore, since the late 1990s the number of groups taking up social issues of poverty, marginalization and health has spiralled. China is now home to cancer groups; voluntary schemes in rural areas; prisoners' wives' groups; HIV/AIDS associations; migrant workers' clubs; diabetic societies; initiatives to assist orphans and poor, rural girls; and so on. This contrasts with the 1980s when the main forms of organizing gravitated around the winners of the reform process – namely, the professionals, intellectuals and businesspeople.

The emergence of a layer of organizations concerned with issues of socioeconomic inequalities, social justice and social welfare is not coincidental. As noted earlier, it reflects a deliberate strategy by the party/state to encourage the development of non-governmental welfare provision, both as a way to absorb surplus employment from the closure of state enterprises and to create a new system of urban social welfare. It also reflects the increasing socioeconomic disparities that have accompanied the process of rapid modernization and a deep concern amongst top party leaders that such disparities are potentially destabilizing. It is thus all the more remarkable that, given the continuing constraints on organizing in China, new forms of association have emerged around issues that touch upon social and political sensitivities. In order to understand why and how this is happening and the significance of this for the developing contours of civil society in China, the next section focuses on two types of organizing – namely, around HIV/AIDS and female migrant workers.

Organizing around HIV/AIDS and female migrant workers

The issue of HIV/AIDS has proved sensitive in China not only for the usual reasons encountered in all countries of social taboos around sexuality and sexually transmitted diseases (STDs), but also because addressing this also publicly exposes other social problems such as drug addiction, exploitation of commercial sex workers, rural poverty, and local government complicity in the transmission of the virus through blood-collecting facilities. Similarly, female migrant workers not only are marginalized from mainstream urban society because of their social categorization as rural and migrant, but also encounter the rough edge of exploitative workplace practices, particularly acute in small-scale Korean and overseas Chinese enterprises. Drawing attention to such practices throws into question not only the role of the official trade union but also the contradictions inherent in a political party on the one hand still proclaiming allegiance to communist ideology and on the other hand presiding over a dynamic but ruthless capitalist economy.

Though non-governmental action around HIV/AIDS has emerged in the late 1990s, the number of registered organizations operating in this field is much smaller compared to women's organizations, environmental groups or business associations, for example, reflecting the social taboos and political concerns around this issue. The main organizations include the China AIDS Network, founded in 1994 and comprising professionals of various disciplines engaged in advisory work, action research and health awareness; Beijing Aizhi, a group created on the internet that played a key role in exposing the devastating spread of HIV/AIDS amongst rural villagers in Henan through government-run blood plasma factories; and the China Foundation for the Prevention of STDs and AIDS, a registered foundation of public health professionals involved in research, public education, and intervention, started in 1988.

Legal constraints and social stigma make it difficult for people living with HIV/AIDS or their carers, or commercial sex workers and drug addicts, to form self-help groups or to speak openly and publicly about their needs. However, attempts are being made to create spaces for the voices of people living with HIV/AIDS to be heard. In 1994 a group of activists and researchers in Yunnan province set up the Yunnan HIV/AIDS Care Network, publishing four newsletters and holding several meetings. A lack of sustained resources and energy led to the closure of this network after two years. In 2001 there was only one self-help group for people living with HIV/AIDS, which was linked to the special HIV/AIDS ward in a Beijing hospital. In the spring of 2002 a person living with HIV/AIDS set up Mangrove Support Group. Since then other self-help groups have sprouted up in Sichuan, Yunnan, Shanxi and Xinjiang provinces, as well as Guanzhou and Shanghai cities.

Given the difficulties of registering organizations, many medical professionals, social scientists and activists deploy a number of strategies for organizing around the issue of HIV/AIDS. These include using existing registered associations as a platform from which to engage in HIV/AIDS-related work. The prestige of such associations and their network of links with government officials can provide an important protective shield as well as legitimacy for professionals working on HIV/AIDS issues. Internationally funded projects are important avenues for raising awareness about HIV/AIDS and for addressing the needs of commercial sex workers and drug addicts. For example, international funds have supported the establishment of a pilot centre in Hainan province to provide advice and counselling on HIV/AIDS to sex workers. Participating in international projects has been a crucial way for activists, researchers and professionals to gain experience and to promote new practices, and for some it has been a strategic step towards setting up a non-governmental organization.

Organizing around the needs and interests of female migrant workers has also been challenging, not least because any attempt to organize around labour issues is deeply disturbing to the top leadership. Nevertheless, it is of interest that there have been several initiatives in this domain. Most prevalent amongst these are the non-governmental legal counselling centres for women, of which there are at least eight in China. Though these tend to address a range of gender issues such as domestic violence, rape and divorce, as with the Beijing University Women's Legal Counselling Centre, some also address specifically the needs of working women, be these laid-off female workers, migrant workers or the victims of labour rights violations. Examples of the latter include the Shenzhen Women Workers' Centre and Fudan University Women's Legal Counselling Centre. Established upon the initiative of a group of Hong Kong women activists, the Shenzhen centre is unique in that it sets out not only to provide advice but also to empower women migrant workers by providing them with negotiating skills and the confidence to organize in the workplace. Through its mobile bus it is able to distribute information about labour rights to female migrant workers in different factories, organize discussion groups, and promote the setting up of mutual support groups. In 2003 it started preparations for a consumer cooperative, enabling female migrant workers to purchase essential goods at low-cost prices (Interview, November 2003, Hong Kong).

Apart from these legal counselling centres, there is also the Migrant Women Workers' Club (*dagongjie zhi jia*) in Beijing, established in April 1996, which serves as a meeting-place for female migrant workers, organizes social activities, and provides a platform for the discussion of gender issues. For example, in October 2000 the Club invited a young domestic worker who had suffered physical abuse at the hands of her employer to recount her experiences and seek public support for the legal action that she was taking (Interview, October 2000, Beijing). In 2003 a second migrant workers' club was also set up in Beijing, carrying out similar work and activities. With the support of international donors, Rural Women Knowing All – a non-governmental women's agency, which publishes a magazine of the same name for rural women – set up a training school outside Beijing for enhancing the skills of female migrant workers.

Given that labour issues are highly sensitive for the party/state in China, it is curious that it seems to be easier to organize around female migrant workers than labour rights in general. There are no specialized non-governmental counselling and legal advice centres for workers, despite attempts to establish these. Any moves to set up autonomous associations of laid-off workers or migrant workers, or to distribute pamphlets about labour grievances and violations, are rapidly stamped upon by public security agencies. Organizing around female migrant workers has been relatively easier for two reasons. First, it is closely related to the way the Chinese Communist Party has historically constructed women as a social group. Though women are portrayed as in need of liberation from the oppressive weights of feudalism and patriarchy, they are also constructed as a group in need of protection because of their biological condition as the 'weaker' sex. Second, organizations and groups focusing on the rights of women in general, and female migrant workers in particular, have addressed these issues in terms of the legal rights of women rather than linking them to any broader political demands for independent trade unions or political reform.

These moves towards organizing around politically and socially sensitive issues such as HIV/AIDS and female migrant workers are both innovative and instructive. The opening up of spaces for organizing around social welfare and justice concerns has made possible experimentation with new methods of treatment, fostered more participatory approaches to research, and focused attention on the needs of different groups. It is instructive because it gives some insight into the changing values of society, the emerging patterns of wealth and power, and the changing dynamics of civil society in China. In the next section I reflect more broadly on the implications of this for the future direction of civil society.

Implications for civil society

The emergence of this new layer of organizing around issues of marginalization, social justice and inequality is significant on a number of counts for the future development of civil society and processes of governance in China. First, many of these new organizations have skilfully avoided the requirement of official registration by operating as units or centres attached to larger institutions, as third- or fourth-level associations, as projects, or as networks. This suggests that the extent of non-governmental organizing is much larger than can be read from official statistics of registered organizations, which in any case are incomplete. It also indicates that the government system designed to 'manage' this new sphere of intermediary organizing cannot keep pace with the growth of non-governmental initiative. At the same time it also points to increasing local government tolerance of such initiatives, where these are perceived to benefit local society. The truce between the party/state and civil society since 1989 is thus constantly being renegotiated and challenged.

Second, most of these new organizations and initiatives rely upon international donor funding. This raises crucial issues not only around the financial sustainability of these organizations, but also the potential risk of such groups orienting their priorities and activities to the agendas of donor agencies, as often occurs in other aid contexts. It potentially lays these groups open to charges that they are products of external forces, a critique that, though not yet mounted, can easily be levelled, should the party/state wish to discredit any such group. The strong ties with external funding also highlight the extent to which China has become entangled in the global political economy, a trend that is likely only to increase. This could make it more difficult for the Chinese party/state to resort to repressive measures to control civil society as developments in China become increasingly open to global scrutiny.

Third, this contestation of the space for autonomous organizing takes place also at the discursive level. The first national conferences on NGOs were held from the late 1990s onwards. These preferred to speak in terms of the 'third sector' *(di san bumen)* or 'non-profit organizations' *(fei yingli jigou)*, thus avoiding the more politicized overtones of various other translations of civil society. This rendering of the notion of civil society in turn dovetailed well with the party/state's vision of an apolitical, intermediate realm of service delivery organizations, which would play an important role in the institutional redefinition of social welfare provision. For neoleftists these sanitized terms were a useful shield for pushing open the boundaries of critical debate and autonomous action.

Finally, there is an important class dynamic to civil society that is overlooked by homogenizing accounts of civil society. Civil society is not an even playing field. It mirrors and reproduces the deep fissures of the socioeconomy and provides a stage upon which contesting visions of the world and power relations are played out. The rapid process of socioeconomic transformation in China since 1978 – and in particular the crystallization of new classes of a domestic bourgeoisie, rural proletariat, and middle class – are becoming manifest in the contours of civil society. In the 1980s the main actors forming more independent organizations were the main winners in the reform process, namely, the intellectuals, professionals and business classes. From the mid-1990s onwards the spaces for more autonomous organization are also being used to address the needs of and give voice to those who are losing out more in the reform process, such as the new urban poor, migrant workers, and marginalized groups. Moreover, new property owners, such as residents of private compounds, are also using new openings to form property owners' associations to protect their interests *vis-à-vis* unscrupulous management and construction companies and local governments (for a fascinating case-study of this see Zhang 2003). In the future we can expect the growing complexity of society, and especially the sharpening socioeconomic divisions, to find organizational expression in the spaces of civil society. For observers of China the contested spaces of civil society will deserve at least as much attention as the relations between party/state and civil society.

Note

I am grateful to the Department for International Development, UK, for providing an ESCOR small grant to conduct this research.

References

Howell, J. (1997) 'Post-Beijing reflections: creating ripples, but not waves in China', *Women's Studies International Forum*, 20 (2): 235–52.

——(2003) 'New directions in civil society: organizing around marginalized interests', in J. Howell (ed.), *Governance in China*, New York: Rowman and Littlefield Publishers.

Hsiung P.C., Jaschok, M. and Milwertz, C. (eds) (2001) *Chinese Women Organising. Cadres, Feminists, Muslims and Queers*, Oxford: Berg.

Li X.J., (1993) 'Xin shiqi funu yanjiu he funu yundong zhi wo jian' [My views on women's studies and the women's movement in the new era], in *Zhongguo Funu yu*

Fazhan. Diwei, Jiankang, Jiuye [*Chinese Women and Development. Status, Health and Employment*], Tianjin Shifan Daxue Special Conference Publication.

Liu B., (1995) 'Zhongguo funu yanjiu qushi' [Trends in China's women's studies], *Funu Yanjiu Luncong*, 1, 9–11.

Tan S., (1995) 'Funu yanjiu de xin jinzhan' (New developments in women's studies), *Shehui xue Yanjiu*, 5(59): 66–74.

White, G., Howell, J. and Shang X., (1996) *In Search of Civil Society. Market Reform and Social Change in Contemporary China*, Oxford: Oxford University Press.

Zhang J. (2003) 'Neighbourhood-level governance: the growing social foundation of a public sphere', in J. Howell (ed.), *Governance in China*, New York: Rowman and Littlefield Publishers.

14 Central Asian fragmented civil society

Communal and neoliberal forms in Tajikistan and Uzbekistan

Sabine Freizer

Since the collapse of the Soviet Union, Central Asian states and societies have sought to (re)affirm their identity and position in a highly contested region. Central Asia is generally considered to include Kazakhstan, Kyrgyzstan, Tajikistan, Turkmenistan and Uzbekistan, while Afghanistan and Mongolia may sometimes be included. Tensions between European vs. Asian, rural vs. urban, secular vs. religious, democratic vs. autocratic, capitalist vs. socialist, and individualistic vs. communal values, ways of life and modes of governance confront the region's citizens and leaders. The tensions extend to civil society. In this edited volume, it is notable that the chapter on Central Asia has been included in the section on 'Asia'. While geographically firmly grounded in the Asian continent, much of the region's population has felt a strong pull from Imperial Russia since the nineteenth century. Within the USSR, the populations of Central Asia belonged not only to a common political and economic system, but also to a social and cultural space that linked them to the Caucasus, the Baltics and Central Europe. Since the USSR's break-up much of this space has dissolved. Central Asia has gained its own specificity as a vast, postcommunist, largely Muslim territory, composed of countries following increasingly divergent development paths. As generalizations between the region's states are difficult to make, this paper will focus on Tajikistan and Uzbekistan, which historically, geographically and culturally are more closely linked with each other than with the three other states of the area.

In discussions on civil society in Central Asia two conceptualizations of the term are of special relevance: communal civil society and neoliberal civil society. The form of civil society that is most deeply embedded in Tajikistan and Uzbekistan can be termed 'communal'. According to proponents of the communal definition, civil society is composed of a host of informal group activities and meeting places that connect individuals, build trust, encourage reciprocity, and facilitate exchange of views on matters of public concern (Varshney 2002: 46). It 'argues for a more inclusive usage of civil society, in which it is not defined negatively, in opposition to the state, but positively in the context of the ideas and practices through which cooperation and trust are established in social life' (Hann and Dunn 1996: 14, 22). One of the distinctive characteristics of the communal definition is that it is less about state–society relations and more concerned with relations within society, with community solidarity, self-help and trust. It is not normatively grounded. It 'contains repression as well as democracy, conflict as well as cooperation, vice as well as virtue' (Robinson and White, quoted in Van Rooy 2000). Communal civil society is a space of public and collective activity – made up of organizations as well as highly informal modes of interaction – where people come together to meet their self-prescribed goals or defend their interests in solidarity. Most often it is bound by a set territory and focused within the local community.

Since the mid-1980s and the advent of glasnost, closely followed by the engagement of international development agencies in Tajikistan and Uzbekistan, a second form of civil society that can be called neoliberal has expanded rapidly. This civil society is conceptualized as 'the realm of autonomous voluntary organizations, acting in the public sphere as an intermediary between the state and private life' (Diamond and Plattner 1996: xxii). It is best represented by non-governmental organizations (NGOs). This form of civil society is voluntary and independent of state, family and local community bonds (Gellner 1994: 33). It is the product of Western European processes of modernity, and tends to promote values linked to the protection of individual human rights and private property. This definition also interprets civil society as being related to the not-for-profit or *voluntary sector* made up of organizations that are private, non-profit-distributing, self-governing and voluntary (Salamon and Anheier 1996).

The resilience of communal civil society in Tajikistan and Uzbekistan

In Tajikistan and Uzbekistan trust and solidarity networks are primarily built around kinship ties. Many theorists exclude kinship as a basis for the development of civil society because it leads to the 'tyranny of cousins' (Gellner 1994). Yet in Tajikistan and Uzbekistan kinship served as an important mobilizing factor through which individuals were able to express and defend their common interests. Abdullaev (2002: 1) argues that in Uzbek and Tajik society 'the dominant institution of power was the *avlod* – an ascent patriarchal extended family ... For generations, this *avlod* system provided survival, autonomy, and adaptability to its members, serving traditionalism and sustainability of the society.' The *avlod* extended its membership through marriage, and today the *avlod* continues to provide protection and assistance to obtain housing, employment, marriage partners, and in certain instances political influence.

Communal civil society based on kinship was strengthened by links based on proximity. In the pre-Soviet era *mahallas* developed in urban areas as relatively independent associations of citizens. *Mahallas* brought people living on the same territory together on a voluntary basis, along interest lines based on profession, ethnic origin, or good neighbourliness. *Mahalla* members gathered regularly to exchange information, decide community problems, and define public opinion in neighbourhood tea-houses (*chaihana*). *Mahallas* were self-governing and served as a forum where local values, rules of behaviour and common needs were defined. To regulate personal and family problems inhabitants turned to councils of elders (*aksakals*), who helped organize traditional feasts and gatherings (*maraka*) to celebrate births, marriages, and funerals. The traditions of community voluntary action (*hashar*) and community giving to help those in need (*sadaqa*) were largely maintained in the Soviet era. *Mahallas* and their leaders had the ability to organize voluntary forms of service provision and resolve community disputes. In Soviet Central Asia *mahallas* often functioned in symbiosis with communist institutions. For example, Tajikistan's Karategin Valley *mahallas* organized a host of capital improvement works in the mid-1980s. According to a former *mahalla* head in the village of Shulmak (Garm district, 1,300 pop.) the local *chaihana*/mosque and school were constructed in 1980–83 with community members' voluntary contribution of labour (*hashar*) and funds, while the collective farm (*kolhoz*) provided the heavy machinery (Alimordhon Rakhimov, personal communication, 30 July 2002). In the postindependence period, *mahallas* continued to have relevance in Tajikistan, and especially in Uzbekistan where they gained legal status as institutions of local self-governance since 1999.

Community civil society in Tajikistan and Uzbekistan was extremely resilient to external influences. Distrust reigned supreme outside networks based on family, proximity and religion. Relations that did not follow these lines were held suspect. Uzbek and Tajik communal civil society is thus mainly inward looking, constructed along horizontal personalized relations – often grounded in face-to-face encounters. Its value base is inherently conservative and its interests local. Groups within communal civil society are disconnected from national-level politics and tend towards communalism and traditionalism.

Glasnost: a moment of opportunity to extend communal civil society

The political openness that accompanied glasnost offered the public space for the expansion of communal civil society institutions as well as the creation of new civil society organizations. Like in many countries of Central Europe and the Soviet Union, movements protesting environmental degradation were some of the first autonomous politicized groups to form in Uzbekistan and Tajikistan (Carley 1995; Howell and Pearce 2001: 196–7; Watters 1999). The ideas and activism of the early glasnost-era civil society organizations attracted mainly the urban middle classes – scientists, professors, teachers and students – and bypassed many rural communities. Some of these individuals were dissidents and strongly believed in the need for fundamental change in the governing system. But overall the new civil society organizations were not in opposition to the state and defended local concerns and interests. They tended to be small urban-based national and cultural associations. In this they were more like an extension of *mahallas* than true political movements. One such group was Ehyoi Khojand, founded in September 1989 by city intellectuals, journalists and artists, who successfully organized a referendum in 1990 to return the original name of Khojand to what was then called the city of Leninabad (Sughd region).

In the late 1980s and early 1990s political entrepreneurs – regional postcommunist leaders and traditional Sufi leaders of popular Islam – were more successful in mobilizing rural communities around issues pertaining to religion and regional identity or *localism*. In a period of mounting political and economic instability these elites acted through traditional solidarity structures of communal civil society, appealing to citizens' local-level grievances and search for identity. As of 1990 in Tajikistan the Islamic Republican Party (IRP) began successfully mobilizing traditional groups using kin- and territory-based networks especially in the Vaksh and Karategin Valleys. In Uzbekistan the Uzbek IRP, and subsequently the Adolat (Justice) movement (in 1992), attempted to do the same in the Ferghana Valley but were violently repressed by the government. By 2003 the IRP was the only representation of political Islam officially recognized in Central Asia. It was registered as a political party though the Tajik government also persecuted its leaders and members. It has a national newspaper, offices in major cities, women's groups, as well as resources to provide scholarships for Tajik students attending universities abroad.

Glasnost also provided intellectuals and urban-based elites with a unique opportunity to confront national-level problems and promote solutions that rivalled those offered by the state. In 1988 Uzbekistan's first non-governmental political group with a nationalist agenda, Birlik (Unity), was created by scientists and other members of the intelligentsia. One of the organization's first goals was to improve the position of the Uzbek language (Fierman 1997). It did not shy from organizing and participating in public demonstrations. In Tajikistan Rastokhez (Renaissance), formed in September 1989, was the first sophisticated civil society organization to develop with an extensive republican-level programme. Birlik and Rastokhez were created in part based on the model of People's Fronts operating since 1986 in the Baltics. There was much experience sharing, communication and support exchanged between Rastokhez civil activists and their Baltic counterparts. Rastokhez's and Birlik's programmes gave great weight to ecological problems, education, language, national cultural renaissance and the national interests of the republic as a whole (Niyazov 1993; personal communication, 8 August 2002). Interestingly both Birlik and Rastokhez tried to influence policy and politics through the electoral process, their leaders setting up

Democratic Parties for the 1991 elections in both countries (Atkin 1997; Fierman 1997). Eventually the Democratic Party of Tajikistan and the IRP would join forces during the 1992–97 Tajik civil war.

During the 1990s the civil war in Tajikistan, and severe government repression in Uzbekistan, significantly weakened Birlik and Rastokhez. Since then no republic-wide autonomous organizations with national-level political agendas have resurfaced. Several of Birlik and Rastokhez's leaders went into exile. Others who remained in Tajikistan and Uzbekistan established human rights organizations including the Human Rights Society of Uzbekistan, the Independent Human Rights Organization (Uzbekistan) and the Human Rights Centre in Khojand, which are barely tolerated by the authorities, and have little organizational capacities or funding.

Civil society divided between communal and neoliberal forms

The most significant postindependence development in civil society's evolution has been the rapid growth of the non-governmental sector. The International Centre for Not-for-profit Law (ICNL) estimates that in Tajikistan a total of 1,241 NGOs were registered in 2002 compared with 33 groups in 1993. According to the 1998 NGO Sustainability Index for Uzbekistan there were 74 officially registered groups, and 456 unregistered active NGOs. In 2002 this figure was estimated at over 2,000. NGOs were generally started by members of the urban elite – who had the education and linkages to establish something new and obtain support from external donors. They were based in cities, and even ten years after the NGO sector began to form, large swaths of mainly rural territory remain untouched by the NGO phenomenon in Tajikistan and Uzbekistan. The NGOs were fundamentally different from the early glasnost-era organizations because they did not rely on communal civil society to mobilize supporters; and rather then being advocacy based, they became heavily engaged in service delivery. Few of the programmes that NGOs implemented sought to address clearly identified local grievances, or to protect community interests; instead they focused on universal issues such as women's rights, civic education, media, health care, language and computer skills development. Funding, skills development and access to broader NGO networks were provided by international development agencies – thus accountability to the community often shifted upwards to international partners.

In 2003 within neoliberal civil society – especially between the new NGOs and the human rights organizations that developed out of Rastokhez and Birlik – cooperation is extremely limited. A key dividing line is separating the advocacy-orientated human rights groups and service-delivery NGOs. For NGOs that are seeking to develop partnerships with government there is a wariness against being perceived as supportive of any groups that openly criticize the government.

In Tajikistan and Uzbekistan there are also few linkages between communal and neoliberal forms of civil society. The values, interests, tactics, networks, structures and resources of communal and neoliberal groups are distinct. There are as yet no mass movements driven by rural inhabitants and few urban groups with supporters in rural localities. Is it because of a lack of interest or because of irreconcilable differences between the two representations of civil society? On one hand, community-level activists who rely on kinship- and territory-based structures for their status and security risk losing their place within that structure if they shift their interests to universal problems and allegiances away from the community. On the other hand, NGO staff who attempt to develop strong community-based networks may be called to address local grievances and adopt more conservative modes of behaviour. In doing so they may alienate their international partners and educated urban colleagues.

Under these conditions a handful of Tajik and Uzbek neoliberal civil society groups have sought to bridge the divide that separates them from communal civil society. In part they are following a shift in international priorities within the UN, the World Bank and USAID to support community-driven development; also, they are expressing a true commitment to breaking down existing barriers. In Tajikistan NGOs based in Khojand and Kurgan Tuppe have shifted their mission to supporting community-based groups, providing them with information, skills and access to funds to meet local needs. In Uzbekistan similar efforts are being made by NGOs implementing programmes in cooperation with local *mahallas*. Working on the same territory, NGOs have found a rise in local inhabitants' and authorities' understanding and receptiveness to their actions. In addition to these links being formed between NGOs and community-based groups, other ties are being created between human rights defenders and religious organizations. In Tajikistan and Uzbekistan the trials that human rights groups monitor, the violations that they report on, the policies that they attempt to change, increasingly involve religious believers.

Conclusions

Theorists remain divided on the strength and nature of civil society in Central Asia (Akiner 2002; Atabaki 1998; MacFarlane 1999; Roy 2002). I argue that civil society does exist in the region though it is deeply divided and faces a host of challenges. To shed some light on the debate about Central Asian civil society, the conceptual distinction between neoliberal and communal forms can help us better understand civic groups' evolution in Central Asia. History shows that the two forms of civil society largely developed in parallel with little mixing of goals and approaches. Territory, religion and more recently nationalism provided normative frameworks and focal points for social mobilization. Commitment to individual human rights and increased popular participation in national-level decision-making were rarely driving forces behind popular organizing in the region. Since the break-up of the Soviet Union Central Asian civil society has faced a hostile environment. The lack of democratic states, the absence of human rights protection and the rule of law, low economic growth, NGOs' dependency on international donors, all pose obstacles to the future development of a strong civil society. Most detrimental to civil society's expansion, however, is the factionalism and rivalry that exists between local groups – particularly between communal and neoliberal civil society forms. The principle opportunity for civil society actors to exert influence on politics, economics or society depends on their willingness or ability to bridge this gap. A competition to define the future nature of communal civil society has already started. On one hand the authoritarian governments of the region are trying to appropriate communal forms of civil society and transform them into obedient clients of the state, as has been done in Uzbekistan where *mahallas* have legally become state institutions. On the other hand western donors with local NGO partners are seeking to introduce neoliberal values to communal forms of civil society. These two projects risk coming into conflict with destabilizing consequences for civil society and the broader political environment.

Note

1 In the most recent incident on 30 May 2003, IRP deputy chairman Shamsiddin Shamsiddinov was arrested and charged with organizing an armed group as well as participating in a variety of crimes, including murders.

References

Abdullaev, K. (2002) 'Current Local Government Policy Situation in Tajikistan', mimeo, Dushanbe, Tajikistan.

Akiner, S. (2002) 'Prospects for civil society in Tajikistan', in A.B. Sajo (ed.), *Civil Society in the Muslim World: Contemporary Perspectives,* London: I. B. Tauris Publishers, in association with the Institute of Ismaili Studies.

Atabaki, T. (1998) 'The impediments to the development of civil societies', in T. Atabaki and J. O'Kane (eds), *Post-Soviet Central Asia,* London: Tauris Academic Studies.

Atkin, M. (1997) 'Thwarted democratization in Tajikistan', in K. Dawisha and B. Parrott (eds), *Conflict, Cleavage, and Change in Central Asia and the Caucasus*, Cambridge: Cambridge University Press.

Carley, P. (1995) 'The legacy of the Soviet political system and the prospects for developing civil society in Central Asia', in V. Tismaneanu (ed.), *Political Culture and Civil Society in Russia and the New States of Eurasia*, New York: M.E. Sharpe.

Diamond, L. and Plattner, M.F. (eds) (1996) *The Global Resurgence of Democracy*, Baltimore: Johns Hopkins University Press.

Fierman, W. (1997) 'Political development in Uzbekistan: democratization?', in K. Dawisha and M. Turner (eds), *The International Dimension of Post-Communist Transitions in Russia and the New States of Eurasia*, New York: M. E. Sharpe.

Gellner, E. (1994) *Conditions of Liberty: Civil Society and its Rivals*, London: Hamish Hamilton.

Hann, C. and Dunn, E. (eds) (1996) *Civil Society: Challenging Western Models*, London: Routledge.

Howell, J. and Pearce, J. (2001) *Civil Society and Development: A Critical Exploration*, Boulder CO: Lynne Reinner Publishers.

MacFarlane, N. (1999) *Western Engagement in the Caucasus and Central Asia*, Central Asian and Caucasian Prospects project, London: Royal Institute of International Affairs.

Niyazi, A. (1993) 'The year of tumult: Tajikistan after February 1990', in V. Naumkin (ed.), *State, Religion and Society in Central Asia: A Post Soviet Critique*, Reading: Ithaca Press.

Niyazov, J., personal communication, 8 August 2002 in Khojand.

Roy, O. (2002) 'Soviet legacies and Western aid imperatives in the New Central Asia', in A.B. Sajo (ed.), *Civil Society in the Muslim World: Contemporary Perspectives*, London: I.B. Tauris Publishers, in association with the Institute of Ismaili Studies.

Salamon, L. and Anheier, H.K. (1996) 'Social origins of civil society: explaining the non-profit sector cross-nationally', *Voluntas*, 9(3).

Van Rooy, A. (ed.) (2000) *Civil Society and the Aid Industry*, The North–South Institute, London: Earthscan.

Varshney, A. (2002) *Ethnic Conflict and Civic Life: Hindus and Muslims in India*, New Haven: Yale University Press.

Watters, K. (1999) 'Environmental NGOs and the development of civil society in Central Asia', in H. Ruffin and D. Waugh (eds), *Civil Society in Central Asia*, Seattle: The Centre for Civil Society International in association with the University of Washington Press.

Part VI

Africa

Civil society as neocolonialism?

15 On the evolution of civil society in Nigeria

Ṣọlá Akínrìnádé

Despite the pessimism expressed by scholars such as Ernest Gellner (1994), Adam Ferguson (1980) and Adam Seligman (1992) about the utility of the concept of civil society as an analytical variable in discourses on non-Western societies including Africa, studies of civil society in Nigeria have blossomed particularly from the early 1990s. The resurgence of prodemocracy movements and human rights organizations following the country's stalled transition to civil rule programme from the mid-1980s was the launching pad for most of the new works on civil society in Nigeria. This should not be a surprise; after all, 'civil society' became the buzzword in social science circles in Europe and North America in the post-1989 period following the successful struggle to dislodge communist rule and military oligarchy in Eastern Europe and Latin America. The emergence of similar trends in Africa in the 1990s, with the opening up of the democratic space in various countries on the continent, similarly produced a wave of studies that presumably *inadvertently* reinforce the conceptualization of civil society *solely* as the domain of free association in independent opposition to the authoritarian state. This partly explains the needless epistemic hurdle that Gellner's proposition, if fully subscribed to, constitutes to the existence and/or discourse of civil society in non-Western societies including Nigeria.

Gellner's assertion about the inapplicability of the concept of civil society to African, or any non-Western, societies is based on his erroneous assumption that what he considers the equivalent of civil society in Africa is 'imposed by birth or sustained by awesome ritual' or 'made stable through being linked to a whole inside set of relationships' (Gellner 1994: 103, 100). This essay proceeds simply on the conceptualization of civil society as the realm of the society minus the state: in other words, the realm of free association organized outside the purview of the state, and, *in the political context*, the domain of independent opposition to the authoritarian state. The essay seeks to locate civil society in Nigeria within the discourse on the relationship between state and society, between the private and the public. While scholarly discourses on civil society in Nigeria emerged in the 1990s and coincided with developments in the political sphere, associational life and organization outside the realm of the state has a longer history. Thus, the question here is neither that posed by Makumbe (1998): 'Is there a civil society in Africa?', nor that of Orvis (2001): 'Is there an African civil society?' Rather, it is the more appropriate one that Woods (1992) has sought to put: how has civil society evolved in Africa and what are the elements of continuity and discontinuity in the process? Civil society in Africa demonstrates essentially the same characteristics as in most other societies; however, allowance must be made for demonstrable peculiarities of each society.

Historically, the tendency to form associations and corporations is very strong in many Nigerian societies but particularly so among the Yoruba of the southwest and the Igbo of the southeast, two dominant ethnic groups in the country. The associations are formed for the purpose of promoting and protecting common interests in diverse fields including economics, politics, religion, and even recreation and enjoyment (Fadipe 1970). Naomi Chazan (1982) has identified two types of associations in Africa: voluntary associations of an interest-group type, and ascriptive or primary associations. Interest-group associations include trade unions, women's associations, professional associations, associations of chiefs, youth and student groups, literary societies, religious societies, self-help groups, rotating credit associations, sports clubs and so on. Primary or ascriptive associations include ethnic associations, traditional political units, and kinship associations. These associations are 'networks through which social values are constituted and resources independent, relatively speaking, of the state are exchanged' (Woods 1992: 93).

Nigeria: beginnings of modern civil society

In Nigeria, the emergence of a *modern* social space that is distinct from the state and family or kinship groupings could be traced to the era of colonial rule. The colonial period coincided with a rapid spread of urbanization in various parts of the country. As new urban centres emerged, more people migrated into them. This migration was accompanied by the emergence of voluntary associations that sought to meet the various needs and demands of the new urban residents (Balandier 1955; Woods 1992). Ethnic associations were very prominent and they played important roles in the new urban centres.

The transformation of the urban centres into a constituted public sphere during the colonial period cannot be separated from the role of the first generation of indigenous intellectuals who helped organize and lead voluntary associations. The crystallization of the public sphere during the period could also not be separated from the failures of the colonial state in various areas such as the economic, educational, and social welfare. In different parts of the country but particularly in the southeast and southwest, regional, ethnic, development and welfare associations sprang up to fill the vacuum created by the failure of the colonial state. One notable area was the provision of education.

The failure of the colonial government stimulated considerable activity on the part of the people in the provision of educational opportunities, setting a pattern for civil society involvement in the provision of education for years to come. The pattern of community and/or voluntary association involvement in the provision of education was set in Lagos during the nineteenth century and this soon spread to the rest of southwestern Nigeria and then other parts of the country. Community groups and voluntary associations teamed up with various Christian missions to establish and run schools at both primary and secondary levels. Some schools operated independently of both government and the missions (Fajana 1978).

Community initiative similarly played a crucial role in the provision and expansion of higher education. Indeed, the efforts of the community in arranging for students to travel outside the country for the purpose of higher education, and the outcome, made nonsense of the position of the colonial government that there was no real need for the provision of higher education in the country. The first set of medical doctors, lawyers, teachers, engineers, architects, surveyors, magistrates and so on who played important roles in Nigerian public life were all trained through private and community initiatives. Again, the Yoruba example was soon followed by other ethnic and regional associations such as the Ibibio Union and the Ibo State Union, who sent groups of students overseas mostly to institutions in the UK and Eire but also to the United States. The point we are trying to make here is that organized civil society and its activities is not a recent phenomenon in Nigeria, nor are its initiatives limited to the political sphere.

Indeed, associational life was such a crucial feature of Nigerian societies in the colonial period that even the pattern of nationalist political activities was influenced by it. For example, membership of the leading political parties of the period including the National Council of Nigerian Citizens (NCNC), formerly the National Council of Nigeria and Cameroon, was institutional. Individual membership of the party was procured through membership of a voluntary association. Likewise, politics in the immediate postindependence period was dominated by the presence on the political sphere of a multitude of voluntary associations who sought to make their impact felt on political life but not necessarily at the national level. At the time of the first military *coup d'état* in January 1966, almost a hundred of these associations were proscribed by the new military regime, which argued that their presence had contributed significantly to the loss of a sense of belonging to a nation because each group was concerned with gaining the best advantage for its particular sphere of interest. But one should not ignore the fact that the military were also aware of the possible mobilizing impact that these organizations could exert if permitted to continue functioning.

State failure, authoritarianism, and awakening of the activist civil society

The proscription of these associations constituted a major setback in the development of civil society in the country. The long years of military rule witnessed continued repression of all forms of civil society, particularly where its activities sought to expose the failures of military rule. Ironically, it was the particular failure of the postcolonial state under the military that allowed the emergence of new civil society organizations, notably those concerned with delivering those services that the state had failed so woefully to provide and which were dedicated to finding 'grassroots solutions to economic and social problems' (Grindle 1996; Ikelegbe 2001). Thus emerged various non-governmental organizations (NGOs) and community-based organizations (CBOs) dedicated to social and economic development and welfare projects at various micro levels. The involvement of international aid donors in the development initiatives of the country facilitated the progressive growth of these civil society organizations. For various reasons – including corruption at all levels of government, gross inefficiency and bureaucratic failures, limited funds and the inability to make a national impact with limited resources – donor funding for development purposes were directed at local NGOs and CBOs who could make the desired impact at these various microlevels.

But 'civil society' in the general parlance is more easily identified with the political engagements of the private sphere in dealing particularly with authoritarian governments. Indeed, the failure of the postcolonial authoritarian state stimulated the growth of civil society in the political sphere. However, there was a conscious programme of undermining civil society through 'strategies of restructuring, control and repression of labour, media houses, and social critics' that were employed to 'weaken and undermine civil society' (Ikelegbe 2001: 7).

The period from the mid-1980s witnessed serious political ferment in Nigeria. There was a more vigorous personalization of power, authoritarianism and popular repression, hegemonic and patrimonial agendas, and clientelism that had accompanied military incursion into and dominance of the Nigerian political process. The outcome was an intolerance of civil society and 'restriction of space for autonomous action, civil rights and rule of law' (Ikelegbe 2001: 7–8). Nevertheless, the military could not completely subordinate civil society as 'elements of confrontation, peaceful and violent, persisted' in the relations between state and civil society (Abutudu 1995: 7).

The awakening of the political and activist civil society in Nigeria during this period was partly the unintended effect of government's attempt at deceiving the populace into believing its opinion was being taken into consideration in the formulation of state policies. First, in 1985, the Babangida regime had initiated public debates regarding whether the government should take loans from the International Monetary Fund. The 'IMF debates' were followed in 1986–87 by the public debates on the political future of the country, also initiated by the government. These officially sanctioned public debates provided great opportunities 'for civil associational life to flower, as numerous associations including labour, religious, student, women's, artisan and professional associations emerged to proffer and canvass positions' (Ikelegbe 2001: 8) on the economic and political future of the country. And once set in motion the process was difficult to reverse. Indeed, it was the several problems that state policies had inflicted on the people that provided the second platform for the awakening of popular civil society at this time. The response of the government to the pervasive economic crisis was the imposition of a Structural Adjustment Programme that imposed hardships and aroused a restive civil population. By 1987, growing popular discontent with the economic situation, and the sufferings it brought, climaxed in public protests and social violence that the military regime put down with unprecedented severity. However, civil society was to manifest its strength and tenacity in the subsequent months as widespread organized protests continued between 1988 and 1990.

Failed transition and the crystallization of radical civil society

It was the gerrymandering associated with the political transition programme, its numerous weaknesses and inconsistencies, and the unbridled prosecution of a self-succession agenda that gave the ultimate fillip to the crystallization of a radical civil society in Nigeria in relation to the democratic agenda. Babangida's 'multiple summersaults' (Obadare 2002: 555) on the transition programme finally came to a head with his annulment of the results of the 12 June 1993 presidential election. This action, more than any other, served to radicalize civil society groups in the country. In addition, a hitherto aloof political society that had severely been compromised through manipulation and intimidation found its voice and joined civil society in the popular struggle.

For its part, confronted with greater challenge from the civil society and the political class, the state became more repressive and sought with greater severity to destroy organized popular resistance against it. Hence, the civil terrain 'was subjected to considerable harassment, arrests and detention, raids and searches of offices, disruption of activities, brutalization, proscription, shut down of media houses, and seizure of newspapers and magazines' (Ikelegbe 2001: 8–9). But it was in this environment that organized civil society blossomed as it tried to redefine the Nigerian political landscape and prepare it for the democratic agenda. From June 1993, protests and strikes were organized on a continuing basis by civil rights and professional groups, as well as trade unions, to challenge the annulment of the elections, and demand its reversal and an end to military rule. The activities of civil society served to put pressure on the military government and compel degrees of economic and political reforms, and maintained the pressure for a redemocratization of the polity.

Five strands of expression of civil society organization could be identified during this period (Ikelegbe 2001). First were those concerned with monitoring and protecting civil rights and liberties. Among these were the Civil Liberties Organization (CLO), established in 1987, the Committee for the Defence of Human Rights, and the Constitutional Rights Project, an offshoot of CLO. Second, there were the prodemocracy agitation groups that numbered in their fold the Campaign for Democracy (CD), the first to be established in May 1991; the Democratic Alternative, an offshoot of CD; United Democratic Front of Nigeria; National Liberation Council of Nigeria; United Action for Democracy; and Association of Democratic Lawyers of Nigeria. These groups all sought to mobilize the civil population to resist government subversion of the transition to democracy programme.

Third were professional and labour associations that took a more active interest in social and political developments in the country. These included the Academic Staff Union of Universities, a constant voice in the country's social struggles; the National Union of Petroleum and Natural Gas Workers and the Petroleum and Natural Gas Senior Staff Association, the two major labour unions in the energy sector; the Nigerian Union of Journalists; Nigerian Bar Association; Nigerian Medical Association; and the National Association of Nigerian Students. Fourth were associations and groups concerned with the protection and projection of specific economic, social, cultural and gender interests such as the Manufacturers' Association of Nigeria, Women in Nigeria (WIN), and a host of NGOs dealing with various issues ranging from development to reproductive health. In the fifth and final category were associations of a religious, ethnic, sectional and cultural nature, which committed themselves to the struggle for democracy and good governance, equity and justice in the country. Among these were the Christian Association of Nigeria, Catholic Bishops' Conference, Northern Elders' Forum, Afenifere, Middle Belt Forum and Southern Solidarity Front. All these groups participated in one degree or the other in the struggle to protect civil rights and restore the country to democratic rule. In the final analysis, despite the severe and several challenges that it confronted including widespread state repression, the civil society held on to the struggle for civic rights and democratization and made possible the transition to civil rule following the assumption of office by General Abdusalami Abubakar in June 1998.

Civil society in the post-transition period: the uncivil face of civil society

The contribution of civil society to democratic consolidation projects is usually taken as given. It is within civil society 'that public opinion is formed and it is through independent associations that individuals can have some influence on government decision making' (Woods 1992: 94). The literature on other parts of the continent suggests that 'independent groups are redefining the pattern of governance in Africa by seeking to limit the arbitrary nature of paternalistic rule through the articulation of a public opinion' (Woods 1992: 95). The presence of a viable civil society is thus considered a crucial force in the agenda for democratic consolidation. However, in the post-transition period, the activities of many civil society groups such as the O'dua People's Congress, Arewa People's Congress and the Ijaw National Front, rather than fostering a development of the democratic system actually constitute a threat to its survival. In the period since 1999, these ascriptive groups have emerged as 'champions of ethnic sentiments' and their activities 'reflect ethnic militancy, regional and ethnical nationalism and separatist tendencies' (Ikelegbe 2001: 18). The violent clashes generated by the activities of these groups constitute a threat to democratic survival. Such was the situation the federal government at various times threatened to declare a state of emergency in certain states of the country affected by the activities of these groups.

Conclusion

Since the late 1980s, civil society in Nigeria has confronted several problems. Among these is the proliferation of civil society groups of different hues but with similar objectives and activities. Inevitably, their activities were marked by wastage, dissipation and inefficiency. Secondly, some groups depend solely on foreign funding for their operations. Thirdly, there were splits, particularly among the prodemocracy and civil rights groups, which weakened their structures. Furthermore, many organizations also confront the challenge of internal discipline, lack of accountability, manipulation and needless squabbles (Jega 1997; Kukah 1997). Civil society as outlined in this chapter is not an alien phenomenon but has a long history in Nigeria and became awakened from the late 1980s. Its radicalization since the early 1990s reflects its frustration with the authoritarian state and the failure of the democratization agenda.

References

Abutudu, M.I.M. (1995) *The State, Civil Society and the Democratization Process in Nigeria,* Dakar: CODESRIA Monograph Series, 1/95.

Balandier, G. (1955) *Sociologie des Brazzavilles noires,* Paris: A. Colin.

Chazan, N. (1982) 'The New Politics of Participation in Tropical Africa', *Comparative Politics*, 14(2): 169–89.

Fadipe, N.A. (1970) *The Sociology of the Yoruba*, edited with an introduction by F.O. Okediji and O.O. Okediji, Ibadan: Ibadan University Press.

Fajana, A. (1978) *Education in Nigeria, 1842–1939: An Historical Analysis,* Lagos: Longman.

Ferguson, A. (1980) *An Essay on the History of Civil Society*, with a new introduction by Louis Schneider, New Brunswick: Transaction Books.

Gellner, E. (1994) *Conditions of Liberty: Civil Society and its Rivals*, London: Hamish Hamilton.

Grindle, M.S. (1996) *Challenging the State: Crisis and Innovation in Latin America and Africa,* Cambridge: Cambridge University Press.

Ikelegbe, A. (2001) 'The perverse manifestation of civil society: evidence from Nigeria', *Journal of Modern African Studies*, 39(1): 1–24.

Jega, A.M. (1997) 'Organising for popular democratic change in Nigeria: options and strategies', *Strategic Planning Workshop on Democratic Development in Nigeria: Report of Proceedings*, London: Centre for Democracy and Development.

Kukah, M.H. (1997) 'State of current actors: an overview of human rights and democratic development in Nigeria', *Strategic Planning Workshop on Democratic Development in Nigeria: Report of Proceedings,* London: Centre for Democracy and Development.

Makumbe, J.M. (1998) 'Is there a civil society in Africa?' *International Affairs*, 74(2): 305–17.

Obadare, E. (2002) 'Civil society in Nigeria: conjectures and refutations', in T. Falola (ed.), *Nigeria in the Twentieth Century*, Greensboro: University of North Carolina Press.

Orvis, S. (2001) 'Civil society in Africa or African civil society?', *Journal of Asian and African Studies*, 36(1): 17–38.

Seligman, A.B. (1992) *The Idea of Civil Society*, New York: The Free Press.

Woods, D. (1992) 'Civil society in Europe and Africa: limiting state power through a public sphere', *Journal of Modern African Studies*, 35(2): 77–100.

16 Civil society in South Africa

Deborah James

Much has been written about the slipperiness of the civil society concept. The term's cross-cultural relevance, according to some commentators, lies more in its ability to evoke an aspired-to normative ideal than in its provision of an analytical model: originally coined in a context of European social transformation, the idea of civil society becomes reinvoked at similarly transitional moments in other parts of the world (Comaroff and Comaroff 1999). However fierce the debate about its applicability to non-Western settings, the term has been so often strategically invoked by protagonists in some of these that its normative purchase cannot be denied. South Africa is one of these. During the late 1980s and early 1990s 'civil society' – referring specifically to township civic organizations (Seekings 1992), the labour movement and non-governmental organizations (NGOs) – was a key ingredient of political speeches and academic papers alike. The term was often used in contexts where the boundaries between social analysis and activism were blurred (see Glaser 1997).

There are two sets of reservations over whether these struggle-era organizations qualified to be described as, or mobilized in the name of, 'civil society'. First, since they were mostly political oppositional forms in another guise, they were political, even 'state-like', rather than 'civil' in nature. Given the banning of the ANC, and in the absence of legitimate local authorities or a legitimate legal system, they assumed functions ranging from the regulating of community affairs to the meting out of justice. (These functions continued into the post-transition period despite the state's attempt to institutionalize justice, revenge and retribution via its Truth and Reconciliation Commission (TRC) (Wilson 2000).) Neither the civic associations nor the trade unions thus seemed to approximate to a pluralist public sphere (Hefner 2000), independent of political interest or influence, 'protected by the state and open to use by equal citizens' (Glaser 1997).

It is claimed by some – including Mzwanele Mayekiso, a civics leader from Alexandra township near Johannesburg and self-styled cofounder of a global 'working class civil society' (Glaser 1997) – that the civics movement remains a force to be reckoned with. But this movement, however resilient, faces an intractable opponent. The ANC government has increasingly concentrated its power centrally while leaving the local state largely incapacitated. In this setting of centralization, according to one commentator, 'authentically independent' groupings have 'wilted' and their members – attracted by government salaries, houses and other perks – have been 'coopted' through inclusion into specific state programmes (Marais 2001: 63, 262). In the post-1994 period it was presumed, says Marais, that 'all the contradictions which fuelled resistance' would dissolve 'into common endeavours': as a result, he claims, 'civil society collapsed into the post-apartheid state' (Marais 2001: 284). The cooption was not as uncomplicated as this suggests, however. As personnel and expertise drifted between the public, non-governmental and private sectors, people often occupied roles in a variety of arenas simultaneously, or received payment from the state while working as private consultants. But this overall blurring of boundaries between public and private has not necessarily increased the pool of expertise overall: 'it has left some organizations incapacitated while giving others the edge in the increasingly competitive bids being made for limited sources of funding' (James 2002; Marais 2001: 285). All in all, the process is seen as having resulted in a loss of 'institutional memory and experience' (Marais 2001: 283).

Moving in to take the place of the former civics, a series of single-interest social movements has emerged, including the AIDS-oriented TAC (Treatment Action Campaign) and the LPM (Landless People's Movement). These have acquired a high profile in the international arena. The LPM, by allying itself with its equivalents in Brazil and Palestine, and by holding mass demonstrations during the 2001 UN Conference on Racism or the 2002 Earth Summit, has 'globalized' itself, and in the process has caught the attention of the media and of the wider world. Responding to the state's disparagement of their cause, protagonists in these movements validate their struggle by emphasizing its transnational character. As Dennis Brutus said at the 2001 meeting:

> President Mbeki says that the people who are protesting, and invading land, are not those who suffered in the struggle. But we are in the struggle now, and the struggle is not yet over. The struggle continues. Our struggle for land is the struggle that is happening in other parts of the globe.

While some optimistically see such movements as capturing the spirit of South Africa's pretransition civics, sceptics dismiss them as being 'guided by identity politics that tend to gravitate less around ideologies and programmes than around "an amalgam of slogans and emotions"' (Marais 2001: 140). Whatever the interpretation, these movements are either thought of as completely political or not political enough: in neither case do they appear to fill the requirements of a genuinely independent and pluralist public sphere.

In the vacuum left by the fading influence of trade unions and civic organizations, a variety of groupings such as 'family and kin groups, "traditional authorities", church organizations such as the Zionist Christian Church ... and other informal organizations' have charged themselves with maintaining order (Thornton 1999: 95, cited in Von Schnitzler *et al.* 2001). Given the alleged ineffectiveness of state functions such as policing, the vacuum has also been filled by vigilante groups. These range from informal local operatives acting against criminal behaviour (Jensen 2003) through to highly organized associations such as the infamous Mapogo a Mathamaga. In the context of a weak criminal justice system, Mapogo started as an informal response to crime in one of the former homeland areas, Lebowa (now Limpopo Province), and later achieved success as a business venture offering protection, among other things, to white farmers vulnerable to ever-increasing farm attacks. A recent report on the organization points out that 'while the group espouses a "crime fighting" discourse, ... many of its "crime fighting" methods and various members are themselves criminal' and draws attention to the problematic nature of 'crimes committed for personal gain beneath the banner of "justice"' (Von Schnitzler *et al.* 2001). Although such organizations – and less formalized kinds of self-protection that border on the criminal – have emerged in part to compensate for the inadequacies of the public sector, they raise questions about 'what civil society could possibly mean here with neither an effective state nor effective political organizations' (Thornton 1999: 95, cited in Von Schnitzler *et al.* 2001).

The second of the two sets of reservations mentioned above arises from doubts about whether South African society, overall, is modern enough to sustain a pluralist 'civil society', given its former bifurcation – augmented during apartheid – into urban/modern and rural/traditional sectors. The apartheid version of indirect rule legislated that rural Africans be members of separate ethnically defined territories, living on communally held land and hence materially and politically dependent on chiefs. Thus was the social landscape fundamentally divided by being 'mapped ... according to a whole new conception of the innate relationship of people to place' (Ashforth 1990: 158). This, according to Mamdani's well-known account, made them subjects rather than citizens able to engage or be protagonists within civil society (1996: 21–2). But this analysis of pretransition South Africa as a 'bifurcated state', while suggestive in its analysis of the *intended* policy concerning citizenship, disregards the proliferation of *actual* social arrangements during a century of rapid social change. South Africa's transition to capitalist industry and agriculture twinned with a reliance on rurally based labour (Bernstein 1996; Marks and Rathbone 1982) resulted in multiple connections between labour migrants' rural and urban forms of identity: Africans who were 'subjects' at the rural pole of their existence were more like 'citizens' in an urban setting as a result of their experiences as members of the unionized workforce, supporters of political parties, Christian town dwellers, and the like. And, as social historians and anthropologists have shown, migrants moving from city to country carried these modern experiences and political involvements with them (Delius 1989, 1990, 1996; James 1999). In the experience of Pedi migrant labourers, as Delius shows in his work on the social history of the former reserve area of Sekhukhuneland (in Lebowa, now Limpopo Province), rural resistance against the apartheid state's restrictions on stock and land was inextricable from, and gave succour to, their involvement in the broader world of ANC politics. At the same time, these migrants' associations occupied themselves with other matters – such as dancing, social clubs, burial ceremonies – which were not explicitly political in nature.

By problematizing a kind of bifurcation other than the citizen/subject one, namely the idea that public organization must *either* be pluralist and hence truly 'civil' *or* explicitly political, social historians' writings also address the first of the reservations mentioned earlier. A recent book demonstrates how Zulu activist/intellectuals of the early twentieth century intertwined the two inextricably. Straddling both rural/urban and proletarian/middle-class divides, and developing a kind of cultural nationalism that hybridized Christian and traditionalist ideas and practices, they variously founded independent churches, formed landholding syndicates and unions, initiated cooperative movements, and authored works of history, as well as being founder members of the overtly political SANC (South African Native Congress, forerunner of the ANC) (La Hausse de Lalouvière 2000).

An examination of present-day society in the light of historical antecedents – and the careful and nuanced researching of postapartheid biographies – will surely reveal similar forms of boundary-blurring. In South Africa's present and future, just as much as in its past, civil society will have its sources in the intertwining of its citizens' multiple sources of identification and experience. As much as it cannot be sought wholly within the political realm, it cannot lie wholly beyond it.

References

Ashforth, A. (1990) *The Politics of Official Discourse in South Africa*, Oxford: Clarendon Press.

Bernstein, H. (1996) 'South Africa's agrarian question: extreme and exceptional?' *Journal of Peasant Studies*, 23(2/3): 1–52.

Comaroff, J. and Comaroff, J.L. (eds) (1999) *Civil Society and the Political Imagination in Africa*, Chicago: Chicago University Press.

Delius, P. (1989) 'Sebatakgomo: migrant organisation, the ANC and the Sekhukhuneland revolt', *Journal of Southern African Studies*, 15(4): 581–616.

——(1990) 'Migrants, comrades and rural revolt: Sekhukhuneland 1950–1987', *Transformation* 13: 2–26.

——(1996) *A Lion amongst the Cattle*, Johannesburg: Ravan Press.

Ferguson, J. (forthcoming) 'Transnational topographies of power: beyond "the state" and "civil society" in the study of African politics', in J. Vincent and D. Nugent (eds), *The Anthropology of Politics*, Oxford: Blackwell.

Glaser, D. (1997) 'South Africa and the limits of civil society', *Journal of Southern African Studies*, 23(1): 5–26.

Hart, G. (2002) *Disabling Globalisation: Places of Power in Post-Apartheid South Africa*, Berkeley and Pietermaritzburg: University of California Press and University of Natal Press.

Hefner, R.W. (2000) *Civil Islam: Muslims and Democratization in Indonesia*, Princeton: Princeton University Press.

James, D. (1999) *Songs of the Women Migrants: performance and identity in South Africa*, Edinburgh: I A I and Edinburgh University Press.

——(2002) '"To take the information down to the people": life skills and HIV/AIDS peer-educators in the Durban area', *African Studies*, 61(1): 169–91.

Jensen, S. (2003) 'Through the lens of crime: land claims and contestations of citizenship on the frontier of the South African state', mimeo, CDS, Denmark.

La Hausse de Lalouvière, P. (2000) *Restless Identities: Signatures of Nationalism, Zulu Ethnicity and History in the Lives of Petros Lamula (c1881–1948) and Lymon Maling (1889–c.1936)*, Pietermaritzburg: University of Natal Press.

Mamdani, M. (1996) *Citizen and Subject: Contemporary Africa and the Legacy of Late Colonialism*, Princeton: Princeton University Press.

Marais, H. (2001) *South Africa: Limits to Change: the Political Economy of Transition*, London and Cape Town: Zed Press and University of Cape Town Press.

Marks, S. and Rathbone, R. (1982) 'Introduction' to S. Marks and R. Rathbone (eds), *Industrialisation and Social Change in South Africa: African Class Formation, Culture and Consciousness 1870–1930*, London: Longman.

Seekings, J. (1992) 'Civic organisation in South African townships', *South African Review Service*, 6: 216–38.

von Schnitzler, A., Ditlhage, G., Kgalema, L., Maepa, T., Mofokeng, T. and Pigou, P. (2001) 'Guardian or gangster? Mapogo a Mathamaga: a case study', *Violence and Transition*, 3 (May), available at www.csvr.org.za/papers/papvtp3.htm (accessed 20 April 2004).

Wilson, R. (2000) 'Reconciliation and revenge in post-Apartheid South Africa: rethinking legal pluralism and human rights', *Current Anthropology*, 41(1): 75–98.

17 Civil society in West Africa

Between discourse and reality

Ebenezer Obadare

A superfluous debate?

The discursive field in West Africa is best placed within the continental stream (Harbeson *et al.* 1994; Monga 1996; Onwudiwe 1998). This is only natural since one is obviously folded into the other, and it also gives us a good backcloth upon which our analysis can be anchored. Since there is little space for an elaborate dissection, I will outline what I consider to be the central problems. Three broad scholarly attitudes to civil society can be identified, ranging from absolute scepticism cum rejection (Callaghy 1994; Mamdani 1997) to conditional acceptance (Blaney and Pasha 1993; Ekeh 1992; Mustapha 1998) and positive affirmation (Chan 2002; Comaroff and Comaroff 1999). The major dilemmas, in my opinion, have invariably centred on civil society's 'polysemous elaboration', its 'historically specific baggage', and the recurrent claim that it is not applicable to 'segmentary non-Western societies ... outright dictatorships or patrimonial societies' (Gellner 1994: 43, 103).

For a concept so belaboured, it ought to be admitted, civil society has not fared badly. Indeed, its popularity seems to have grown in inverse proportion to the quite legitimate worry about its meaning and usefulness. Perhaps this should not come as a surprise. On a recent research visit to parts of the subregion, the researcher did not fail to notice a certain wanton, even happy, ignorance of the rarefied intellectual debate regarding its progeny, even among the diligent activist champions of civil society. Rather, in a reminder of the curious admission by a senior official of Britain's Department for International Development (DFID) at a Development Studies Association conference in London in 2000 (Crowther 2001: 2), they seemed to be more interested in 'strengthening' civil society than defining it. In the searing heat of the tropical sun, on the streets of Lagos, Dakar and Accra, the academic crossing of swords described above was a distant and vanishing echo. A partisan might see this as just deserts, another example of 'Gellner mugging' (Loizos 1996), or simply another evidence of how reality can exist in utter contempt of theory. What is beyond doubt is that in West Africa today one searches in vain for the classical meaning(s) of civil society. I will even argue that it is irretrievably lost, as one might expect to happen when a notion of civil society's infinite nuances comes into contact with the political and cultural kaleidoscope that exists in West Africa and the rest of the continent in general.

So one does nod politely at the existence of the debate on the provenance and meaning of civil society – but perhaps it is a moot point. Such is its popularity today that greater intellectual capital might be accumulated from focusing on what is slowly crystallizing as 'the broader meaning of civil society', which can be 'fruitfully explored in all types of human society' (Hann and Dunn 1996: 20). This is without disputing the validity of many of the objections articulated even by people who are ordinarily enthusiastic about the possible virtues of civil society, but are wary of its cynical hijack and uncritical veneration by international 'development' agencies that are apparently all too ready to prostitute it to suit their own ambiguous agendas. In my view the analytic challenge is, in the words of the Comaroffs, to 'disinter the cultural seedbeds and historical sources of anything that might be regarded as an analogue of civil society in Africa' (1999: 23), while still acknowledging the inescapable limitations imposed by its history, cultural origins and ontological indeterminacy. In essaying to explore the imaginings and reality of civil society in West Africa, these brief reflections are in keeping with this mandate.

Ideas versus images

> Even political formations in West Africa lacking any consolidated form of the state reveal 'some space for manoeuvre between the personal and the public'. They too have specific norms and normative codes through which people are made accountable and responsible to other members of society. This is the broader meaning of civil society, and it can be fruitfully explored in all types of human society
>
> (Hann and Dunn 1996: 20)

> However, it is the subcontinent of West Africa that currently commands international attention – and for the wrong reasons. Here, a fault-line of failed and failing states is clearly discernible ... From Liberia which has collapsed for a second time, Côte D'Ivoire which is practically dismembered, Guinea and its terminally ailing leader, Togo and its restive populace under the hammer of a vicious despot, recuperating Sierra Leone, to a democratically challenged Nigeria and its riverine insurgents, the picture is very bleak indeed
>
> (Williams 2003: 11)

Most scholarly commentaries on civil society are plagued by a recurrent affliction – the failure to delineate between civil society as a concept, as a description of a state of affairs (whether past or present), or even as a normative project. This is partly responsible for the messy state of knowledge on the subject. Here, I intend to straddle the fuzzily charted borderline between civil society as an idea (a platform for halting the excesses of an overbearing state) and as a living reality (the Wildean 'world of implications' that encompasses the reality of everyday life), and the permanent struggle for order even as postcolonial West Africa continues to stagger from one mishap to another. The two extracts above appear to capture this duality well.

One speaks rather eloquently of the historicity of civil society in West Africa (defined as 'codes through which people are made accountable and responsible to other members of society'). The other paints the altogether unnerving (but true) picture of the same codes rapidly disintegrating, and Kaplan's worst horror of anarchy without seams pounding insistently at the door. Either holds some essential truth, and together they offer the observer a window into the multilayered tableau that is the West African subregion.

A condensed history

To put this duality in its right context, some historical perspective is necessary. When the notion of civil society entered the African/ist scholarly discourse in the late 1980s and early 1990s, the West African subregion was on the cusp of fundamental social and political transformations. The contradictions of the postcolonial state had reached a head, or so it seemed, and authoritarianism's days appeared obviously numbered. *Anciens régimes* across West Africa faced a robust challenge to their powers, both from urban-based middle-class elements prickled by their rapid proletarianization and the erosion of long-secured economic advantages; and rural dwellers who have historically (and stoically) borne the major brunt of the political elite's economic mismanagement. The consequences of this seething discontent were always going to be unpredictable. In Nigeria, although demonstrations against the Structural Adjustment Programme (SAP) by a coalition of workers, students and professionals (what a commentator memorably referred to as the army of Nigerians in contradistinction to the Nigerian army) were ruthlessly smothered by the military-dominated state, the momentum for democratic liberalization was already in full flush.

Throughout the subregion – in Togo, Benin Republic, Liberia and Sierra Leone to name a few – ossified regimes struggled with unprecedentedly virulent demands for an expansion of the democratic space. The results were uneven – a pact-based civilian regime in Nigeria, further consolidation of popular democracy in Mali, a much-desired end for the Jerry Rawlings regime in Ghana, a still evolving seesaw between progress and relapse in Benin Republic, and the continued success of Senegal's Maraboutist democracy. In Liberia, Sierra Leone and Côte d'Ivoire, popular rage had exploded into armed insurrection, the collective result of which has been states trapped in the unseemly penumbra between an armed juvenile warlordism and complete chaos.

It is common to attribute these rapid transformations, especially in the domain of the state, to the newfangled ebullience of 'civil society'. Yet this ebullience was everything but new, though part of the inspiration might have emanated from processes in Eastern Europe, most especially the powerful symbolism inherent in the fall of the Berlin Wall in 1989. In truth, state and society in Africa have always existed in some mutual suspicion, if not antagonism, especially when one considers Mamdani's apparently valid argument (1997) that one was actually conjured into existence in seeming opposition to the other. In which case, civil society in Africa has always existed to patrol its borders with the state, to paraphrase Bayart (1986: 111–16).

If 'civil society', emerging in the light of the preceding as 'the venue for the aggregation and communication of societal interests' (Green 1999: 2) (a clear reminder of Dahrendorf's (1997) conceptualization of civil society as the 'anchorage of liberty') is of ancient pedigree in (West) Africa, certainly the same cannot be said of the terminology itself. The essence may be old, but the term itself is comparatively recent. As Hann has noted, 'some space for manoeuvre between the personal and the public' has been a feature of West African communities right from precolonial times. In the precolonial era this space opened or closed according to the balance of social forces, the caprice of the monarch, and the courage of what Habermas (1989) calls, in a different context, the 'political public'. In all cases, culture and tradition provided a limiting framework, the dimensions of 'civil society' being defined in accordance with the principles of an essentially patriarchal social order. To be sure, what existed then was not the state as it is currently understood. The Westphalian architecture was part and parcel of the baggage of colonialism (some would say its lightning rod), and with it came the integrated process described so painfully well by Mamdani: the creation of an urban 'civil society' and the subjectivization of the rural mass. Villalon (1995: 20) seems to have been making the same point when he noted that 'the organising principles of the colonial state were formulated primarily in accordance with metropolitan, rather than indigenous, interests and constraints'.

All told, it was the rump of this 'civil society' that took over the reins of authority from the colonialists, inheriting, in the process, the traditional animosity that the 'uncaptured' rural subjects have always had towards it.

This is probably not the best place and time for a lavish recapitulation, but an awareness of this process should help put in historical perspective the dynamics of contemporary intercourse between the state and civil society in West Africa. Because the substitute elite, the 'civil society' created by the colonial order, has hardly deemed it fit to reform the state structures it took over from the colonial overlords, antistatist (even subversive) activity from below has been a major feature of political life in postcolonial West Africa. This was the energy that the civil discourse tapped into after its sensational career in Eastern Europe and Latin America in the mid-1980s (see Havel

1985). Still, this falls short of actually explaining the altogether favourable reception that the idea received. This is what I consider next.

Why civil society?

> We've not learnt to trust the government ... government is the enemy of the people. My relationship with the state is war
>
> (Olorunyomi 2003)

Civil society, as expressed earlier, did not make its way into the African discourse until the late 1980s and early 1990s. Comparatively unpacked, it was used to describe the broad opposition to military and other forms of hegemonic rule, and even at this early stage its emancipatory imagination was already evident. The researcher's personal experience is instructive in this regard. Reporting underground for *TEMPO*, the leading anti-military newspaper in Nigeria in the early 1990s, I was asked by a correspondent of a foreign newspaper what I thought the consequences of our struggle (my newspaper had been shut down, following which, in defiance, we continued reporting with mobile logistics) would be in terms of energizing 'civil society'. I could not give the correspondent a coherent answer, for it was the first time I had heard about civil society. But I did not miss the presumed association of civil society with democratic liberalization, and the possibility of a more open society.

Across the West African subregion in the early 1990s, the association of civil society with democracy, or at least the possibility of its achievement, was common indeed. Many freely conflated the two, and the popular media treated them as though they were synonyms. To be sure, civil society did seem to have a romantic appeal to it – here at last the pluralist paradise! Beyond this easy association, there was something definitely positive about an idea that seemed to capture the essence of the people's struggle against their preternatural enemies (see the quotation above). Civil society was not only a convenient nomenclature; it was also a platform for social mobilization. Everyone with one grievance or another against the state (also generally understood as the government) rallied in the name of civil society. In the popular imagination, the government and the state are one and the same thing, fused as the realm of 'the other': it is where 'they' make policies to govern 'us'. It was only a matter of time before forces traditionally hostile to the state in individual countries and across the subregion had a common umbrella: civil society organizations (CSOs).

The antistatist conception of civil society is putatively traced to the writings of Thomas Paine, and more recently Antonio Gramsci, and it was this conceptualization that so animated scholars, professionals, students and human-rights activists across the subregion. If any proof was needed at all about the promise of civil society, it seemed to have been supplied by the events in Eastern Europe where civil society had been used successfully to challenge hegemonic practices. But this was not the only inspiration. Civil society also seemed to suggest something about civility, an element that was believed to be in short supply in the overall relations between the state and society across the subregion. This particular struggle for 'civility' meshed with human-rights activists' outstanding claims of for institutional accountability and the upholding of the rule of law. Beside the state, civil society also seems to be useful as a rallying point against the perceived irresponsibility of multinational and other powerful businesses. What immediately comes to mind is citizen organizations across the subregion (cocoa farmers in Côte d'Ivoire, say) mobilizing for social justice and a vision of social development that regards them as partners. Significantly, when mobile phone subscribers in Nigeria decided to switch off their phones on 19 September 2003 in protest against alleged mistreatment from the communications companies, their mobilization took place under the banner of civil society.

There was also something in the material conditions of the different countries that seemed to have contributed to the popularity of civil society, especially among the urban middle class. If there is anything that is common to West African countries in general, it is their general poverty. As several studies have shown (Mustapha 1998; Olukoshi 1993), members of this middle class were terribly hit by the new economic regime that followed the implementation of the SAP across Africa in the mid-1980s. They saw in the emergence of the idea of civil society not only a political strategy for ousting an unfavourable regime – that was always there – but more significantly an economic strategy for private resource accumulation. This explains the huge increase in the number of NGOs and other seemingly public institutions with the hidden agenda of, to stand Ulrich Beck on his head, 'using a systemic strategy to solve autobiographical problems'. Many of those on the ground are weak, institutionally speaking, and in parts of Western Nigeria many of those that I visited operated under false identities to protect themselves from the larger public whose interests, ironically, they were established to advance.

In short, while there was an objective social situation necessitating the emergence of civil society, the idea was also a godsend for a cross-section of an economically wounded middle class in search of personal, not even group, salvation.

Partial responsibility for this equivalent of a gold rush was borne by the so-called international development organizations, many of which had their own ideas (or none at all) about what civil society is (remember our DFID official?), the strategies for 'empowering' or 'strengthening' it, and sufficient funding to back up such vision. As it happens, many 'civil society organizations' mushroomed across the subregion to quite literally cash in on this, a good number of them receiving huge sums of money to implement programmes with no direct relevance to the society. For example, when asked what they understood by civil society, a large number of civil society entrepreneurs, as defined by Larry Diamond, that I spoke to admitted that they really didn't have the foggiest idea, but that they had fallen in love with the subject only after persistent requests by international funding agencies that they include it in their reports and proposals for funding (Howell and Pearce 2001: 184–9).

Conclusion: what is civil society useful for?

We should not allow the reality of civil society entrepreneurship to distort the reality of massive developments taking place throughout the West African subregion. That is not my intention. On the contrary, I have merely tried to *look through* the predominant roseate picture of civil society that many are used to by indicating the simultaneous existence of what we may call 'the other face' of civil society, despite its ugliness.

Yet, there is cause for cheer. To begin with, there is the consolation that this development is not by any means unique to West Africa or the continent at large. Studies on civil society in Latin America (see for example Boussard 2002) have indicated the existence of the same phenomenon. In any case, it would appear that civil society entrepreneurship is an excellent guide to the political economy of the states under consideration and a useful illustration of how dominant social classes struggle to preserve their advantages. The final related point is about the limits of foreign assistance especially for troubled countries of the Third World, which seem to be perpetually needy. What seems to be the apparent wisdom (and Boussard has underscored this) is that aid to civil society might actually have a deradicalizing effect on authentic representatives of the people. There is a legitimate fear in many parts of West Africa that international financial support for emergent NGOs and CSOs may have produced a situation whereby real agendas for change are shunned in favour of those cobbled together by civil society entrepreneurs ensconced in 'remote' urban offices. At all events, there is sufficient evidence that NGOs and CSOs are themselves weakened by continued reliance on international financial support as, over time, they tend to become dependent and totally drained of all initiative (for further expatiation see Van Rooy 1998).

This is a bleak picture indeed. What, you wonder, is the fate of civil society if the constituent organizations themselves are in such dire need for reformation? Fortunately, associations and organizations, no matter how useful, visible or powerful, are not the exact equivalent of civil society. They may well be the building blocks of civil society, but at the end of the day civil society is more than the sum of its constituent organizations. As I have argued, in West Africa, the authentic spoors of civil society are best traced to those 'norms and normative codes through which people are made accountable and responsible to other members of society' (Hann and Dunn 1996: 20). These seem to have endured despite the depredations of 'modernity'. Seinde Arigbede, a development activist in Ibadan, Nigeria, likes to argue (and I believe he has a point) that the sentiment civil society seeks to capture can be found in the Yoruba proverb *Igi kan kii da igbo se* (one tree does not a forest make), an enunciation of a cosmology that places ontological priority on the public at the expense of the individual and prefigures what might be called a Yoruba theory of civil society.

The recent incarnation of civil society of course has different social roots (or so it seems) but the continuity with existing norms and normative codes cannot be dismissed. The enduring ethos is that of creating an awareness of the problems of society and looking for a common platform to tackle them. In many cases, this has involved the transformation of supreme challenges into splendid opportunities. A good example is the SAP, which, among other things, can be said to be the immediate precursor to the emergence of the contemporary civil society movement in West Africa. While, as admitted earlier, it generally pauperized the people, it also served, by default it seems, to 'hasten, reinforce and intensify the radicalisation of professional associations' across the West African subregion (Olukoshi 1996: 460). This is the idea of civil society as countervailing power, and it is the one that seems to be most relevant to the contemporary needs of West Africa.

References

Bayart, J. (1986) 'Civil society in Africa', in P. Chabal (ed.), *Political Domination in Africa: Reflections on the Limits of Power*, New York: Cambridge University Press.

Blaney, D.L. and Pasha, M.K. (1993) 'Civil society and democracy in the third world: ambiguities and historical possibilities', *Studies in Comparative International Development*, spring, 28(1): 3–24.

Boussard, C. (2002) 'Civil society and democratisation: conceptual and empirical challenges', in O. Elgstrom and G. Hyden (eds), *Development and Democracy: What Have We Learned and How?*, London: Routledge.

Callaghy, T.M. (1994) 'Civil society, democracy and economic change in Africa: a dissenting opinion about resurgent societies', in J. Harbeson, D. Rothchild and N. Chazan (eds), *Civil Society and the State in Africa*, London: Lynne Rienner.

Chan, S. (2002) *Composing Africa: Civil Society and Its Discontents,* Tampere Peace Research Institute Occasional Papers Series No. 86, pp. 1–82.

Comaroff, J.L. and Comaroff, J. (1999) (eds) *Civil Society and the Political Imagination in Africa: Critical Perspectives*, Chicago: The University of Chicago Press.

Crowther, S. (2001) 'The role of NGOs, local and international, in post-war peace building', a paper presented at a workshop organised by the Committee for Conflict Transformation Support, CCTS, held at Islington Town Hall, London.

Dahrendorf, R. (1997) *After 1989: Morals, Revolution, and Civil Society,* Basingstoke: Macmillan Press in association with St Antony's College, Oxford.

Ekeh, P.P. (1992) 'The constitution of civil society in African history and publics', in B. Caron *et al.* (eds), *Democratic Transition in Africa,* Ibadan: CREDU.

Gellner, E. (1994) *Conditions of Liberty: Civil Society and Its Rivals*, London: Hamish Hamilton.

Green, A. (1999) 'A cross-regional analysis of civil society and democratic development', Columbia International Affairs Online Working Papers, September.

Habermas, J. (1989) *The Structural Transformation of the Public Sphere: An Inquiry into a Category of Bourgeois Society*, Cambridge: Polity Press.

Hann, C. and Dunn, E. (eds) (1996) *Civil Society Challenging Western Models*, London: Routledge.

Harbeson, J., Rothchild, D. and Chazan, N. (eds) (1994) *Civil Society and the State in Africa*, London: Lynne Rienner.

Havel, V. (1985) *The Power of the Powerless: Citizens Against the State in Central-Eastern Europe*, London: Hutchinson.

Howell, J. and Pearce J. (2001) *Civil Society and Development: A Critical Exploration*, London: Lynne Rienner.

Loizos, P. (1996) 'How Ernest Gellner got mugged on the streets of London, or: civil society, the media and the quality of life', in C. Hann and E. Dunn (eds), *Civil Society Challenging Western Models*, London: Routledge.

Mamdani, M. (1997) *Citizen and Subject: Contemporary Africa and the Legacy of Late Colonialism*, Princeton: Princeton University Press.

Monga, C. (1996) *The Anthropology of Anger: Civil Society and Democracy in Africa*, Boulder CO: Lynne Rienner.

Mustapha, A.R. (1998) 'When will independence end? Democratization and civil society in rural Africa', in L. Rudebeck, O. Tornquist and V. Rojas (eds), *Democratization in the Third World: Concrete Cases in Comparative and Theoretical Perspective*, Basingstoke: Macmillan.

Olorunyomi, S., Coordinator, Information Aid Network (IFANET), Ibadan, Nigeria. Personal communication 15 June 2003.

Olukoshi, A. (ed.) (1993) *The Politics of Structural Adjustment in Nigeria*, London: James Currey.

——(1996) 'Associational life', in L. Diamond, A. Kirk-Greene and O. Oyediran (eds), *Transition Without End: Nigerian Politics and Civil Society under Babangida*, Ibadan: Vantage.

Onwudiwe, E. (ed.) (1998) *African Perspectives on Civil Society*, New York: Tri-Atlantic Books.

Van Rooy, A. (1998) *Civil Society and the Aid Industry: The Politics and Promise*, London: Earthscan.

Villalon, L.A. (1995) *Islamic Society and State Power in Senegal Disciples and Citizens in Fatick*, Cambridge: Cambridge University Press.

Williams, A. (2003) 'A Trojan horse for Africa', *Africa Today*, 9(7): 10–11.

Part VII

The Middle East

Civil society as emancipation?

18 Civil society in Iran

Past, present and the future

Ali Paya

A very brief overview

By 'civil society' I mean 'social institutions', which act as a buffer between the individual and his or her 'social environment', and create breathing spaces for the individual *vis-à-vis* other individuals and powerful social institutions or socially constructed entities. States and their various apparatuses as well as large business corporations are amongst the most important social institutions against whose excesses 'civil society' would operate.

As a 'social construct', 'civil society' undergoes continuous changes, both conceptually (intensionally) and extensionally. Social agents with fresh 'collective intentionalities' should or will be able to come up with improved models of 'civil society'.

Historical background

From the middle ages until the late nineteenth century a number of institutions can be discerned as precursors of the modern concept of 'civil society' in Iranian society. The institutions in question are: clerics, sanctuaries and the places of refuge, *khaneghahs*; the elders, tribes and clans, *ayiarraan*; peasant groups, and *Asnaf*.

Clerics, especially those of the rank of Shi'ite *Mujtahids* (jurists), have always played a moderating role in taming the power of the state. Moreover, the Islamic *Fiqh* (or *Shari'ah*: religious legal system), with its emphasis on the support of private ownership, has provided individuals with a reasonable degree of freedom for economic and social activities within the rigid structure of the political despotic and authoritarian order of Iranian society over the past several hundred years.

Sanctuaries – in the shape of holy shrines, mosques and other places of worship, mausoleums, and residences of eminent religious or political personalities – provided some forms of safeguards against the authorities for those individuals or groups who were vulnerable or unprotected. Other institutions with dual religious or temporal functions – such as *khaneghahs*, which are non-orthodox places for worship and socializing – provided believers with alternative forms of religious life that were much more liberal in their outlook and rituals than those enforced by *Shari'ah*.

Tribes were large social groups consisting of extended families, which provided all sorts of supports for their members (Beck 1995). In rural regions peasant groups were small village organizations that acted on behalf of individual peasants in a wide range of issues from paying taxes and duties to getting their fair share of water to defending their realms. The elders – as locally respected figures whether in a tribe, a rural area, a town or a city – had an important social role in interceding with the authorities on behalf of individuals. They were also involved in other areas of the community. In the cities, *ayiarraan* or *ayyarun* were also important in this respect. They were urban groups of brave and astute individuals who 'seem to be more closely linked with the local bourgeoisie in support of a native prince, ... Sometimes the bourgeoisie relied on them in resisting the authorities ... , in the majority of towns which had no *charta* (police force), they formed an indispensable local militia, ... upon whom the race of the city relied' (Massignion 1935: 962).

In more urban settings *Asnaf* (sing. *Sinf*) functioned, to some extent, rather like the European guilds. They provided a public sphere for the activities of their members. There were however, some noticeable differences between these bodies and their European counterparts. *Asnaf* had more social functions than the guilds, whereas the economic power of the guilds and their control over professional matters were much stronger (Ashraf 1995).

Guilds usually consisted of merchants, craftsmen and artisans, whereas *Asnaf* embraced a wider variety of professions and even included the *Sinf* of dancers and the *Sinf* of beggars. Heads of *Asnaf* had the dual responsibility of representing their own members as well as carrying out the duties assigned to them by the town or city authorities. They were, for example, responsible for collecting taxes on behalf of the authorities. In contrast, heads of the guilds did not have such responsibilities.

Whereas members of each guild elected heads of their respective guilds, heads of *Asnaf* were appointed by the town or city authorities with the endorsement or consent of the members of each *Sinf*. Due to the geographic location of their trades, which were near the Grand Mosque or other mosques in the cities, and also to the particular social circumstances of Islamic lands, *Asnaf* had close links with the religious authorities. Such a close relationship with the Church was not a characteristic of the European guilds.

Guilds acted in a social environment in which there was a substantial division between the burgeoning cities and the old villages. The former were representatives of emerging industries and businesses, while the latter were under the control of great landlords who were living in their own castles. In the cities of the Middle East, in contrast, city or town authorities and the great landlords lived side by side and exerted their control over the inhabitants of various districts of the cities that were occupied by both peasants and the members of *Asnaf*. Such a situation, on the one hand, would limit the freedom and autonomy of *Asnaf* and, on the other, would prevent polarization between the village and city forms of life, a polarization that was instrumental for the birth of capitalism in the West.

Throughout the nineteenth century and until 1906 Iranian society's increased exposure to Western ideas and models resulted in a greater demand for sociopolitical reforms. People's struggles to change the political system, which culminated in the Constitutional Revolution of 1906, paved the way for the emergence of the first modern instances of 'civil society', as well as more active and thorough involvement of some of the older forms of civil society institutions. In addition, these institutions greatly helped the people to expand their share of the public sphere through these mediums of social change.

Of the indigenous precursors to civil society, the two institutions of *Asnaf* and the clerics not only retained their past significance but also assumed new sociopolitical roles. However, the other earlier forms of civil society either faded away or lost their important position. In their place, new types of institutions, such as political associations and political parties, appeared on the scene. Among these latter-day institutions, the role played by the printed media was of great importance. Early Iranian journalists made a significant contribution to the process of educating the society at large and promulgating the ideas and ideals of civil society.

The two autocrat shahs of the Pahlavi dynasty (1925–78), Reza khan and his son Mohammad Reza, tried in direct or indirect ways to weaken the budding civil society. To this end, they created state-supported civil institutions such as the Supreme Council of *Asnaf*, Chamber of *Asnaf*, and various professional unions that were instruments of the regime. They also supported the activities of cultural institutions such as Franklin Publication House and Shiraz International Annual Art Festival, which were related to the royal court. At the same time, the activities of popular political parties were declared unlawful, while a number of subservient parties were allowed to appear on the political scene. The pressure on the independent clerics, and intellectual and political activists was also systematically increased and the free press was to a large extent silenced or coerced to toe the line. In the absence of free media, the official media, including the national radio and television stations and the printed press with large circulations, were acting as the loyal mouthpieces of the regime, promoting, among other things, the views and profiles of proregime intellectuals.

In the meantime, the opposition groups, in their struggle for survival, tried to create independent bodies that would represent their views and positions. Amongst the better-known institutions of this kind one can mention the Writers' Union, Associations of Lawyers, Students' Associations, and independent *Asnaf*. The clerics also managed to make use of the large network of mosques all over the country to put their message across (Khaniki 2002).

Civil society in Iran since the Islamic Revolution (1978)

The Islamic Revolution, Iranians' second popular attempt in the lifetime of three generations at changing an autocratic system, was the result of many factors, including the royal regime's own efforts for a speedy but ill-planned modernization. In the years that followed the revolution, along with Iranian society itself the institutions of civil society underwent profound changes. We can quickly trace these changes in the following three phases.

In the immediate wake of the revolution society experienced a degree of freedom unheard of for decades. The various political and social groups that mushroomed in the aftermath of the fall of the *ancien régime*, the number of newspapers and journals that flooded the market, and the sheer volume of previously banned books that saw the light of the day, all were clear testimony to the emergence of a truly pluralistic society. Amongst the more significant social changes in the early days, there was a shift in the public perception away from the values and merits of the working class – which had been the ideal norms for all prerevolution populist social and political movements, secular or religious alike – towards the values of the middle class. It is in this context that the notion of the 'civil society' gained some prominence in the early days of the revolution. This happy state of affairs was not to last long. The invasion of the Iraqi Ba'athist regime in 1981 pushed the state to centre stage, a move that inevitably caused the newly emerged discourse of civil society to gradually fade away.

However, even during the Iran–Iraq war, the more traditional clerics who were anxious that a powerful state might be tempted to opt for a centralized, planned economy of the type operative in the communist bloc did their best to slow down all the government's moves towards controlling the market and curtailing the influence of their *Bazari* (merchant) allies. The traditional alliance between the more conservative clerics, who were sensitive towards any infringement of the rights of individuals to produce wealth and to preserve their private properties, and the *Bazarirs*, who were the main financial backers of the traditional clergy, proved to be too much of a burden for a state that had to coordinate all the war efforts in the country, including a fair distribution of basic goods. Ayatollah Khomeini, in a historic edict, tried to outmanoeuvre his conservative fellow-clerics. He stated in 1986 that 'The Islamic State, which is a part of the absolute guardianship of the Prophet, is one of the primary principles of *Shari'ah*, and as such takes priority over all the secondary principles even the Prayer, the Fast, and the Pilgrimage to Mecca … . The State can stop any practice, related to religious rituals or otherwise, whose implementation is against Islam's [i.e., Islamic State's] interest until this remains the case' (Ayatollah Khomeini 1989). The edict had many other ramifications apart from its immediate target. Among other things, it paradoxically paved the way for the emergence of a secular state that is more sympathetic towards institutions of modern civil society.

The reason for such a paradoxical move is not hard to explain. Ayatollah

Khomeini, as a Grand Ayatollah in charge of the Islamic state, had a dual responsibility. On the one hand, he was the representative of the Prophet and Shi'ite Imams, and in this capacity had absolute authority over the system of *Fiqh* and the *Shari'ah*. He could introduce new religious laws and rulings in the same way that the Prophet and the Shi'ite Imams would do. On the other hand, he had acquired his power and legitimacy through a 'social contract' with the faithful. In this role he was the representative of the people and the symbol of national sovereignty and was obliged to look after national interests and the public good. However, to do his job as the representative of people, the Ayatollah had no choice but to resort to pragmatic measures in conducting the affairs of the state. Here the notion of utility took precedence over all other values. But since he was also representing the realm of the sacred, his recourse to pragmatic measures drove a wedge between his responsibilities towards the state, as the manager of worldly affairs, and the more spiritual and personal religious aspects of his position. This therefore sped up the process of introducing modern institutions (Hajjariyan 2001; Paya 2004a).

At the end of an eight-year sanguinary war which, thanks to the full support given by the Western and Eastern blocs to Saddam and his regime, resulted in an stalemate with no clear winner, but caused more than a million casualties and produced widespread political stagnation. Hashemi Rafsanjani, a shrewd clergyman who was close to Ayatollah Khomeini, was elected as president (1989–97). Coming from a landowner and merchant family, he was in favour of open market policies. At the same time, he was very fond of being in full control of the affairs of the state and was averse to any political criticism or opposition, even within the boundaries set by the constitution and other laws of the land. As a result he opted for a two-tier programme of free-enterprise economics and political closure.

Freedom of speech, which had been restricted during the war, did not receive a significant boost. Plans concerning the resumption of political parties' activities, which according to the constitutions should have started their functioning years before, were once again put on hold. Otherwise loyal groups that opposed the clergy were placed in jail and, worst of all, clandestine semi-official armed groups from the Ministry of Information embarked on a project of physical elimination of those intellectuals deemed 'undesirable elements'. Some of these intellectuals were actively campaigning for the restoration of the institutions of civil society.

Mohammad Khatami, an unlikely candidate for presidency, who was not enjoying the support of the powerful religious conservative establishment, won a surprising landslide victory in the 1997 presidential elections. Apart from his personal charm, his winning policy was advocating a programme of social and political reform whose main element was the re-empowerment of civil society. However, in order not to offend the conservative clerics and their traditional followers for whom all mention of concepts such as civil society were sign of 'Westoxication' and a lack of adequate Islamic commitment,

Khatami initially introduced his idea under the guise of 'Islamic civil society', an invention that was criticized by liberal-minded intellectuals (Paya 1998; 2000a). Nevertheless, the idea of effecting reforms through the empowerment of the populace was not only warmly received by intellectuals but also enjoyed an enthusiastic acceptance by the ordinary public (Organization for Cultural Documents 1997).

One of the immediate and startling results of Khatami's reform programme was the release of an immense amount of social energy in the form of people's wholehearted participation in programmes suggested for the expansion of 'civil society' in a multitude of ways. For the first time since the early days of the revolution, a free quality press reappeared on the scene. Intellectuals, as if freed from a tight shackle, exuberantly embarked on the production of ideas and theories that would provide a theoretical basis for a freer and fairer society; non-governmental organizations made their debut; elections for local councils in cities and town were successfully carried out, thus fulfilling one of the neglected aspects of the constitution (as a result of this election more than 33,000 councils were formed in town and cities all over the country: of 4,600 city councillors, more than 300 were women, a record for a system that until then had often paid not more than lip service to women's rights); and an overwhelming majority of the voters elected pro-Khatami's candidates for the *Majlis* (Parliament) to assist him in pushing forward his reform agenda (Paya 2000b).

Despite the concerted efforts of conservatives to derail Khatami's reform project, he was once again voted into office by a huge margin in the 2001 presidential elections. However, since then the uphill struggle for him and his followers has become even more strenuous. The conservatives, who had lost not only public trust but also control over the executive and legislative powers, have used the non-elective judiciary to put maximum pressure on Khatami and his allies and to bring his reform project to a halt. A large number of proreform papers and journals have been closed since the 2001 elections, and many journalists, intellectuals, activists, lawyers, and even university professors have been given long-term jail sentences after 'trials' that are at best poor simulacrums of the genuine judicial procedures.

As Khatami approaches the last days of his final term in office, due to end in June 2005, it seems a good deal of the momentum that was created when he was first elected has disappeared. A sense of frustration appears to be gripping the public, and there are good reasons for this: despite the earnest efforts of proreform intellectuals as well as the public to support ideas such as associational autonomy, rule of law, freedom of expression, inclusive citizenship, transparency and accountability and the like, there is no doubt that what they have achieved falls far short of their ideals. The large number of cases of colossal financial corruption gradually being brought into the limelight, the continued violent actions of vigilante groups against the reformers, the opaque activities of powerful financial and economic private foundations that are not accountable to the government, the arbitrary ways in which the judiciary appears to be operating, and the like, are all clear indications of the fact that Iranian citizens, notwithstanding their great achievements since the 1990s, still have a long way to go.

The future of civil society in Iran

Although the seemingly sizable list of the setbacks in the road towards a just, free and fair society gives cause for concern to all those who are sincerely trying to bring about genuine changes in Iranian society, the complex realities of modern Iran leave enough room for being optimistic about the future of civil society in Iran.

In considering such a future, it must be borne in mind that Iranian society is still suffering from the impact of a long and brutal tradition of despotism. When the Shah's regime was toppled, people were half-jokingly telling each other that there are small shahs hidden inside each of us, which are yet to be ousted. The fact that people have warmly responded to Khatami's reform programme, however, is a testimony to their readiness to rid themselves of the old habits.

The Shi'ite religion, which is the religion of the vast majority of Iranians, with its emphasis on individualism, elitism, abstract and theoretical thinking and sense of mission (Enayat 1982), and its endorsement of the spirit of free enterprise in the realm of economic activities (Hajjariyan 2000; 2001), creates a favourable environment for active participation of the people.

However, there are some built-in mechanisms in *Shi'i Fiqh* that might act as an impediment. For example, the Institution of Emulation in the *Shi'i Fiqh,* which regulates the relationship between the lay believers (the emulators) and their Grand Ayatollahs (the sources of emulation) in all practical (in other words non-doctrinal) aspects of life, would mean that there are some barriers to the creation of political parties: the emulators are more likely to listen to their Ayatollahs than their political leaders.

Some other factors could also impede the consolidation and proper functioning of civil society in Iran. For instance, the fact that Iran is a vast country with diverse ethnic groups surrounded by neighbours with little or no democratic credentials means that, among other things, a powerful state needs to be in control to ward off any threat to national security and territorial integrity. The gradual emergence of a new logic of cost and benefit amongst the Iranian intelligentsia, which is replacing the original logic of sacrifice and selflessness prevalent in the early days of the revolution, could also act as a hindrance. Fewer people are nowadays ready to risk their livelihood, let alone their lives, for the sake of consolidating the institutions of civil society, in the face of menacing reactions from the more conservative classes.

Notwithstanding these negative factors, the potential for the formation of a fully fledged civil society in Iran remains quite strong: whereas, according to some writers, many of the nations in the Middle East region are not well acquainted with modernity (Ajami 2003), Iranians are at home with modern ideas and institutions. This internal propensity is also being assisted by two external factors: the phenomenon of globalization, among other things, has facilitated the introduction of new ideas and models to Iranian society, and recent international developments, especially the fall of the Ba'athist regime in Iraq, have had a significant impact on the views and attitudes of Iranians at all levels. All in all, it does not seem far-fetched to predict that, given all the forces operating within and without the ecosystem of Iranian society, the future evolutionary path of this society leads towards emergence of a more robust and effective civil society (Paya 2004b).

References

Ajami, F. (2003) 'Iraq and the future of Arabs', *Foreign Affairs*, January/February, 82: 1.

Ashraf, A. (1995) 'Sinf system and the civil society', *Iran Nameh*, 14(1): 5–40.

Beck, L. (1995) 'Tribes and the civil society', *Iran Nameh*, 14(1): 523–56.

Enayat, H. (1982) *Modern Islamic Political Thought*, London: Macmillan.

Hajjariyan, S. (2000) *Republicanism: Demystification of Power*, Tehran: Tarh-e Nou.

——(2001) *Sacred in the Secular Age*, Tehran: Tarh-e Nou.

Khaniki, H. (2002) *Power, Civil Society and the Press*, Tehran: Tarh-e Nou.

Khomeini, A.R. (1989) *Sahifeh Nur* [Book of Light], Tehran: Vezârat-e Farhang va Ershâd-e Eslâmi, Vol. 20.

Massignion, L. (1935) 'Sinf', *Encyclopaedia of Islam*, Brill: Leyden, Vol. II.

Organization for the Cultural Documents of the Islamic Revolution (1997) *The Realization of the Civil Society in the Islamic Revolution of Iran: An Anthology*, Tehran.

Paya, A. (2000a) 'Muslim identity and civil society: whose Islam? Which society?', a paper presented at the International Conference on Muslim Identity in the Twenty-First Century: The Challenges of Modernity, University of London (SOAS), October–November 1998, and published in the proceedings of the conference: London: Book Extra Publications.

——(2000b) 'The future of democracy in Iran', *CSD Bulletin*, 7(2): 15–17.

——(2004a) 'Modern trends in Shi'i thought: variations on the same old themes or revolutionary break from the past?', *International Journal of Middle East Studies*.

——(2004b) 'The future of civil society in Iran', *American Journal of Islamic Social Sciences* (forthcoming).

19 Contractions of a sociocultural reflex

Civil society in Turkey

Hakan Seckinelgin

This discussion can be approached from many directions. Given the limited size of this chapter I will only focus on the conditions under which the idea of civil society is discussed in Turkey. Also, I will be looking at the specific background conditions that are mobilized by various actors when they are threatened. I call this mechanism the sociocultural reflex. The concept of 'civil society' has an interesting resonance for Turkey. The adjective 'civil' is translated into Turkish as *sivil*, that which is not related to military. In this context civil society, *sivil toplum*, has represented until very recently a debate and a mobilization for democratic politics and their establishment due to the several military interventions that occurred between 1961 to 1980. The actors in this debate included politicians, trade unions and numerous sectoral associations or clubs (*dernekler*). These actors contested the position of the military in assuming the ruling of the country from the view of democratic freedoms and democratic solutions. After the last military intervention in September 1980, military generals in 1984 transferred the governing powers to the elected parliament (under a number of restrictions on electoral rights). Civil society actors were among those who pushed the military authority for this end. Since this, the system seems to have moved on to a position where the importance of political process and democratic procedures are recognized by the military. The voice of civil society in this process has been contributing to the change. In this sense civil society has a particularly political nature in the Turkish context.

Generally the following institutions are seen as taking part in civil society: foundations (*vakıflar*), whose traditions have existed for centuries; the clubs bringing internal migrants from similar areas together in large cities (*Hemşeri dernekleri*); sectoral associations or chambers (*odalar*); bar associations (*barolar*); universities, journalists and trade unions (*sendikalar*). Traditionally, many of these organizations are formally established and since their establishment have represented the interests of their members in the political and legal processes (Bora 2000). *Hemşeri dernekleri* are mostly concerned with social relations, while *vakıflar* have traditionally provided more of a service role in health or education sectors. The others constitute the formal actors of civil society with a political voice. This suggests that the role of civil society in the sociopolitical debate has a formality and certain agreed parameters.

However, as democratic ideals are taking deeper root and the military, despite its continuing pre-eminence in society, is becoming more respectful of these ideals, the idea of civil society has become much more nuanced. In this, several other factors are important – both the impact of the concept's global resurgence and of organizational forms and the Turkish aspiration to become a member of the European Union have brought about a certain change. The number of non-governmental organizations (NGOs) has increased, and their areas of interest have diversified: from various women's issues to the environment, from gay and lesbian rights to homelessness, from language rights to ethnic groups to prison-reform associations. In other words, the civil society scene is becoming less formalized, and as a result is becoming more diffused than is possible within the more bureaucratic structures characteristic of traditional organizations. Therefore, the recent increase in the numbers of organizations that can be seen as NGOs is changing the reach of civil society while also altering its characteristics. Although this change is neither very rapid nor widely observable outside large urban settings, various groups are emerging with political agendas and demands to make of the system. The question here is whether both new and traditional groups have a similar voice in terms of the sociopolitical debate, and the reach of this voice in the system.

It is at this juncture of the new and the traditional that the existing traditional tacit understanding between the formal civil society and the state is exposed. What can be called a social contract that commits the society to a particular model of *Turkishness* is questioned. At the same time this questioning can be seen as another step towards deepening society's democratic ideals. However, despite representing two offshoots of an ongoing process of democraticization, they sit uncomfortably with each other.

Ne Mutlu Türküm Diyene! ('Happy is one who can say one is a Turk')

This statement is taken to be the defining expression of Turkish nationalism. The idea expressed here moves beyond race or ethnicity-based ideals of nationhood. It locates nationalism in particular sociocultural characteristics that need to be accepted in order to secure membership of the nation. In this way, it does not credit any exclusivity to any particular race or ethnicity in the claim to be Turkish. This contractual concept may be seen as an interesting construction to hold together a polity after the collapse of what was then a multinational (*millet*) political structure, the Ottoman Empire. Although it addressed the problem at hand in the early 1920s, the question now is whether it can still be relevant today, 80 years later.

The question is raised not in terms of the structure of this nationalism but in terms of its contents. Clearly the contractual mechanism makes it amenable to change while the contents that substantiate the nature of *Turkishness* create certain limitations. This substantiation is generally considered under the *Kemalist* project, after the founder of the Turkish republic, Mustafa Kemal Atatürk. The most striking characteristics of this project are its total commitment to a Western secular society (most importantly breaking the link between religions and the judicial system), a state feminism that promotes the rights of women in public life, a strong emphasis on economic modernization, and an important commitment to Western civilization in both social and political spheres. Ernest Gellner (1981: 68) considers this Kemalist secularism as a didactic secular project that is applied to and permeated through society by the means of education and changes in public life (adaptation of modern marriages, and Western time, metric measurements, clothing and alphabet). One also observes in this, as Gellner suggests, a particular ethical outlook about life that is defended and implemented. In other words the Kemalist project commits the society and its people to a particular way of being. Therefore the changes initiated in the early republic were mechanisms to construct such social identities. However, secularization is also seen, as Nur Vergin suggests, as the sign of power and the existential reason (*hikmet-i hükümet*) for the new republic (2000: 36). The position of women must be seen central in this process; it was used as one of the most important interventions to initiate this process. As Nilüfer Göle suggests, the increased visibility of woman in public life both as a body and as an actor establishes one of the central guarantees of the Kemalist commitment to the modern civilized world (2000). Therefore, a link between the status of women and the core ideal of the reason of state are closely identified. In this way activist women and their groups have always seen as one the faces of the secular civil society.

Thus, one can observe the organic relationship between what is seen as an essentially political struggle to create a new form of polity and what is a social construction of a particular cultural identity. The relationship was a political one in the sense that the cultural change and measures that were committing the society to a particular mode of being civilized were (and are still) seen as anchoring the political regime, which would move gradually towards a democratic system. This assumption linked social life and identities with the political commitments of Kemalist project. In this environment, although Islamic and other forms of traditional associations and their activities were removed from public life, new republican forms of associations moved into their places. There is no doubt that one would have observed, in the early years of the republic, a dynamic civil society emerging with a strong commitment to the Kemalist project. However, it is in this context that one can also observe the political agenda merging with the social agenda, creating a particular understanding of the civil society space. Furthermore, the process also committed civil society to becoming a defender of a particular form of life in the sociocultural sphere. In the process, civil society has gained two roles: making sure on the one hand that the state is democratically responsible and on the other hand that society develops within the Kemalist lines.

Why does this matter?

These origins matter since, as from the mid-1980s onwards Turkish society has become much more democratic, the cultural identity of the society constructed in this political manner has not been responsive to the changing nature of the deepening democracy that is creating new opportunities in the civil society space. Nevertheless, the sociocultural reflex of society is still based on the cognitive map provided by the outward signs, such as changing attire, of the earlier cultural commitments discussed above. The close correlation between the political form and the cultural attributes of *Turkishness* are considered to be essential for the continued well-being of the society. It is also clear that this is leading to a particular overlap between civil society and the state. They are both committed to a particular nationalist project, though the former questions certain state interventions in social life. As a result the deepening democracy and the new groups emerging in the process are finding themselves in a rather precarious position.

In most cases civil society shares the precepts of the Kemalist project, or it is assumed that it should, and aims to help deepen the democracy by defending it (in its particular form). Although the state tends to argue and discuss with civil society in a confrontational manner, from the larger perspective I consider in this chapter the position of civil society is acceptable to the state: civil society can disagree on everyday political issues and economic management, and can advocate new laws. Gradually many groups even question the conditions of prisoners, while others fight for a more open society in terms of freedom of expression, and question the legality of the State Security Courts (*Devlet Güvenlik Mahkemeleri*) established during the military interventions. Nonetheless, when the questioning addresses what is seen as the core values of the Kemalist project – around the issues of Islam (in particular in terms of headscarves), ethnic languages, human rights issues (since the 1970s, both of these have been mostly related to Kurdish issues) that are testing the accepted norms, or whether the country should consider a federal structure – the sociocultural reflex contracts. When this happens, both civil society and the state protest with one voice to defend a particular way of life. This creates an amalgamation of the political nationalist feelings expressed both by the state – for example by the military and the judiciary and those who adopted the Kemalist project as society's cultural identity – and outside the state – such as the universities, trade unions and Kemalist NGOs (Erdoğan 2000). With this, the newly emerging groups and demands have to adopt the ethical outlook shared through the Kemalist ideals in order to be included. Groups or people failing to do so risk being seen as traitors (*bölücüler*) rather than being seen from any of the civil society perspectives available. Those who are seen in this manner find themselves outside society as offenders of the national psyche.

This situation has been experienced more and more since the end of 1980s with the emergence of rather vocal Islamic groups and of groups questioning the ongoing military involvement, its grounds and implications, in the southeast throughout the 1990s. These newly established groups find it difficult to enter the civil society space as agents for social debate. This is due to the existing national sociocultural reflex, which contracts at any sign of these groups participating in a debate with social demands. It is not uncommon to see this reflex in newspaper headlines reporting from national unity demonstrations in spaces that are symbolically associated with Kemalism. The process works on the basis of demonstrating what *Turkishness* should be like as well as acting as a deterrent for these new groups. The match between the political identity of the state and the cultural identity of people, particularly a certain social consensus among the educated elite, is used as a reflexive restriction for the space of civil society. In this way, those excluded are constructed as socially irrelevant and politically suspicious.

In terms of civil society this poses a difficulty. The sociopolitical space is occupied with agents who fundamentally agree on their identities and do not recognize other participants as agents in this space. Ultimately this creates social frustration as spaces of political debate and social recognition for many groups are closed.

It is important to realize that this reflex I am talking about has been contracting more frequently in the first few years of the twenty-first century than it did in the last thirty years of the twentieth. The emergence of politicized religious groups (with or without a human rights focus) in particular motivated such situations. The Turkish political scene has changed since the National Salvation Party (*Milli Selamet Partisi* – MSP) was established in 1972 to represent the socially more conservative Islamic view, and these new groups want to take part in a much larger sociopolitical debate than was provided by the MSP. These views are very much articulated by the Justice and Development Party (*Adalet ve Kalkınma Partisi* – AKP), which was elected as the majority government in 2002.

One of the clearest examples of these newly emerging groups can be seen in relation to women who would like to experience their religion by wearing headscarves. The issue of women's attire is related to one of the most important precepts of Kemalism. The removal of religious clothing from society was one of the ways to *free* women and also teach westernization to society. In this sense it is at the core of being Turkish as well as constituting the ideal of a civilized woman's identity. Although the use of scarves in rural areas, by mostly uneducated or older women, has long been accepted practice, a demand for headscarves from the younger generation and the educated is seen as a political manoeuvre to reverse the Kemalist project. The debate over the issue still continues, with influential women's organizations protesting against allowing women to use headscarves as they consider it demeaning to their Kemalist identity. In the process a number of NGOs have been established to promote this demand on the basis of human rights (Çayır 2000; Pusch 2000). In particular the election of AKP as the government in 2002 – considering that most ministers' wives, including the Prime Minister's, wear headscarves – made this reflex much clearer. In April 2003, the President of the Republic refused to attend a reception in parliament for the anniversary of its establishment because the speaker of the parliament, who was hosting the event, has a wife who wears a headscarf. Most *secular* politicians participated in this protest, supported by many representing the Kemalist elite, who were offended by a host who might have worn a headscarf in parliament. As a result of this protest no women with headscarves appeared in the reception. An important debate followed, in which the president, the former head of the constitutional court, argued that wearing headscarves was fine in one's personal life but was not acceptable in public spaces and could not be allowed. This understanding was adopted and has been applied at two other national days since then. Those dignitaries who are known to have wives with headscarves are invited without their wives. In this the understanding of the public space and those who can participate in this space to have a voice is very important. It restricts access and voice in the political and social spheres by an appeal to the Kemalist project and its resulting sociocultural prejudices.

This line of argument is not only applied in relation to religious issues but also in judging certain international actors funding NGOs in Turkey. Those organizations that are funding explicitly Kemalist organizations seem to proceed without too much attention as they provide funding to bolster *democracy* and market economies, as was the fashion throughout the 1990s. However, some other organizations are seen as interfering with the integrity of the nation as they talk to or fund those groups that are not within the civil society vision of the state. Such groups can vary from groups related to Islamic women or Kurdish language to community groups. One such group is a group of villagers that has been protesting against an Australian company's excavation of gold with arsenic in their village in Bergama (Hablemitlioğlu 2001). This protest is perceived as being manipulated by international environmentalists and funders against the interests of the nation. In the same way, the activities of some international foundations working in Turkey are seen as divisive and their activities are challenged in state security courts. Another example of this expression can be observed in the following. In April 2003 the secretary general of the National Security Council (*Milli Güvenlik Konseyi*), a high-ranking general, visited several western European countries, and in these visits he proposed the creation of an umbrella organization to bring together all civil society groups established in Europe by migrant Turkish people (some of the Islamic groups were not included in these discussions).

He argued that all of these groups should coordinate their work to support Turkish national interests. This can be seen as demonstrating a restricted understanding of civil society that considers it as an extension of the specific interests of the state. In turn the interests of civil society becomes relevant provided that they match the national interests set out in Kemalism and defended (and to a degree interpreted) by the state and sociocultural Kemalists.

Some conclusions

In this short piece I have outlined an important sociological mechanism that restricts civil society's identity in Turkey. I also argued that this is being challenged as the democratic process is establishing itself. However, the present paradox will take a long time to be resolved. It is possible to argue that the process through which democracy is becoming deepened is calling the sociocultural reflex into question. However, while Kemalism's democratic ideals are becoming a reality and taking shape, its cultural identity is limiting the democratization process and its outcomes. As a result many people are still construed as a threat to the continuity of the republic. While their voices are not considered in terms of actors in civil society trying to participate in a debate of social political issues, those who are considered as representative of civil society find themselves intentionally or unintentionally aligned with those actors that present a culturally nationalist frame of reference, such as the military. For democracy to function and to become the organizing principle of society, the basis of the sociocultural reflex needs to be discussed. In this way, it is not only the state but also ordinary people, those who are seen as the proverbial soldiers in the Kemalist project, who need to rethink the sociopolitical limitations that are internalized if they are also aspiring to achieve the main Kemalist aim of becoming a modern democracy.

References

Bora, T. (2000) 'Professional chambers and non-voluntary organisations: the intersection of public, civil and national', in S. Yerasimos, G. Seufert and K. Vorhoff (eds), *Civil Society in the Grip of Nationalism*, Turkey: Orient-Institut.

Çayır, K. (2000) 'İslamcı Bir Sivil Toplum Örgütü: Gökkuşaği İstanbul Kadın Platformu', in N. Göle (ed.), *İslamın Yeni Kamusal Yüzleri*, Istanbul: Metis Yayınları.

Erdoğan, N. (2000) 'Kemalist non-governmental organisations: troubled elites in defence of a sacred heritage', in S. Yerasimos, G. Seufert and K. Vorhoff (eds), *Civil Society in the Grip of Nationalism*, Turkey: Orient-Institut.

Gellner, E. (1981) *Muslim Society*, Cambridge: Cambridge University Press.

Göle, N. (2000) (ed.) *İslamin Yeni Kamusal Yüzleri*, Istanbul: Metis Yayınları.

Hablemitlioğlu, N. (2001) *Alman Vakfları ve Bergama Dosyası*, Istanbul: Otopsi.

Pusch, B. (2000) 'Stepping into the public sphere: the rise of Islamist and religious-conservative women's non-governmental organisations', in S. Yerasimos, G. Seufert and K. Vorhoff (eds), *Civil Society in the Grip of Nationalism*, Turkey: Orient-Institut.

Vergin, N. (2000) *Din, Toplum ve Siyasal Sistem*, Istanbul: Bağlam.

20 Unfulfilled aspirations

Civil society in Palestine 1993–98

Salma A. Shawa

The concept of civil society gained ground during the 1990s in the Palestinian Territories among political activists, non-governmental organization (NGO) leaders, international donors and even, to some degree, within the Palestinian governing authorities. This chapter reports findings from empirical research on the organizational dimensions of local and international efforts to 'strengthen' Palestinian civil society between 1993 and 1998, based on detailed organizational case studies of four Palestinian NGOs working in the rural development and social sectors. The study explored the reasons for increasing interest in the civil society concept, and found explanations at both local and international levels (Shawa 2001). The aim of the research was to analyse the changes experienced by the sector during and after the transfer of authority and to explore the roles played by NGOs as actors engaged in a self-styled process of 'building' civil society.

There has been a longstanding presence in Palestine of a range of associations, service providers and community organizations such as women's groups, charitable associations and cooperatives. However, the tendency to refer to this public sphere as 'civil society' only really became apparent in the period following the three peace agreements achieved between 1993 and 1995. The emergence of this new discourse was in part a consequence of the creation of a Palestinian National Authority (PNA), which was envisaged as having a distinct range of civic functions that would operate alongside the authorities of the Israeli occupation. This new institutional presence allowed existing Palestinian non-governmental social actors to begin to widen their roles within the public sphere, such as the provision of expanded service delivery roles and the possibility of contributing to policy formulation. The limited transfer of power to a new authority also further opened up Palestinian society to the influence of international development agencies. These agencies generally favoured stronger roles for NGOs, which were seen as potentially efficient private agents of development and as possible catalysts for strengthening democratic political processes. As a result, many Palestinian NGOs began to internalize and communicate 'new' values of transparency, accountability and professionalism that many hoped would help strengthen their legitimacy.

Formal NGOs had begun to emerge in Palestine during the 1970s for purposes of development and as vehicles for political mobilization primarily among women, students and the professional classes. During the first Intifada (uprising) between 1987 and 1993, voluntary committees were established to provide relief services to populations enduring particular hardships under the occupation (Barghouthi and Giacaman 1990). It was the Madrid peace process in 1992 which finally allowed Palestinian NGOs to turn their attentions more closely to questions of social and economic development and the new challenges of nation-building. Funding for NGOs reached a peak in 1990–92 with between US$170 and US$245 million per year (Clark and Balaj 1996: 3).

The signing of the Declaration of Principles in 1993 by the Government of Israel and the Palestine Liberation Organization (PLO), which became known as the Oslo I Agreement, led to the formal establishment of the PNA in 1994. The PNA was given jurisdiction over most civic affairs in the main towns of the Gaza Strip and in the town of Jericho in the West Bank. At this time it was estimated that Palestinian NGOs, in the absence of official provision, had been providing 60 per cent of Palestine's health care, 50 per cent of hospital services, 100 per cent of disability care, at least 95 per cent of agricultural extension and around 30 per cent of educational services (Claudet 1996). These efforts had begun attracting increased international recognition and support from external agencies, but once the PNA was established NGOs quickly began to lose ground again as international donors quickly shifted their focus to the new authority. This change particularly affected those NGOs involved in service delivery (UNSCO 1995). At the same time, NGOs also lost access to much of their funding from the Palestine Liberation Organization (PLO) on which they had previously heavily depended (Sullivan 1996). As a result, the World Bank introduced the idea in 1996 of an NGO Trust Fund to assist NGOs, with an allocated budget of US$14 million.

The establishment of the PNA led to a major policy debate on the role of NGOs and civil society within the new arrangements (PNGO 1995; 1997). This debate was conducted among leftists, nationalists, international NGOs and international donor agencies within a flurry of workshops, conferences and meetings that took place on this theme. The various participants reflected a range of different views and ambitions for actors within the new landscape. Multilateral agencies were keen to stress aspects of the 'reconstruction' and 'good governance' of Palestinian society after the long years of occupation and began to fund various types of 'democratization' projects (Carapico 2002). Many NGOs worried that they could lose their sources of funding as a result of the shift of resources to the PNA. Some Palestinian political factions feared that they would lose ground after being excluded from the peace negotiations (Hammami 1995). Many observers feared the emergence of an undemocratic state (Hammami 1995; Hilal 1998; Sullivan 1996, 2000). There was also a view in some quarters that real civil society in the Occupied Territories could still not emerge because it required the tence of democratic citizenship as a precondition, and there was still no authentic Palestinian state (Bishara 1995: 135–60).

NGO roles in 'building' civil society

Despite the debates about civil society taking place at this time, the transitional period in Palestine did provide new space for NGOs to contribute to the changing institutional landscape in the Occupied Territories. How did NGOs see themselves as contributing to this process of building civil society after the transfer of authority? A primarily ethnographic approach was adopted for the study. This made it possible to observe the ways in which NGOs attempted to institutionalize their new roles, the informal interactions that took place between people in different sectors of society, and to gain insights into people's changing perceptions of authority and power. Four well-established NGOs were selected and analysed, referred to here anonymously in view of the current political sensitivities and uncertain political climate. Each NGO aimed to eradicate inequalities by focusing on a particular disadvantaged section of the population: women in rural areas (Organization 1), women and children from poorer families (Organization 2), education and cultural needs of poor women and children (Organization 3), and the elderly and the disabled (Organization 4).

The first aim emphasized by the NGOs was that of building social equality through strategies of 'sustainable development', with each NGO defining such strategies differently. For Organization 1, sustainable development could be pursued on three levels: within the agricultural sector, within Palestinian society more widely, and within the organization itself through staff and clients' efforts to work together to strengthen local institutions of democracy and civil society – by combining economic development with democracy and civil society goals. For Organization 4, the challenge was to build social equality through organizational transformation. After the Oslo accords, it moved from a traditional associational model towards a new identity as a 'developmental charitable organization'. Organization 3 placed gender and class at the centre of its strategy and supported economic, educational and cultural activities alongside provision of women's health services. All of the NGOs except Organization 4 considered gender support to be an essential component of 'building civil society'.

The attempt to build democracy was seen as complementary to that of strengthening civil society and there was a strong emphasis among the NGOs on the idea of 'community participation'. Community participation was defined as having three components: increasing the involvement of beneficiaries in public and community decision-making, involving the community in the decision-making of organizations, and empowering the community at large. Organization 3 showed the strongest emphasis on promoting participation in public decision-making through its central focus on culture and gender equality. For example, the establishment of a cultural centre for girls and boys in a culturally relatively conservative area reflected this commitment to challenge wider social and cultural beliefs. The NGO's members were actively involved in the preparation for a Women's Model Parliament, a project that initially started as collaboration between women's organizations in Jerusalem and West Bank to articulate their expectations of the future personal status law. These efforts eventually led to the formulation of a personal status law and its adoption after extensive lobbying efforts, as well as contributions to extensive press debates on the subject at this time (Moussa 1998; Sharida 1998).

The first two organizations also participated in the Women's Model Parliament and were concerned about debating social issues more publicly. Organization 2 facilitated the emergence of a public space for school children by establishing a library in one of Gaza's most crowded refugee camps. The library then served as a meeting place for both local children and NGO members. The children also utilized the library for social and recreational activities, since there was an acute lack of suitable public space within the refugee camp. Some organizations were also interested in enlarging 'public space' within their own organizational structures. Organizations 1 and 3 both issued newsletters and set up bulletin boards through which their members could express their views. There were also lectures and seminars organized by Organization 3's members on general topics, which were not necessarily dedicated to the formal objectives of the organization. Organization 4, despite the difficulties of the cases that it served, had recreational and sports tournaments, but these were confined to male staff.

The organizations in the study all mentioned the importance of improving legal codes for regulating relationships between NGOs, the PNA and the political opposition, and between wider civil society and the authority. However, only Organization 1, as a member of the Palestinian NGO Network, was specifically active in lobbying efforts to institutionalize progressive legislation for NGOs. Organization 4's interviewees emphasized the importance of progressive regulation, believing that this would reduce the likelihood that some PNA personnel could abuse their powers and mistreat NGOs, and that it could also protect them from pressure from the Israeli authorities. There have been several cases in which charitable societies have been shut down by security forces on the pretext that they were affiliated with Islamic factions.

The expectations of international agencies led to pressure on Palestinian NGOs to improve the values and practices of 'transparency', 'professionalism' and 'accountability'. For Organization 1's interviewees, NGOs could only be regarded as a part of civil society if they could effectively demonstrate transparency. It was suggested that NGOs could achieve this by publishing their annual reports and budgets in the newspapers to show their openness and lack of secrecy. Many NGOs also began to stress 'professionalism', which was usually taken to mean that they should not behave in a clientelistic way with political parties to which they were sympathetic, a practice for which NGOs had been criticized during the Intifada. Professionalism was also understood as meaning that NGOs considered issues of sustainability and long-term strategy as far as possible, and this led to broader discussions of institutionalization. Professionalism led also to the introduction of business management practices into the work of NGOs, such as the gaining of ISO certification by Organization 1. Another concept gaining ground among NGOs was that of legitimacy, understood as gaining trust from the members of communities in which they worked. This credibility also gained strength from the growing acknowledgement of many PNA officials of the value of NGO services.

By 1997–98, the first three case-study NGOs were each working hard to improve their profile and image by stressing transparency, professionalism and accountability, seen by the NGOs as key instruments in their struggle to present themselves as legitimate 'civil society organizations'. However, the more charitable, religious section of the NGO community as exemplified by Organization 4, which had an Islamic religious background, placed less emphasis on these values than did the more political and secular NGOs. Part of the reason for this was that it was the latter NGOs which received the bulk of the international funding that became available to Palestinian civil society, and with these funds came both pressure and encouragement to stress NGO accountability, transparency and professionalism.

Conclusion: continuing constraints

NGOs' attempts to build civil society were curtailed by the intensification of Israeli occupation, problems with relations with the PNA and decreases in access to economic and social capital. After the interim agreement Oslo II, Palestinian land was divided into three categories of control so that land in many territories was formally shared with the Israeli military. Such a division severely restricted the PNA's powers during this transitional period and also impacted negatively on the work of the NGOs. For example, Organization 1, which worked on agricultural development, experienced new difficulties in working with rural communities because the PNA was not the sole authority in charge of land within the West Bank and Gaza. The borders with Israel also remained closed for Palestinians. This affected the work of most organizations under study with headquarters in the West Bank or Jerusalem, and it also constrained their ability to network with other similar organizations. In addition, it restricted communication between like-minded organizations located in the West Bank and Gaza. Deteriorating economic conditions caused by the border closure, especially in the Gaza Strip, led NGOs to carry out new tasks, which were not always firmly within their organizational capacities. For instance, Organizations 1 and 3 – which worked predominantly in agriculture and culture respectively – began to organize free medical camp days with other local NGOs to provide free health services for residents.

Relationships between NGOs and the PNA were also problematic. The continuing lack of legal codes restricted NGO room for manoeuvre in relation to the PNA and there was no clear division of responsibilities. Initiatives of PNA ministries towards NGOs depended on the people in charge rather than on clear policies. Even 'well-intentioned' or sympathetic officials found it difficult to overcome the organizational and bureaucratic limitations within their ministries. Indeed, all of the NGOs under study complained of inconsistencies in the policies of the PNA towards them and their work. The decrease in economic and social capital impacted negatively on civil society by weakening individual NGOs and also by undermining the ties between them, thus affecting the whole sector. Competition for scarce resources was also intensified by donors' exacting funding requirements. The demand for greater professionalism caused many NGOs to focus on efficiency while ignoring aspects of building firmer social and moral values within the sector (Cameron 1999). In this way, the efforts of NGOs to strengthen new aspects of their organizational capacities under external pressure led many to endanger aspects of their older social capital in the form of already existing trust, rootedness and relationships.

The contribution of NGOs to the wider effort of strengthening civil society in Palestine can be usefully seen as a process of negotiation and struggle in which NGOs have attempted to carve out a larger public space. Despite the wide-ranging political and historical constraints within the Palestine context, NGOs have managed to secure roles in public service provision, expanded the public sphere and have begun to influence legal codes. However, progress has been hindered by the PNA's overall lack of sovereignty, which ultimately led it to seek tighter control over whatever resources it could command, and it has used monitoring and sometimes coercion to this end. The PNA and the NGOs are also both subject to the power of the Israeli Occupation, which has struggled to control the actions of both.

The process of strengthening civil society has been severely limited by the gradual decrease in economic resources available to the NGOs and by the relative weaknesses of networks of social capital within wider civil society. In view of these limitations, progress has been slow in terms of building a political movement towards a higher degree of democratization (as many Arab writers have described civil society). However, the dynamism of non-governmental social actors in the Palestinian areas may yet contribute to such processes in the future. The cultural and historical presence of NGOs in the Palestinian areas will continue to combine with the ongoing political and social needs of local communities.

References

Barghouthi, M. and Giacaman, R. (1990) 'The emergence of an infrastructure of resistance', in J. Nassar and R. Heacock (eds), *Intifada: Palestinians at the Crossroads*, New York: Praeger.

Bishara, A. (1995) 'Democratisation in the Middle East context', in J. Hippler (ed.), *The Democratisation of Disempowerment: The Problem of Democracy in the Third World*, London and Amsterdam: Pluto Press with the Transnational Institute (TNI).

Cameron, J. (1999) 'Generating national NGOs: a comparison of national NGO support activities in Ethiopia, Nepal, and Palestine', unpublished paper presented at the Development Studies Association (DSA) Conference, University of Bath, UK.

Carapico, S. (2002) 'Foreign aid for promoting democracy in the Arab World', *The Middle East Journal*, 56(3): 379–95.

Clark, J.D. and Balaj, B. (1996) *NGOs in the West Bank and Gaza*, Washington DC: World Bank.

Claudet, S. (1996) *The Changing Role of Palestinian NGOs since the Establishment of the Palestinian Authority (1994–1996)*, Washington DC: World Bank.

Hammami, R. (1995) 'NGOs: the professionalization of politics', *Race & Class* 37(2): 51–63.

Hilal, J. (1998) *The Palestinian Political System: Organisation after Oslo*, Ramallah, West Bank: Institute for the Study of Democracy.

Moussa, E. (1998) 'And the Palestinian model parliament wins', *Al Hayat Al Jadida*, p. 20.

PNGO (1995) 'A suggested framework for relations between Palestinian NGOs and the Palestinian Authority', Perspective on the PNGO Network Newsletter, PNGO, I.

——(1997) 'More on legislation concerning charitable societies, social bodies and private associations', Perspective on the PNGO Network Newsletter, PNGO, III.

Sharida, M.H.A. (1998) 'Quiet dialogue on the Women Model Parliament: women and legislature', *Al Ayyam*, p. 11.

Shawa, S.A. (2001) *Building Civil Society: Case Studies of Four Palestinian NGOs*. Unpublished PhD dissertation, London School of Economics.

Sullivan, D.J. (1996) 'NGOs in Palestine: agents of development and foundation of civil society', *Journal of Palestine Studies* 25(3): 93–100.

——(2000) 'NGOs and development in the Arab world: the critical importance of a strong partnership between government and civil society', www.mideastinfo.com/arabngo.htm (accessed 30 March 2004).

UNSCO (1995) *Putting Peace to Work*, Gaza: United Nations Office of the Special Coordinator in the Occupied Territories.

Part VIII

The case for global civil society

21 Globalization and civil society

Mary Kaldor

The reinvention of civil society in the 1970s and 1980s has to be understood in the context of the process we call globalization. We tend to think of globalization in terms of the spread of multinational corporations or of global culture, but during this period the term 'civil society' was resurrected to mean a new form of non-party politics – the so-called new social movements, the dissidents in Eastern Europe, the new focus on single issues such as human rights, the environment or women. This new wave of activism developed new forms of organizing as a way of getting around the dominance and conservatism of political parties and of finding new avenues for political influence and social change. In effect, the political parties controlled access to the state, so the new activists sought to influence society directly through their own actions or they tried to influence political institutions at global and local levels. By linking up with similar groups and individuals across borders, by promoting global norms and rules, civil society actors, like multinational corporations or the stars of sports or popular music, became agents of globalization.

Some authors in this book have argued that civil society is a Western concept that is being imposed on the rest of the world with undesirable consequences for social justice, notions of community, and for the diversity of cultural values. Some suggest that the concept should be abandoned and political activists should re-emphasize the role of the state and political parties. Others propose that the term should be adjusted to different cultural contexts, so as to reflect more communitarian tendencies in other parts of the world.

In this chapter, I want to defend the concept. To be sure, it has its origins in the Western Enlightenment. It is true that Western donors promote a neoliberal understanding of civil society that is used to spread market economies. Nevertheless, it is a term that has an emancipatory potential as a way of developing progressive global governance and, in particular, for minimizing war. Precisely because the term is so widely accepted, it can be utilized in a subversive way, to open up public space for the poor and excluded.

To develop this argument, I will briefly discuss the meaning of the concept. I will then discuss how the term is applied in the current global context, and its relevance for different political streams of thinking.

The changing meanings of civil society

The concept of civil society has changed since it came into widespread use in the late seventeenth century (for an elaboration of this discussion, see Kaldor 2003). For early modern thinkers, there was no distinction between civil society and the state. Civil society was a type of state characterized by a social contract. Civil society was a society governed by laws, based on the principle of equality before the law, in which everyone including the ruler (at least in the Lockean conception) was subject to the law – in other words, a social contract agreed among the individual members of society.

It was not until the nineteenth century that civil society became understood as something distinct from the state. It was Hegel who defined civil society as the intermediate realm between the family and the state, where the individual becomes a public person and through membership in various institutions is able to reconcile the particular and the universal. Hegel's definition of civil society included the economy and was to be taken up by Marx and Engels, who saw civil society as the 'theatre of history'.

The definition narrowed again in the twentieth century, when civil society came to be understood as the realm not only between the state and the family but between the market, state and family – in other words, the realm of culture, ideology, and political debate. The Italian Marxist Antonio Gramsci, the thinker most associated with this definition, drew the distinction between hegemony, based on consent, and domination, based on coercion.

Despite the changes in usage of the term, I want to suggest that all these different definitions had a common core meaning. They were about a rule-governed society based on the consent of individuals, or a society based on a social contract among individuals. The changing definitions of civil society expressed the different ways in which consent was generated in different periods and the different issues that were important. In other words, civil society, according to my definition, is the process through which individuals negotiate, argue, struggle against or agree with each other and with the centres of political and economic authority. Through voluntary associations, movements, parties and unions, the individual is able to act publicly. Thus in the early modern period the main concern was civil rights – freedom from fear. Hence civil society was a society where laws replace physical coercion, arbitrary arrest, and so on. In the nineteenth century, the issue was political rights and the actors in civil society were the emerging bourgeoisie. In the twentieth century, it was the workers' movement that was challenging the state and the issue was economic and social emancipation – hence the further narrowing of the term.

Not only did all these definitions have this common core of meaning, but also they all conceived of civil society as territorially tied. Civil society was inextricably linked up with the territorial state. It was contrasted with other states characterized by coercion – the empires of the East. It was also contrasted with premodern societies, which lacked a state and lacked the concept of individualism – Scottish Highlanders or American Indians, for example. And, above all, it was contrasted with the sphere of international relations, which was equated with the state of nature because it lacked a single authority. Indeed, it can be argued that the achievement of civil society depended in part on war and imperialism. The social contract that underlay the development of civil society in Western states could be interpreted as a bargain hammered out in wartime. As Tilly has argued, states were able to raise taxes and recruit soldiers in wartime in return for great civil, political and eventually economic and social rights (see Tilly 1990).

Moreover, the emergence of civil society in Western Europe, linked to the rise of capitalism, cannot be disentangled from increased coercion elsewhere. Mamdani has shown how the rights enjoyed by Europeans in towns in Africa were associated with the imposition of a coercive interpretation of customary or tribal law in the hinterland (Mamdani 1996). Likewise, the second serfdom in Eastern Europe, or the spread of slavery in the Americas, has to be understood both as a reaction to and a condition for the development of Western Europe. This widening gap was increasingly expressed in the discourse of civil society; notions such as 'orientalism' were invented to explain the 'backwardness' of other societies.

The revival of civil society

The revival of the idea of civil society in the 1970s and 1980s, simultaneously in Latin America and Eastern Europe, broke the link with the state. In both cases, the term 'civil society' proved a useful concept in opposing militarized regimes. Latin Americans were opposing military dictatorships; East Europeans were opposing totalitarianism – a sort of war society. Both came to the conclusion that overthrow of their regimes 'from above' was not feasible; rather it was necessary to change society. For both, civil society referred to autonomy and self-organization. The emphasis was on withdrawal from the state – creating islands of civic engagement – a concept shared by both East Europeans and Latin Americans. East Europeans also used terms such as 'antipolitics', 'living in truth' – the notion of refusing the lies of the regime – or 'parallel polis' – the idea of creating their own Aristotelian community based on the 'good', in other words moral, life.

As well as the emphasis on autonomy and civil organization, civil society also acquired a global meaning. This was a period of growing interconnectedness, increased travel and communication, even before the advent of the Internet. The emergence of 'islands of civic engagement' was made possible by two things. The first was the formation of links with like-minded groups in other countries: the Latin Americans were supported by North American human-rights groups; the East Europeans made links with Central European peace and human rights groups, who supported them materially and publicized their cases, and put pressure on governments and institutions. The second was the existence of international human-rights legislation to which their governments subscribed and which could be used as a form of pressure. For Latin America, it was the human-rights legislation that was important; for East Europe, the Helsinki agreement of 1975 in which East European governments signed up to human rights provided a platform for new groups such as Charter 77 or the Workers' Defence Committee (KOR) in Poland.

In other words, through international links and appeals to international authorities, these groups were able to create political space. Keck and Sikkink (1998), in their book on transnational activism, talk about the 'boomerang effect' whereby instead of addressing your government directly, appeals to the international community bounce back, as it were, and put pressure on governments to tolerate certain activities.

This transnational or global aspect of the new understanding of civil society was widely neglected by Western commentaries of the period, perhaps because they understood civil society within their own traditions of thought. Yet it was stressed by the new thinkers themselves, certainly in East Europe. George Konrad, the Hungarian writer, and my favourite of these thinkers, used the word 'globalization' in his book *Anti-Politics* written in 1982. Václav Havel talked about the 'global technological civilization'.

Thus the new understanding of civil society represented both a withdrawal from the state and a move towards global rules and institutions. Civil society still has that common core of meaning, as the medium through which a social contract is negotiated, pressed for, debated with the centres of political and economic authority. But nowadays, the centres of political and economic authority are global as well as national and local. They include international institutions and multinational corporations. Essentially civil society today has to be understood as the medium through which a set of global rules and a framework for managing global affairs are being constituted. Linked to this is the erosion of absolutist concepts of sovereignty, the idea that the state is increasingly subject to global rules that its own citizens can influence, at least in principle. In other words, the new meaning of civil society had the potential for overcoming the distinction between domestic civil society and external war as well as between consensual and coercive societies. It is sometimes said that there were no new ideas in the 1989 revolutions – that they just wanted to be like the West. But I think this new understanding of civil society was the big new idea, an idea that was to contribute a new set of global arrangements in the 1990s.

Political positions on globalization

Globalization is often depicted as an anarchic process – an inexorable, deterministic phenomenon. One of the advantages of analysing the role of civil society is that it allows us to locate agency. Globalization is shaped by rules set by governments and international institutions, even if those rules take the form of deregulation. Key to our concerns about globalization is the changing role of the state as a rule-making institution.

Global Civil Society 2003 (Kaldor, Anheier and Glasius 2003) sets out four political positions on globalization, positions that relate to the future direction of rule-making. Each of these positions has different versions of the concept of civil society. The first position is the *Supporters*. These are the people who declared that the 1989 revolutions were a triumph for the West and opened the way for the spread of the Western system – representative democracy plus market economies. They understood civil society as what the West has – a passive phenomenon that eases the functioning of elections and market reform, and that provides a social safety net for the victims of market reform. In principle, they support free trade, free capital movements, as well as free labour movements and human rights, and many envisage the eventual demise of the nation-state. (In practice, many merge into the neo-conservatives described below in that they only accept part of this agenda.) These are the people associated with the neoliberal version of civil society, which has been described in other chapters of this volume. They provide funds to Western NGOs to spread Western ideals throughout the world. Indeed, those who insist that civil society is a Western concept are usually criticizing a neoliberal version of civil society.

The neoliberals are often confused with the neoconservatives in the USA. However, the neoconservatives are not supporters of globalization *per se* – rather they can be described as *regressive* globalizers. The *Regressives* are those who support globalization when the rules favour particular groups of people, when globalization benefits the few. Thus the neoconservatives favour free trade and free capital movements only when it benefits US trade and capital. They are usually negative about the free movement of people or about a global human-rights regime. Neoconservatives favour globalization in so far as it benefits the USA. They also want to spread the US system but they believe it has to be done through force. Part of the neoconservative narrative is the idea that the USA brought democracy to Europe as a result of World War Two. They are trying to do the same thing in Iraq today.

Regressives also include the various religious and nationalist movements that have increased in importance since the early 1990s. These groups see civil society as a bounded concept either in terms of the state or in terms of ethnicity and/or religion. Some groups tend to have an old-fashioned view of sovereignty; in general their aim is to capture state power in the name of an ethnicity or religion and to exclude others from citizenship. It is often said that Israel is the only democracy in the Middle East. Israel does, of course, have a lively civil society but it is a bounded civil society based on war against and exclusion of other ethnicities. Some regressive groups have more global aspirations in that they favour transnational Islamic states – for example, Al Qaeda favours the restoration of the Caliphate in the Middle East – and some have a less statist orientation. Thus Ali Bulac, a Turkish scholar, identifies civil society with the Islamic community and sees it as a counter to the state. According to Bulac, 'This modern state developed into a monster which controls all aspects of social and cultural life: law, education, art, religion. It imposes a common nationality on many ethnicities; the logic of the state is ethnic cleansing internally and nationalist wars globally'(quoted in Zubaida 2001: 238). The individual has to be freed from the state not as the atom of liberal theory but as part of an Islamic community. Bulac envisages coexisting self-governing religious communities, rather, it seems, on the model of the Ottoman Empire. He cites *Medina Vasikasi*, the charter drawn up by the Prophet to regulate the relations between the new Islamic community and other tribes.

Many of these groups use violence as a deliberate strategy for achieving their goals and many reject notions of individual rights in favour of notions of community. For this reason, it is often argued they cannot be considered part of civil society. Yet bounded civil societies in the West historically involved similar contradictions. In wartime, Western citizens became communitarians and their ideas of individual rights did not extend beyond borders.

I call these groups regressive rather than rejectionist because although they favour bounded communities, they also make use of global infrastructure and spread their messages across borders. Typically they are organized both through more traditional hierarchical structures and through global networks linked to diasporas. Many of these networks involve state structures or bits of state structures. Often they amount to a kind of parallel society, involving different components for finance, welfare, education or communication. Many of these groups have special schools (Madrassahs, the new Hindu schools in tribal areas, or Christian schools in America, for instance) and humanitarian NGOs who provide social security to, for example, newly arrived immigrants. They make use of the 'new media': Internet, circulation of videocassettes, TV and radio. Finance often consists of criminal activities, diaspora support, or plunder.

A third group is the *Rejectionists*. These are the groups who want to roll back globalization and restore the nation-state. They argue that it was neoliberal governments that introduced new rules allowing for the free movement of trade and capital and that these rules can be reversed. Often these groups are left-wing and believe that only the state can provide social justice. They are deeply sceptical of civil society, viewing it as a bourgeois concept designed to favour capital, and which therefore blocks full human emancipation. Human emancipation must involve economic and social emancipation and, on this line of thinking, the abolition of private property. Like the Regressives, the Rejectionists are also communitarians favouring community over individual rights. Of course, they are in favour of political movements of poor people – workers, peasants, students – but they prefer the term 'social movements' to 'civil society'.

The Rejectionists share with the Regressives a bounded conception of civil society. The Rejectionists have a tendency to overlook the violence and oppression of statist solutions, the ways in which preparations for war infringed individual rights – the reasons for the revival of civil society in the first place. Some Regressives may favour rules and rights within the community but view war and violence as legitimate strategies for the protection of those rights. Others, such as Bulac for example, may favour the regulation of communities but limit the freedom of individuals to choose communities or to influence the overall rules. My concern, in the aftermath of 11 September 2001 and the Iraq war, is that these two groups could combine to limit the scope for public debate on a global scale and to reverse some of the achievements of global governance in the 1990s, particularly in the area of human rights. In a world of greater global interconnectedness, it is impossible, and it was always difficult, to establish hard boundaries – notions of a bounded civil society merely mean that more violence is likely to spill over borders. The Bush administration justifies war in the name of spreading an American version of civil society but already the 'war on terror' is circumscribing political tolerance and infringing civil liberties, as in Guantanamo. The Islamic militants regard terrorism as legitimate self-defence against outsiders, but the killing of civilians calls into question the very notion of an Islamic civil society.

The final group is the *Reformers*. These are the people who favour globalization, who believe it carries the potential to end wars and to spread social justice, but only insofar as the rules that shape globalization benefit the many rather than the few. They are the inheritors of the Latin American and East European concepts of civil society. They see global governance as a set of rules necessarily based on consent, which can supplant force as a way of settling international disputes. For them global civil society is necessary as a way of constituting and being constituted by global governance in much the same way that civil society related to individual Western states.

I share the view of Immanuel Kant that civil society, in the sense of rules based on the consent of individuals, can only be achieved in a global context. According to Kant (1992 [1784]: 47): 'The problem of establishing a perfect civil society is subordinate to the problem of a law-governed external relationship with other states, and cannot be solved unless the latter is also solved.' In that sense, civil society has always been an aspiration and what was achieved in the West was always imperfect. In the 1990s, the growth of global civil society did bring us closer to a rule-governed international system, with a series of innovations such as the International Criminal Court or the Kyoto protocol on Climate Change. Of course, it is true that global civil society was dominated by Western NGOs and that multinational corporations and their neoliberal version of civil society had a predominant influence in shaping global rules. But just as political rights gained by the bourgeoisie in the nineteenth century provided space for the workers' movement, so the term 'civil society' legitimizes the participation of marginalized political groups on a global scale.

The growing regressive political currents threaten a roll-back of the global achievements of the 1990s. But there is one significant contradiction in the regressive position. The fact that they use the term 'civil society', even if it has a neoliberal, nationalist or Islamic connotation, offers us a common platform on which those who favour the global, non-violent version based on individual rights can challenge other versions.

References

Kaldor, M. (2003) *Global Civil Society: An Answer to War*, Cambridge: Polity Press.

——, Anheier, H. and Glasius, M. (2003) *Global Civil Society 2003*, Oxford: Oxford University Press.

Kant, I. (1992 [1784]) *Idea for a Universal History with a Cosmopolitan Purpose*, in Kant, *Political Writing*, ed. H. Reiss, trans. H.B. Nisbet, Cambridge: Cambridge University Press.

Keck, M.E. and Sikkink, K. (1998) *Activists Beyond Borders*, Ithaca: Cornell University Press.

Mamdani, M. (1996) *Citizen and State in Africa*, Princeton: Princeton University Press.

Tilly, C. (1992) *Coercion, Capital and European States* AD *990–1992*, Oxford: Blackwell.

Zubaida, S. (2001) 'Civil society: community and democracy in the Middle East', in S. Kaviraj and S. Khilnani (eds), *Civil Society: History and Possibilities*, Cambridge: Cambridge University Press.

22 Global civil society and global governmentality

Ronnie D. Lipschutz

Since the early 1990s, the concept of 'global civil society' has been the focus of a good deal of research and criticism (Colas 2002; Drainville 1998; Hopgood 2000; Korten 1999; Lipschutz 1992; Pasha and Blaney 1998; Walzer 1994), and with good reason. On the one hand, there has certainly been an efflorescence of local, national and transnational activism, lobbying, and volunteerism since the 1980s (Kaldor, Anheier and Glasius 2003); on the other, we face at least two problems in theorizing and assessing the phenomenon. First, as Alejandro Colas (2002) has perceptively pointed out, much of this earlier work (including my own) is ahistorical and divorced from the state. Second, while there has emerged a clear distinction between *transnational civic associations* (here I draw on Paul Wapner's term 'world civic politics'; Wapner 1996), which have a more bureaucratic and bourgeois orientation, and *transnational social activists*, engaged in 'world social activism', and which tend to be more protest-oriented and engaged with the 'political' (Arendt 1958; Wolin 1996), the relationship of both to global politics and economics remains somewhat unclear. Moreover, this division of labour raises the question of how to address those actors that are clearly based in the market yet purport to be engaged in social and political activity (here I refer to corporate associations and the 'corporate social responsibility' movement).[1]

In this chapter, I draw on the work of Michel Foucault (1991) and situate global civil society (GCS) in what is best understood as 'global governmentality'. I argue here that much of GCS is deeply imbricated with the market – perhaps intentionally, perhaps not – and is political only in a rather impoverished sense. Indeed, global civil society is a product of *global* liberalism and stands in a problematic relationship to the international system of states. As I have asked elsewhere (Lipschutz 1999), if there is a *global* civil society, where is the *global* state to which it corresponds? Colas (2002) argues that this civil society is *international* and corresponds to the state system and its national states, while Martin Shaw (2000) posits the emergence of a 'global state' encompassing the industrial heartland of the West, which may offer the political framework for global civil society. I suggest that the hegemony of US neoliberalism expresses itself through governmentality (Lipschutz 2002c), reminiscent to some degree of the Empire of Michael Hardt and Antonio Negri's (2000) eponymous book, and it is this arrangement of global management and order through which global civil society exerts most of its efforts.

Since global civil society has been defined and discussed elsewhere in this volume, I begin this chapter with a discussion of the relationship between global civil society and global governmentality. I then examine what this means in terms of our understanding of politics under contemporary conditions of globalization. Finally, I conclude with some remarks about the implications of this relationship as it concerns the possibility of *political* action by GCS, specifically where global social regulation is concerned.

Governmentality and global politics

As I have argued elsewhere (Lipschutz 2002a; 2004), the global unevenness of social regulation – indeed, its absence in many instances – has led to a transnational version of a phenomenon observed during the nineteenth and early twentieth centuries in most industrial countries: the emergence of populist and social efforts to impose political constraints over the 'self-regulating' markets that have emerged out of the globalization of neoliberalism (Polanyi 2001). As suggested above, *civic action* occurs via 'world civic politics', the activities of increasingly professionalized and bureaucratized non-governmental organizations and corporate actors who deal largely in the formulation, implementation and reform of transnational public policies. These organizations rely on lobbying, influence and expertise to accomplish their objectives (Wapner 1996). *Social activism* takes place largely via transnational social movements, composed of a broad range of individuals and organizations, united through coalitions, intent on mobilizing members and publics so as to induce governments and institutions to change their policies or even reject them (Colas 2002). Coalitions of the latter type have become most visible through their engagement in public protests (which, I would argue, is the only venue currently available for the *demos* to act directly in the political realm) and, more recently, in the World and European Social Forums. But both civic action and social activism take place in relation to global governmentality.

Governmentality, as Michel Foucault put it, is about *management*, about ensuring and maintaining the 'right disposition of things' of that which is being governed or ruled. It is

> the ensemble formed by institutions, procedures, analyses and reflections, the calculations and tactics that allow the exercise of this very specific albeit complex form of power, which has as its target populations, as its principal form of knowledge, political economy, and as its essential technical means apparatuses of security
>
> (Foucault 1991:102)

This 'right disposition' has as its purpose not the action of government itself, but the welfare of the population, the improvement of its condition, the increase of its wealth, longevity, health, and so on (1991: 100; see also Dean 1999, Chapter 1). Anything that challenges this disposition is to be absorbed; anything that disrupts it is to be eliminated. Foucault's notion of governmentality contrasts with that of *sovereignty*, which posits the autonomy of the Prince's person and property from that over which he ruled.

Governmentality is also associated with the practice of *biopolitics*, which, according to Mitchell Dean (1999: 99), 'is concerned with matters of life and death, with birth and propagation, with health and illness, both physical and mental, and with the processes that sustain or retard the optimization of the life of a population'.

Biopolitics must then also concern the social, cultural, environmental, economic and geographic conditions under which humans live, procreate, become ill, maintain health or become healthy, and die. From this perspective biopolitics is concerned with the family, with housing, living and working conditions, with what we call 'lifestyle', with public health issues, patterns of migration, levels of economic growth and the standards of living. It is concerned with the biosphere in which humans dwell (Dean 1999: 99).

Populations, as conceived here, are not composed of sovereign or autonomous individuals, as conceived under liberalism. Rather, they are analysed and treated as homogeneous collections of people moulded into particular categories and forms, who regard themselves as belonging to these categories and forms and behave as such.

Who or what, then, are the agents in a system of governmentality? The biopolitical management of human populations and their environments is the task of both the agencies of government and the populations themselves. The former includes the myriad of governmental and international agencies, public and private associations, and even non-governmental organizations and corporations that populate the globe, each of which has its own instrumental function as well as normative goals. This is not to say that all of these actors are in coherence with one another in either their activities or objectives. They are, however, engaged increasingly in what Kanishka Jayasuriya (2001) and others (Gill 1995; 2002) have described as the instantiation of a global 'economic constitutionalism' associated with neoliberal globalization. As Jayasuriya puts it, 'Economic constitutionalism refers to the attempt to treat the market as a constitutional order with its own rules, procedures, and institutions that operate to protect the market order from political interference' (2001: 452).

The latter, as suggested by the example above, involves populations behaving normally. Individuals comport themselves according to their specific population's standards of 'normality'. The right disposition of things is maintained through the standardization of populations within certain defined parameters, the self-disciplining of their own behaviour by individuals conforming to these parameters, and the disciplining function of surveillance and law that seeks to prevent any straying outside of those parameters. Taken together, these constrain individuals' practices to a 'zone of stability', or 'normality'. Power is then embedded within the hegemonic discourses that naturalize normality and reproduce themselves through associated practices. Resistance is possible, of course, but that risks losing the benefits of governmentality and biopolitics and, indeed, being marginalized completely. It is in this sense, as Foucault puts it (1980: 109–33), that we are the products of power circulating through society in capillary fashion.

It should be evident, perhaps, that the arrangement of rules, regulations and practices characteristic of contemporary capitalist states, operating under and through global neoliberalism, do not and cannot address more than a fraction of the 'welfare of populations'. Much of the remainder of this function is increasingly being provided through civil society, some of which has been drawn into existence in order to address these lacunae. That is to say, the projects of both civic actors and social activists are directed ultimately to the reorganization, stabilization and normalization of conditions that are seen as threats or disturbances to the welfare of those human populations and the 'order of things'. The precise methods of accomplishing these ends, as well as the specific parameters of the ends themselves, may be the focus of intense contestation, but the overall objective is the same: improvement in social welfare. No one is in favour of impoverishment and everyone wants people to be 'better off'. In this sense, much of what appears to be opposition – by civil society organizations in particular – is better understood as integral to governmentality.

One consequence of governmentality, however, is the severe constraints that it imposes upon politics. Although Ulrich Beck (2000) does not use the term governmentality in his work, his concept of 'subpolitics' captures much the same point. Today, many political matters are treated as technical and managerial problems, to be considered and addressed by non-elected experts rather than those who are directly affected. In a system of neoliberal governmentality, the structure of the decision-making process is already established when markets are organized. The markets themselves serve primarily to distribute resources, not for political ends.

To put this point more graphically, market-based, neoliberal democracy focuses on increasing the size of the pie, rather than dividing it fairly, in the view that absolute increases in rewards will limit objections to the process of allocation. This kind of 'politics' is structured to ensure that no one complains about the pie filling, since everyone's piece, however small it might be in comparison to others, is getting larger over time. Furthermore, the distribution of the pie becomes a technical and managerial task: people must fit certain standardized parameters – citizen, single parent, disabled – in order to receive their share. But there are no possibilities for people to decide what kind of pie they might want or, for that matter, whether they even want pie rather than some other kind of pudding.

Under these arrangements, therefore, notions of justice or equity or even politics are subsumed under the beneficent consequences of growth and trickle-down economics which, in turn, are also seen as providing the basis for opportunity. The means by which such growth takes place, and the power relations embedded within these means, are simply taken for granted, as the consequence of the 'natural' operation of markets. That there could be, and have been, alternative forms of economic and social organization, or that politics might encompass more than mere twiddling with the allocation of entitlements within a society, is made to appear as outlandish as (perhaps more outlandish than) discussions about aliens and UFOs.

Politics via markets?

One of the consequences of neoliberal global governmentality is that much civic action and social activism comes to be focused on politics via markets. By this I mean that most contemporary efforts to implement global social regulation utilize consumer pressure on capital and encouragement of 'corporate responsibility' as a means of improving labour conditions in factories, reducing environmental externalities from industry, and controlling production and shipment of various kinds of goods in cross-border commodity chains. Many of these campaigns have been highly successful in achieving their instrumental goals, but they have real limitations in political terms. These limitations become evident in apparel-industry campaigns (Lipschutz 2002b; 2004).

For example, there are at least a dozen civic action and social activism campaigns underway that are aimed at the Nike Corporation (Lipschutz 2002b). All focus on distributive strategies designed to improve health and safety conditions and to provide minimum wages in Nike's 600-odd subcontractors' plants scattered around the world. These campaigns have generated considerable public attention (although it is not clear that they have affected the company's financial performance), and Nike has responded energetically, concerned about its market share, its competitiveness and its image. The company has adopted codes of conduct, contracted out audits of its subcontractors' factories, and permitted independent monitors either to accompany auditors or conduct their own inspections. It has joined the Fair Labour Association and coestablished the Workers' and Communities' Association, as well as taken a number of other steps to improve both conditions of production and its own reputation. And while there apparently remain significant problems in many, if not all, of its subcontractors' operations, there has been a not inconsiderable amount of ratcheting upwards of conditions within the Nike subsystem of global apparel production (Lipschutz 2002b).

But what have been the *constitutive* political effects of these campaigns? How have these campaigns altered either corporation or capitalism in terms of *structure*? Nike offers improved conditions and higher wages to the workers in its subcontractors' factories, but both workers and consumers remain fully integrated into the regime of consumption that constitutes contemporary globalization and subjectifies those workers and consumers. Workers still have no power to make political decisions, and there are no changes either in the position of waged labour or in the structures of capitalism.

What is absent from civic action and from much social activism is any sense of the political inherent in the very notion of social policy or a recognition of the ways in which *power constitutes not only that which activists seek to change but the activists themselves.* Decisions must be made by those who are subjectified about what is necessary for the good and just life (Mouffe 2000; Polanyi 2001: Chapter 3). Instead of this, what we find are versions of what Sheldon Wolin attacks when he writes about 'fugitive democracy' (1996), that is, non-political decision-making, or Ulrich Beck's (2000) 'subpolitics' through markets and expertise, or what Chantal Mouffe (2000) calls the 'democratic paradox', in which liberalism seeks to constrain democracy.

Returning to the case of Nike, for example, there is a widely held expectation that, if the company manages to improve conditions in its subcontractors' plants, other corporations, subcontractors, and factory managers will go along in order to remain competitive. Manufacturers will impose standards on their own businesses in order to maintain the good reputation of their brand, to sustain and even increase profit margins, and because it is the 'right thing to do' (Fung, O'Rourke and Sabel 2001). There is only limited evidence, however, to indicate that such outcomes do follow. Moreover, if political conditions in a particular country are generally unfavourable to unions, collective bargaining and other workers' rights – and this is the case even where countries have ratified relevant International Labour Organization conventions – improvements in individual plants are not likely to have much impact on labour across the country as a whole (Lipschutz 2002a; 2002b; 2004).

Bringing politics back in

These observations reinforce my argument that social regulation and the general relationship between politics and economics are not simply matters that should be left to markets. Regulation of any sort inevitably means that both business and polity will have to pay some costs, which implies that resources must be redistributed. But the arguments and justifications for redistribution – and to whom they will be given and why – must come about through politics and the political, and this can only happen effectively *within* the communities where such laws are made, implemented and monitored, whether that be local or global. The globalization of social regulations is not irrelevant to this point, to be sure. Such rules set normative standards to which states ought to adhere and, having ratified them, citizens can demand that governments observe them (Keck and Sikkink 1998). But it is only through political action *within* political communities that people and societies will come to recognize and acknowledge the need for social regulations and accept them as a necessary part of global industrialization, development and economic growth.

What civil society activists ought to be engaged in, therefore, is 'bringing politics back in', through forms of face-to-face politics. Such politics are not only about the pursuit of shared interests, as collective action theorists generally describe it (Olson 1966), or the mobilization of resources, as some social movement theorists would have it (Tarrow 1998). They are also about productive power, about means as well as ends: *people decide and act*. They discover how power functions and how it constrains yet enables action and, as they act, they assert their political sovereignty and are transformed into sovereign subjects by their action. Examples of such politics can be multiplied manifold, and they are not just manifestations of 'friendly, ultraliberal' towns, such as the one in which I live (Santa Cruz, California). Among them are neighbourhood associations, environmental justice groups, labour unions, educational collectives, low-income housing advocates, renewable energy activists and, yes, even national liberation and resistance movements. Not all such politics are progressive, nor are they all non-violent, especially if we take at face value Foucault's dictum that 'politics is the continuation of war by other means' (Foucault 1980: 61). But better politics than war or governmentality.

Conclusion

The 'problem' of accounting for GCS in its many variants and alternatives, as well as explaining its relationship to global governance, arises for several reasons. First, many scholars are more interested in fostering the efficiency and transparency of non-governmental participation and process. Second, they seek to elucidate and develop mechanisms through which the desires, needs and interests of those blocked by powerful actors can be fulfilled (Keck and Sikkink 1998). They are less interested in the normative implications and consequences of how power is exercised and the results of that exercise (which I take to be the goal of political theory). The focus on efficiency and instrumentalities is a type of theorizing aptly suited to a liberal worldview, which eschews foundational questions of politics and power and deals with distribution rather than constitution. Such a focus accepts the deployment of power as a given and begs for dispensations from the powerful.

From this view, global civil society is less a 'problem' for power than a product of power. It is deeply enmeshed with practices of governmentality and biopolitics. It is a means whereby those matters that cannot or will not be addressed by the agents of the state or interstate institutions will, nonetheless, be dealt with by someone. This view of global civil society does not undermine the concept so much as it forces us to recognize how particular forms of society and governmentality are constituted and reconstituted, sometimes through the very agency that, at first glance, appears to be a means of opposition and resistance, if not liberation. It also motivates us to ask whether it is possible to (re)create forms of political sovereignty that can function, perhaps, in a counterhegemonic way to challenge the discourses of neoliberalism.

Note

1 A longer and somewhat different version of this chapter appears in Michael Barnett and Raymond Duvall (eds), *Power and Global Governance* (Cambridge: Cambridge University Press, forthcoming). The advice and comments of Barnett, Duvall, David Newstone and others has been extremely helpful. Support for this research has been provided by Sokka University America, the Aspen Institute's Non-profit Sector Research Fund, the University of California Institute for Labour and Employment, the University of California Institute on Global Conflict and Cooperation, and the Academic Senate of UC-Santa Cruz.

References

Arendt, H. (1958) *The Human Condition*, Chicago: University of Chicago Press.

Beck, U. (2000) *What is Globalization?*, Cambridge: Polity Press.

Colas, A. (2002) *International Civil Society*, Cambridge: Polity Press.

Dean, M. (1999) *Governmentality – Power and Rule in Modern Society*, London: Sage.

Drainville, A. (1998) 'The fetishism of global civil society: global governance, transnational urbanism and sustainable capitalism in the world economy', in M.P. Smith and L. E. Guarnizo (eds), *Transnationalism from Below: Comparative Urban and Community Research*, New Brunswick: Transaction.

Foucault, M. (1980) *Power/Knowledge*, trans. Colin Gordon, New York: Pantheon.

——(1991) 'Governmentality', in G. Burchell, C. Gordon and P. Miller (eds) *The Foucault Effect: Studies in Governmentality*, Chicago: University of Chicago Press.

Fung, A., O'Rourke, D. and Sabel, C. (2001) 'Realizing labour standards – how transparency, competition, and sanctions could improve working conditions worldwide,' *Boston Review*, 26(1) (February/March), available at www.bostonreview.net/BR26.1/fung.html (accessed 20 April 2004).

Gill, S. (1995) 'The global panopticon? The neoliberal state, economic life, and democratic surveillance', *Alternatives*, 2(1) (January–March): 1–50.

——(2002) 'Constitutionalizing inequality and the clash of globalizations', *International Studies Review*, 4(2) (Summer): 47–66.

Hardt, M. and Negri, A. (2000) *Empire*, Cambridge MA: Harvard University Press.

Hopgood, S. (2000) 'Reading the small print in global civil society: the inexorable hegemony of the liberal self', *Millennium*, 29(1): 1–25.

Jayasuriya, K. (2001) 'Globalization, sovereignty, and the rule of law: from political to economic constitutionalism?', *Constellations*, 8(4): 412–60.

Kaldor, M., Anheier, H. and Glasius, M. (eds) (2003) *Global Civil Society 2003*, Oxford: Oxford University Press.

Keck, M. and Sikkink, K. (1998) *Activists Beyond Borders – Advocacy Networks in International Politics*, Ithaca: Cornell University Press.

Korten, D. (1999) *Globalizing Civil Society*, New York: Seven Stories Press.

Lipschutz, R. (1992) 'Reconstructing world politics: the emergence of global civil society', *Millennium*, 21(3) (winter): 389–420.

——(1999) 'From local knowledge and practice to global governance', in M. Hewson and T.J. Sinclair (eds), *Approaches to Global Governance Theory*, Albany: State University of New York Press.

——(2002a) 'Doing well by doing good? Transnational regulatory campaigns, social activism, and impacts on state sovereignty', in J. Montgomery and N. Glazer (eds), *Challenges to Sovereignty: How Governments Respond*, New Brunswick: Transaction.

——(2002b) 'Regulation for the rest of us? Global social activism, corporate citizenship, and the disappearance of the political', at: www.theglobalsite.ac.uk/press/211lipschutz.htm (accessed 31 March 2004).

——(2002c) 'The clash of governmentalities: the fall of the UN republic and America's reach for imperium', *Contemporary Security Policy*, 24(2) (December): 214–31.

——(2004) 'Sweating it out: NGO campaigns and trade union empowerment', *Development in Practice*, 14(1–2) (February): 197–209.

——with J. Mayer (1996) *Global Civil Society and Global Environmental Governance – The Politics of Nature from Place to Planet*, Albany: State University of New York Press.

Mouffe, C. (2000) *The Democratic Paradox*, London and New York: Verso.

Olson, M. (1966) *The Logic of Collective Action*, Cambridge MA: Harvard University Press.

Pasha, M. and Blaney, D. (1998) 'Elusive paradise: the promise and peril of global civil society', *Alternatives*, 23(4) (October–December): 417–50.

Polanyi, K. (2001) *The Great Transformation*, Boston: Beacon Press.

Shaw, M. (2000) *Theory of the Global State*, Cambridge: Cambridge University Press.

Tarrow, S. (1998) *Power in Movement: Social Movements and Contentious Politics*, Cambridge: Cambridge University Press.

Walzer, M. (ed.) (1994) *Toward a Global Civil Society*, New York: Berghahn.

Wapner, P. (1996) *Environmental Activism and World Civic Politics*, Albany: State University of New York Press.

Wolin, S. (1996) 'Fugitive democracy', in S. Benhabib (ed.), *Democracy and Difference*, Princeton: Princeton University Press.

Index